WILL WILLIMON'S

LECTIONARY SERMON RESOURCE

WILL WILLIMON'S

YEAR
C
PART 1

LECTIONARY
SERMON
RESOURCE

Abingdon Press™
Nashville

WILL WILLIMON'S LECTIONARY SERMON RESOURCE,
YEAR C PART 1

ISBN 978-1-5018-4727-1

18 19 20 21 22 23 24 25 26 27—10 9 8 7 6 5 4 3 2 1

MANUFACTURED IN THE UNITED STATES OF AMERICA

Contents

LENT

EASTER

Introduction

For over three decades *Pulpit Resource* has been helping preachers prepare to preach. Now, in this volume, some of the most helpful resources have been brought together to help you faithfully preach your way through the first half (Advent through Easter) of Year C of the Common Lectionary. This *Lectionary Sermon Resource* doesn't claim to be the sole resource needed for engaging, faithful biblical preaching, but it does give you, the pastor who preaches, accessible, easy-to-use help on your way to a sermon.

No sermon is a solo production. Every preacher relies on inherited models, mentors in the preacher's past, commentaries on biblical texts by people who have given their lives to such study, comments received from members of the congregation, last week's news headlines, and all the other ways that a sermon is communal. Using this resource is equivalent to sitting down with a trusted clergy friend over a cup of coffee and asking, "What will you will preach next Sunday?"

In the sermons that follow, I give you just what you need to begin the journey toward a sermon. I hope that this *Lectionary Sermon Resource* stokes, funds, and fuels your imagination. Rarely do I give you a full sermon in the "Proclaiming the text" section that can be preached verbatim. I've left plenty of room to insert your own illustrations, to make connections that work within your congregational context, and to speak the word in your distinctive voice. Sermons are occasional: God's word spoken in a particular time and place to a particular people. Only you can speak God's word in your distinctive voice to your distinctive context. All I try to do in this volume is to give you my insights and ideas related to a specific biblical text and then leave you free to allow the Holy Spirit to work within you and your particular congregation.

From what pastors have told me, the value of this guide is its simplicity, its unvarying format. Every Sunday you are given the following sections: "Theme" (I still think the time-honored practice of using a theme sentence to begin sermon preparation is a good practice, enabling the sermon to have coherence and unity); "Introduction to the readings" (that can be used as preparation for listening to the texts read in corporate worship); and "Prayer" (because every sermon is a gift of the Holy Spirit). The sections "Encountering the text" (listening to the biblical text, engagement with its particular message, is the first essential step on the way to a faithful sermon), "Proclaiming the text" (my sketch of ideas and movements for developing what I hear in the assigned text), and "Relating the text" (copious illustrative material that helps the sermon hit home) are given on different Sundays.

I'm honored that you have invited me to be a partner in your preaching. It's a demanding, challenging, joyful vocation to which God has called us. Let's work together to make sure God's word is offered in a lively, engaging way to God's people. Onward in the great adventure of preaching!

WILL WILLIMON

First Sunday of Advent

Jeremiah 33:14-16

Psalm 25:1-10

1 Thessalonians 3:9-13

Luke 21:25-36

Interruption

Selected reading

Luke 21:25-36

Theme

Advent is the apocalyptic, eschatological season of the church year. In Advent the church celebrates a God who not only cares but also acts, a God who not only hears but also intervenes, interrupts, and interjects. Herein is our great hope. Jesus Christ, whose advent we celebrate in this season, is the grand, loving, divine interruption.

Introduction to the readings

Jeremiah 33:14-16

"The time is coming," says the Lord, when humanity will see the long-awaited justice and righteousness of God made manifest as God intervenes and saves Israel.

1 Thessalonians 3:9-13

Paul intercedes for the suffering early Christians at Thessalonica, praying that God would strengthen them as they await their full redemption.

Luke 21:25-36

Jesus speaks of "signs in the sun, moon, and stars. On the earth, there will be dismay" when the earth will be radically changed, a time when "your redemption is near."

Prayer

Almighty God, on the whole, we are rather well fixed down here. Our families dwell secure, without great deprivation or danger. Our friends live lives that are reasonably well off. Our church, while it has needs, does not suffer persecution or peril.

The world, this world, has been good to us. Therefore, we praise you for giving us such a good and pleasant time.

And yet, we know that you are not just our God but also God of the whole world and all humanity. Judge us, Lord, for our uncaring and unconcern for the plight of our less fortunate neighbors. Forgive us when we benefit from the status quo without feeling even a twinge of conscience that our benefits are often obtained through the suffering and deprivation of others.

Interrupt our status quo, Living God. Intervene, shake, dismantle, and renew us, we pray. Even if it hurts. Amen.

Encountering the text

One of the things that we do well in the church is continuity. We worship in buildings that look as if they are older than they really are. We do fairly much the same things every Sunday, just like we did them last Sunday. Last year, last century. We call it an "Order of Worship," because that's what it's for—to order our acts of worship into a continuous, flowing whole. Church specializes in continuity.

And here we are, just like clockwork, again at the season of Advent. We could have predicted it. Advent is the beginning of the church's liturgical year, but not much about it feels like a true beginning. It feels like something in the middle, one more thing in the orderly progression of the church's year, which makes all the more remarkable the stories we have to tell during Advent. Advent is God's great discontinuity worked on a world in which many people believed that we were going along rather fine on our own devices. Our Advent texts—especially the texts for this first Sunday in Advent—speak of a God who steps up, steps in, and interrupts the flow of human history.

The apocalyptic, revealing ending that Jesus describes in today's Gospel contains some fearsome, cataclysmic events. And yet Jesus dares to speak of such a time as a time of "redemption." How can it be that the ending of a world, the destruction of the status quo, is a time of hopeful redemption?

Such is the world we live in, which God interrupts in order to intervene.

Proclaiming the text

He was looking forward to a pleasant Saturday morning with the family. On his way to run an unimportant errand, he looked in the sky and saw a passenger jet in flames, soaring across the sky. Was this the work of terrorists, or was this merely a tragedy due to mechanical failure? More important, was this a sign of something larger? Was this only a small, isolated tragedy that would affect only the people on that plane and their families and friends? Or did this mean something else?

This begins a day of interruptions for a man in London in his story told by Ian McEwan. During the course of the day, a deranged man will break into the placid life of this family and change everything. McEwan writes about this in his novel *Saturday*. If you've ever read him, you know that he specializes in observing the disrupted, interrupted lives of people.

In another novel, *Enduring Love*, McEwan tells about an Oxford science professor. The professor is a rational, modern sort of man, who likes his world orderly and explained. And yet, on a fine summer's day, he looks up into the sky and sees a hot air balloon racing out of control across the landscape. A little boy is in the balloon, screaming. A man is dangling from the balloon, trying to stabilize it. A number of onlookers join in and together try to pull the balloon down, but they are unsuccessful. And the man who was holding on to the chord of the balloon falls and dies. The little boy eventually lands safely in the balloon. But all of this proves to be terribly disrupting in the life of this staid Oxford professor. He knows that he will never be the same after that afternoon. Welcome to the world of the novelist Ian McEwan.

In fact, when you think about it, this is a definition for a good story. A good story begins quite normally, and moves along its expected ruts, but then something happens, something intrudes, and things are disrupted, turned upside down.

It is interruption that makes for the stuff of a good story. Interruption surprises, dislodges people, disorients them, and they spend the rest of the story trying to get back into more accustomed locations.

But what if an orderly story with no surprises and interruptions is not only boring but also a lie? What if interruptions are the true stuff of our lives? It is interesting how we like to think of our lives as an orderly progression of birth, childhood, youth, adulthood, and so on. First you have this, and that is always followed by that, and so on.

We say that someone dies "unexpectedly." But is the death of the human animal ever really "unexpected"?

What if our sense of order and progression is only a human delusion? I remember the good but disturbing novel that became a movie many years ago, *Girl, Interrupted*. It is a true story about a young woman's struggle with mental illness. The title suggests that you have a fairly stable young woman who, because of the unexpected assault by mental illness, has her life turned upside down and terribly interrupted. She goes through years of treatments for her illness, eventually survives, comes out on the other side, and resumes her life.

I thought the title was unusual because from everything that I could read in the book, this young girl had never known "normalcy." She had always suffered from severe mental illness. What we call "severe mental illness" was normal for her.

Isn't it interesting how we think of God, when we think of God, as the divine source of order and stability? That's how we generally conceive of what is happening in the first two chapters of the book of Genesis. The world begins out of a "formless void." There is chaos, confusion, and disorder. And then God speaks and there is order, the progression of seasons, seedtime, and harvest. But a closer reading of the text suggests that that is really not the story. God speaks and there is light. Not order but light in the darkness. Presumably darkness can be orderly until light bursts on the scene, and once the light is switched on we discover that the darkness is disordered. So maybe creation is bringing a disorder or at least a different kind of order. Maybe we think of creation as the bringing of order because we sense that there is such disorder in our lives and in our world, or at least not the kind of order we would like.

But in a good novel, or at least in the novels that I like, the story really doesn't get going until something falls from the sky or there is a knock at the door— an intrusion, an interruption that makes the characters' lives, while more difficult, certainly more interesting.

And when you look at scripture from this perspective, including this morning's text, you are reminded how much of scripture deals in interruptions. For our world to fundamentally change, something has got to fall from the sky.

Today's Gospel, and for that matter all of our biblical texts during the season of Advent, speak of a God who loves us enough to interrupt us. Here we are, proceeding down our comfortable runs, creatures of habit and routine, getting by just fine on our own. And then, in a place we don't expect, in a way we don't expect, God comes. God is born among us in a form we didn't ask for.

Emmanuel, God with Us, is God's grand, gracious interruption. There are times when it's as if God disrupts and interrupts in order to make room in our lives, room for God to come among us. Advent points to such moments.

I know that some of you think you are here at church in order to bring some order and stability to your lives. And I hope that church is sometimes that way for you.

But Advent suggests that many of us also yearn for a genuine disruption, for some divinely induced instability too. Many of us are caught in situations for which there is no humanly conceivable way out. Some of you are enslaved to habits that are literally killing you. Others face some dilemma for which there is no answer, at least no answer that is human. We live in a world in which the problems on the world stage are larger than our collective resources for addressing the problems.

And just as we get all settled in and accommodated to things as they are, just when we learn to face facts, to accept reality, to think that this world is as good as it gets, we are surprised by the intrusions of God. Somehow God interrupts our comfortable adjustment to the present and offers us a considerably disrupted future. Our notions of what can and what cannot be are turned upside down. This is Advent.

Advent says that our God not only cares about us but also comes to us. We don't have to get everything together on our own. We don't have to make the world work out right. God moves, acts, creates, and recreates.

A friend of mine says that the main difference between a living, true God and a dead, false god is that a dead, false god will never surprise you. So perhaps Advent is a yearly reminder to our church that God is able to reach in and to surprise us. Perhaps we ought to think of church as training in the skills required for following a living, surprising, interrupting God!

Let us therefore begin Advent with a prayer:

Lord, give us the grace to be prepared for the interruption of your grace among us, give us the courage to receive you when you intrude into our lives, and give us the wisdom to follow you into the future that only you can give. Amen.

Relating the text

Life consists of a series of interruptions. One day you are doing just fine, then there's the telephone call from the doctor after your yearly physical, there is that odd pain in the chest, or you turn on the evening news and some new disaster has just occurred and your world is rocked.

And what do we do at such moments? Most of us reach out or dig down for resources to deal with the crisis in an attempt to get life "back to normal," in order to achieve homeostasis and balance.

Fred Craddock tells of a person who, in a time of crisis, reached down but had no resources upon which to draw:

"I went to see a lady in our church who was facing surgery. I went to see her in the hospital. She had never been in the hospital before, and the surgery was major. I walked in there and immediately saw that she was a nervous wreck. She started crying. She wanted me to pray with her, which I did. By her bed was a stack of books and magazines: True Love, Mirror, Hollywood Today, stuff about Elizabeth Taylor and folk. She just had a stack of them there, and she was a wreck. It occurred to me, there's not a calorie in that whole stack to help her through her experience. She had no place to dip down into a reservoir and come up with something—a word, a phrase, a thought, an idea, a memory, a person. Just empty.

"How marvelous is the life of the person who, like a wise homemaker, when the berries and fruits and vegetables are ripe, puts them away in jars and cans in the cellar. Then when the ground is cold, icy, and barren and nothing seems alive, she goes down into the cellar, comes up, and it's May and June at her family's table. How blessed is that person."

—Fred B. Craddock, *Craddock Stories*, ed. Mike Graves and Richard F. Ward (St. Louis, MO: Chalice Press, 2001), 30

I've got a friend who is one of the most creative biblical interpreters I know. I once asked him what was the most difficult challenge in biblical interpretation.

Mastering Greek and Hebrew? Keeping abreast of the latest trends in biblical scholarship?

No.

"The greatest challenge is not to let your presuppositions, your expectations for what the text says or cannot say get in the way of the revelation of a living God. The most difficult thing is not to stifle God's sovereign freedom with your careful study of the biblical text."

Theologian Karl Barth once said that "Christians go to church to make their last stand against God." In the light of today's Gospel and our proclamation I might paraphrase Barth to say that sometimes we Christians go to church for the purpose of stabilizing and taming the incursions of a living, interrupting God.

How do we pastors, in all sorts of subtle ways, become enlisted by our congregations in that project?

Our Gospel today is from that genre of biblical literature called apocalyptic. Strange images are set before us in Jesus's interpretation of the times. Apocalyptic literature is metaphorical, pushy, symbolically charged, and just plain strange. It's—how shall I say this—unbalanced.

Things are overstated in apocalyptic, the colors are too vibrant and strong, and the tone is too strident. This sort of literature is therefore a challenge for us preachers, not only because it seems primitive and archaic, but also because it is unbalanced. Many of us think our job as preachers is to take a biblical text and explain it, lessen the tension, soften the blow, in other words, to balance out strident, overly pronounced biblical texts with our moderating, balanced sermons.

I've got a friend who is a pastoral counselor. Once I heard her define *balance* as "the illusion that the world is under your control."

Second Sunday of Advent

Baruch 5:1-9 or Malachi 3:1-4

Luke 1:68-79

Philippians 1:3-11

Luke 3:1-6

Advent Anger

Selected reading

Malachi 3:1-4; Luke 3:1-6

Theme

The prophets speak of that day when God will at last come to redeem a lost and fallen world. The world, as it is, is not the world that God intended when God began creating the world. So the prophets preach fierce judgment against our unrighteousness. God is angry at the way we have misrepresented God to the world. There can be no redemption until there is the honest recognition that we are those who need redemption. In order to prepare ourselves for the advent of the Christ, we must face God's judgment against us. God loves us enough not to leave us to our own devices. God comes to us, reveals the truth to us, and enables us to bear the truth in order that we might be able to receive the Christ who comes to redeem us.

Introduction to the readings

Malachi 3:1-4

The prophet Malachi speaks of the one who comes "like a refiner's fire" to purify and redeem Israel.

Philippians 1:3-11

Paul writes to an early Christian congregation from his prison cell, speaking tenderly of his great affection for them.

Luke 3:1-6

John the Baptist appears in the wilderness, "calling for people to be baptized to show that they were changing their hearts and lives and wanted God to forgive their sins."

Prayer

Come, Lord Jesus, not to fulfill our desire for you, but rather in accordance with your desire for us. Be truthful with us, and then give us the grace to be able to endure your truth. Stir up in us fresh desire to meet your expectations for us. Purify us and transform us into the people whom you would have us be. Amen.

Encountering the text

Unfamiliar images of God confront us this Second Sunday of Advent. The prophet Malachi speaks of God as a "refiner's fire." God heats up a fire to burn away impurities. God is coming to judge Israel, to purge Israel's sins. God loves Israel enough not simply to support and affirm Israel but also to call Israel to account, to give the nation the opportunity to be expurgated of infidelity.

Today's Gospel is perhaps more familiar than Malachi but no less challenging. "God is coming," announces John the Baptist. Messianic expectations are being fulfilled. How will the Messiah come to us? John says that Messiah comes not so much to comfort as to bring to account. Messiah will come and enact Malachi's refiner's fire.

God is thus making a case against God's people. To be chosen by God is to be held accountable by God. The wrath of God, the anger of God against our unrighteousness is not a frequent theme in mainline Protestant churches. Let us make it our theme this Advent.

Proclaiming the text

This is an emotion-laden season of the year. People often say, "Christmas is the season of joy." Joy, yes. Growing excitement and eagerness among the children, yes. A church near us has a sign out front that says, "Rejoice!"

But this Sunday I'd like to say a good word for anger. That's right, anger. It's an emotion rarely underscored during this time of the year, which is a bit strange if you are attentive to this morning's scripture. The first word of Homer's Iliad is *menin*, which means "anger." We translate this line, "Sing, o goddess, of the anger of Achilles, son of Peleus," but more accurately it reads, "Anger . . . sing it, goddess, the one belonging to Achilles son of Peleus."

For the early Greeks, anger is a chief impulse of action and a major reason for tragedy. The Homeric hero walks a path between reserved cowardice and blind fury.

However, for the later, more philosophical Greeks, anger is something sub-human that the wise person learns to overcome, to contain, and to harness. Plato said that our souls are like a charioteer who strives to control two horses, each pulling in a different direction. One horse is reason, and the other is emotion. For Plato, the good soul learns to hold the reins in such a way that one horse (reason, of course) is dominant. The wise person learns to keep passion—emotions such as anger, rage, and desire—in check by the moderation of reason.

We are right to be suspicious of anger. In resentful anger, Cain killed Abel. The first time the Bible mentions the emotion of rage is followed quickly by the first fratricide. In anger, Jonah refused to obey God's call to go to Nineveh and instead fled in the opposite direction to Tarshish. Jesus's first sermon, at his hometown synagogue in Nazareth, ended in his listeners' anger. They tried to kill him, so enraged were they by his words. Many terrible tragedies occur through anger.

And yet, even moderate, reasonable Plato had to admit that mere reason is an inadequate motivation for human engagement for good. Reason does a good job of helping us avoid doing wrong, but reason lacks the energy to motivate us to do good. Even Plato said that in order to know a subject, one must become "erotic" about the subject. Eros, fevered desire, is not all bad.

In fact, I think I could argue that some of the greatest good worked in the world is through anger.

Jeremiah the prophet did not really want to speak truth to Israel. He lived in a tragic age. The cruel armies of Assyria had overrun Israel. Jeremiah told Israel that God was punishing Israel for its sin. Can you imagine telling some suffering, hurting person that she is suffering because of her errors of judgment, her mistakes, her sin? Yet the prophets say that sort of thing all the time. Tough words, but true.

In anger, "gentle Jesus, meek and mild" took a whip and drove the money-changers from the temple, knocking over their tables, damaging their goods. Why would a nice person like Jesus do something like that?

"Because passion for your house has consumed me," reads Psalm 69, which the disciples recalled in light of Jesus's actions in the temple. Jesus was acting like a prophet, someone who loves the truth of God more than anything else and who becomes angry when the truth is not honored.

Indignation can be a dangerous emotion. But what about righteous indignation?

We tend to think of the Christian faith in a platonic fashion. Christianity is a religion of peace. Christianity helps sooth ruffled feathers. Christians are those who, from training over a lifetime, know how to sit quietly and listen.

I remember the well-meaning parent who attempted to moderate her young children's voices with, "Shush! Now's the time for church voices! No loud talking. Church voices."

But the man who said "moderation in all things" was a pagan philosopher, not Jesus. Jesus wept for the fate of his beloved Jerusalem, and his loud voice in the temple appealed to unbridled prophetic zeal.

We believe that God loves us. But today's scriptures are a great reminder that God loves us enough to be angry with us. God expects more out of us than we expect out of ourselves, holding us up to a higher standard of righteousness than that whereby we often judge ourselves.

"Messiah is coming!" John the Baptist tells the expectant multitudes. "And is he ever angry! We have not been living as we should."

"What are we to do?" they ask.

"Repent!" John responds, "Change, turn around, live your life moving in another direction."

Relating the text

After the first half of a very tough football game our coach came in and fumed, cursed, and raged, singling out a number of players for particular scorn. Me, a high school junior, sat there in fear and trembling. I had never seen our coach so angry.

On the way out of the locker room, a fellow football player said, "Coach only yells at us because he loves us. All he wants is for us to be the best that we can be."

I didn't really know what he meant until sometime later when I heard a strange preacher shout a sermon in the desert: "Messiah is coming, and is he ever angry!" And all he wants is for us to be the best we can be.

Look! I'm standing at the door and knocking. If any hear my voice and open the door, I will come in to be with them, and will have dinner with them, and they will have dinner with me (Rev 3:20).

The Danish philosopher Søren Kierkegaard, after noting how many people in the nineteenth century had invented all sorts of labor-saving devices, making human life easier in developing countries, said that he would dedicate himself to a life of making people's lives more difficult—he would become a preacher!

Third Sunday of Advent

Zephaniah 3:14-20
Isaiah 12:2-6
Philippians 4:4-7
Luke 3:7-18

The Politics of Advent

Selected reading

Luke 3:7-18

Theme

The Messiah who floods into our world at Advent is more than a spiritual phenomenon: he is also an ethical, moral, political demand. John the Baptist introduces the Messiah who saves by calling forth a new people who not only believe in him but who also follow him down a narrow, sometimes perilous, ultimately life-giving way to freedom. The good news that comes among us at Advent is also demanding news.

Introduction to the readings

Zephaniah 3:14-20

God's prophet speaks words of hope and encouragement for suffering Israel, telling the people, "I will bring all of you back."

Philippians 4:4-7

"Be glad in the Lord always," Paul tells an early congregation. "The Lord is near."

Luke 3:7-18

John the Baptist preaches fierce words to those who come out to the wilderness to hear him preach.

Prayer

Lord Jesus, you were born among us, into a very human family. You took up residence in our world. And that's one reason why we can come to you in prayer. Because you took an interest in us, because you came close to us, we know that you care about us. You stooped to us and reached out to us, so we can reach out to you. We are bold to pray for the needs of those in this congregation, and those in the whole world. We lift up before you especially the needs of those who suffer from the cruelty of unjust governments, who must live amid wars and rumors of wars, who suffer from the effects of civil unrest and social turmoil.

In the name of our Lord Jesus, the Messiah, the one who comes to us in the nativity, the one whom we now await in hope. Amen.

Encountering the text

In last Sunday's Gospel we were introduced to John the Baptist, the one who introduces Jesus the Christ. Today we get the full text of John's sermon about Jesus along with implications for those of us who expect to meet the Messiah when he comes.

Luke subtly depicts the story of John the Baptist against the backdrop of the Roman occupation of Judea. Luke is too good an artist to say upfront, "Now I am going to tell you a story with some very real political implications." Rather, Luke tells a story about some ordinary, lowly, first-century people that is acted out against the backdrop of a violent, threatening world.

To say that the story of the advent of the Christ has political implications is another way of talking about the incarnation. The Christ comes into the world, our world, a world full of violence, of tyranny, of oppression, and of war. That's our world and it is to our world that the Christ comes.

Proclaiming the text

You can't just pick up Homer's old book *Iliad* and read it without some help. The Bible is also a very old book, with the newest parts of the Bible being two thousand years old! When you're reading something that old, it helps to contextualize what you are reading. Permit me to give you the historical context for today's Gospel from Luke 3:7-18.

Tiberius Claudius Caesar Augustus was the successor of the greatest of the emperors, Augustus Caesar, truly one of the greatest of all the Caesars. He was named emperor on September 14, 14 BCE, and fourteen years later Luke's Gospel opens (3:1). Tiberius demurred from accepting the title of "God," though he heartily encouraged continued worship of his stepfather Augustus. Whenever the Gospels refer to "Caesar," they're talking about Tiberius.

Now, Tiberius appointed Pontius Pilate as his lackey (I mean "governor") of all of Judea, and it was then that Herod (a Jew) was assigned to be in charge of Galilee. Pilate watched Herod who watched his own people on behalf of the Roman occupation forces. Pilate is of course vilified in the New Testament—what could you expect from Jews who were suffering under the heel of the Roman occupation forces—but later historians say that Pilate was probably a typical representative of the Roman government occupying Judea. Pilate was probably not a particular villain, just a typical lackey for the emperor in this outpost of the empire. Pilate did what he had to do to keep these Jews quiet. And for one hundred years it worked. Sure, there was an insurgency—in fact, about sixty different outbreaks of violence from these Jews—still Tiberius, Pilate, and Herod had proved to be an effective occupation administration.

And it wasn't only the government that kept these Jews underfoot. I must admit that they had support from the head clergy—high priests Annas and Caiaphas—who worked with Herod and under Pilate to keep everything as smooth as possible up at the temple. There had been a day a long time ago when high priests served for life. But now the Romans installed and removed high priests whenever they wanted to make sure that none of the Jewish clergy dared to challenge Roman power.

The Romans graciously allowed the Jews to practice their religion, as long it was under the watchful eyes of Annas and Caiaphas, and as long as nobody mixed religion with politics or got restless during the temple rituals or dared to question the notion that the God of Israel was all well and good, and as long as Israel's God knew that Augustus Caesar and his stepson, so ably represented by Pontius Pilate, assisted by Herod, backed up by Annas and Caiaphas, were the real power in Judea.

Tiberius, Pilate, Herod, Annas, Caiaphas—all powerful, important men. This is the stuff of history—powerful, important men on top. That's what you read about if you will open up today's newspaper—stories about powerful men who control things from the top.

Then Luke writes, "God's word came to John son of Zechariah in the wilderness" (3:2). Literally in the Greek, "The word of God happened to John." The word of God—the long-awaited, eagerly listened-for word of God happened to "John son of Zechariah in the wilderness." John's Gospel says that the "Word was God" (John 1:1). The Word, God, came to John, son of Zechariah, in the wilderness.

Now, historians can tell you about Tiberius, who Pilate was, as well as who Herod, Annas, and Caiaphas were, but who in the world is this Zechariah or who is his son John to whom God, the Word, happens?

Maybe one reason why neither you nor any historian has ever heard of John is that John, son of Zechariah, is working out in the "wilderness." Unlike Annas and Caiaphas, John does not preach in the urban center of Jerusalem, up at the temple in all of the temple's grandeur. A few verses later, when you hear one of John's sermons in which he calls the congregation "snakes" and dumb and dead as "rocks," you can see why he couldn't get a church anywhere, except way out in the backcountry. Wilderness!

What self-respecting pulpit committee would call a wild man like John to preach in their self-respecting church? John was out in the wilderness.

Ironic, don't you think? Here were trained religious professionals, seminary-educated scholars, spiritual experts—Annas and Caiaphas—working up at the temple, ensconced at Israel's "national cathedral," looking for the "word of God." And the Word, God in the flesh, came to the unknown, un-credentialed, untrained, and unauthorized John, son of Zechariah, who was living off locusts and wild honey in the wilderness. What a way to begin a Gospel.

What a way for God to get close to the world.

Pick up this morning's newspaper. You won't read about people like John in places like the wilderness. You will read about politicians, powerful people in places like Washington, London, and Moscow. Take a course in world history at the college. You won't study about anybody but politicians, powerful people in places like Washington, London, and Moscow. It's famous people like Tiberius, Pilate, and Herod who make world history. And yet says Luke, when it came time for God to make history, God came to none of them.

In the wilderness John quotes the prophet Isaiah with some beautiful poetry about making straight the highway of God, lifting up the valleys, and bringing down the mountains, translated: "God is coming and the whole world is going to change." "All humanity will see God's salvation," says John (Luke 3:6). And that's wonderful, except you and I keep forgetting that the "salvation of God" is not the salvation we thought we wanted. Not only is salvation larger than the personal (it's nothing less than cosmic); but also salvation is preceded by a wild man on the margins, a fierce, demanding preacher of righteousness who is "John son of Zechariah."

John's message is rather simple and direct: "Messiah is coming." *Messiah* is a political designation for a political leader who will come and confront the Romans, who will thereby give Israel a different future.

And to whom and to where will Messiah arrive? He will come out in the wilderness, among ordinary, not-at-all-powerful people. And that's good news for most of us because, let's face it, most of us are not all that prominent. Few of us live in prestigious cities. Our church may be beloved and beautiful, but it is no one's idea of a grand and glorious national temple.

And it was people like many of us to whom John preached, telling them that the long-awaited Messiah was coming to them. And John cared enough to respond to their question, "What must we do?" with specific ethical injunctions, telling them specific things they could do in their ordinary lives that would make them part of the coming Jesus revolution.

Sometimes you come to church and you get the impression that following Jesus is a very extraordinary, heroic sort of thing. Church is where we come to rise above the grubby realities of this earthly life and become "spiritual." To really follow Jesus you have to go be a missionary to Africa or do something spectacularly difficult.

It's odd that we feel this way because Luke's Gospel goes out of its way to demonstrate that the Messiah entered this world and confronted the problems of this world. And Luke begins the story of the Messiah with the story of John the Baptist. John, preaching in the wilderness, says that if you want to greet the Messiah, if you really want to be part of his movement, fine. Then pay attention to what you do with your money and be willing to change the direction in which you are headed and turn into another direction. You already have all that you need in order to follow the Messiah, right here, right now.

And maybe that's why John's sermon, though harsh-sounding, is called by Luke "Good news." Gospel. To all of you who live in some out-of-the-way place, who live ordinary lives, engaged mostly in rather ordinary, everyday affairs, besieged by all sorts of injustices and cares and concerns, there is good news. Messiah is coming and he is coming to you. He calls you where you are to follow him as you are and, in the process, to be what you can be.

This news is good.

Relating the text

About this time of the year, many years ago, there was a new movie, *The Nativity*. I went to see the movie somewhat reluctantly. I was suspicious of any Hollywood attempt to do the gospel, having seen other disappointing cinematic attempts. But despite myself, I loved the movie. It had many virtues, I thought, but none greater than the virtue of a believable, real-life depiction of life in that part of the world in that day.

You could feel the dust in your throat, could hear the hoofbeats of the horses of the Romans. When Mary and Joseph made their way to Bethlehem, they passed the bodies of Jews hanging from Roman crosses. It was all a very real depiction of what life was surely like in the first century near the eastern village that was constantly under the threat of the Roman Empire and its military might. I thought *The Nativity* was a wonderful depiction of the reality of the Word made flesh.

In our scripture reading and preaching, we give specificity and content to the name *Jesus*. Catholic novelist Walker Percy said that you can say *Jesus* so much that it sounds like a cheap product or an advertising slogan, as if you're shouting "Exxon! Exxon!"

—Walker Percy, *The Message in the Bottle* (New York: Picador, 2000), 89

John the Baptist serves a Messiah who comes not only to help us but also to go head-to-head with the political powers that be. This suggests that Christians ought to be profoundly uneasy when the Christian faith is easily meshed with the presumptions of the modern nation.

On September 14, 2001, in the National Cathedral President Bush said: "But our responsibility to history is already clear: to answer these attacks and rid the world of evil."

And in his State of the Union address, January 28, 2003, as we were mobilizing for war in Iraq he said to the nation: "Once again, we are called to defend the safety of our people, and the hopes of all mankind. And we accept this responsibility. . . . We do not know—we do not claim to know all the ways of Providence, yet we can trust in them, placing our confidence in the loving God behind all of life, and all of history. May he guide us now. And may God continue to bless the United States of America."

The war began fifty days later, on March 19, 2003.

America lives with the promise and peril of what Robert Bellah has termed "civil religion"—defined by Gerhard Sauter as "the transfer of religious symbols into national self-understanding."

—H. Stephen Shoemaker, *Being Christian in an Almost Chosen Nation: Thinking about Faith and Politics* (Nashville: Abingdon Press, 2007), 24

Luke ends his talk of John with a brief reference to Herod Antipas (3:19-20) who finally imprisoned and cut off the head of John, son of Zechariah. But pity poor King Herod. He's not as important or as powerful as he thinks. Herod can't shut John up. The word of God has come to John in the wilderness. A wild conflagration has flared up out in the wilderness, among the marginalized and the lowly, a fire that will eventually sweep toward Jerusalem and consume the whole world. The Word has happened to John.

Fourth Sunday of Advent

Micah 5:2-5a

Luke 1:46b-55 or Psalm 80:1-7

Hebrews 10:5-10

Luke 1:39-45, (46-55)

The Invasion

Selected reading

Micah 5:2-5a; Luke 1:39-45, (46-55)

Theme

Into our troubled world, into our dark and disordered lives, a savior has come. Because we, in our sin, could not hope to come to God, God in Christ has come to us, embracing us, redeeming us, claiming us as his own. The advent of Christ is God's invading of our world.

Introduction to the readings

Micah 5:2-5a

In the eighth century the prophet Micah promised suffering Judah God's peace and blessing.

Hebrews 10:5-10

"When Christ came into the world," he became the supreme offering to God in behalf of humanity.

Luke 1:39-45, (46-55)

Mary, told by the angel that she is to have a baby, breaks into song, her "Magnificat."

Prayer

Lord God, at the nativity in Bethlehem you came among us as Jesus, one of us, that we might be brought close to you.

Help us receive him as our savior.

Enable us to listen to him, to hear what he says to us of your truth.

Above all, help us forsake our sin and follow him when he calls us. Help us move from the manger in Bethlehem into the world to tell and to demonstrate that the one who is born in Bethlehem is also the king of the world, the Lord of all life. Amen.

Encountering the text

In this Sunday's first lesson, the prophet Micah speaks to a people who are oppressed. They have experienced military defeat and exile and have suffered greatly. In other portions of the book of Micah, the prophet tells them that they have brought this disaster on themselves through their infidelity.

Today's lesson is more hopeful. Micah evokes the image of the shepherd. In the Old Testament, the shepherd is often spoken of by the prophets as the one who will gather and reconstitute a defeated and scattered Israel. Micah says that this shepherd is coming.

For our purposes of proclamation today, we need to note that these words are addressed to a people in the middle of severe national crisis. They are words that promise divine incursion into a desperate political situation.

They fit well, these politically charged words, with today's gospel, Mary's Magnificat. Mary is told that she is to have a baby by the Holy Spirit, and she breaks into song. But it is no lullaby that Mary sings. It is a war cry, a battle song. Through Mary, God's purposes for suffering Israel will be accomplished. There is nothing spiritual or private, inner and subjective about what God is intending to do, according to Mary's song. God is moving politically, economically, strategically. Those in power are to be cast down. The lowly and the oppressed are to be lifted up. A great transfer of power is being prophesied here.

Advent expects that transition. We have been waiting in these Sundays for this deliverance. Now we stand on the threshold of that expected salvation.

Let this Sunday be a time of claiming the promises of God, of celebration of their fulfillment in the advent of Jesus among us.

Proclaiming the text

"Each night, we secretly huddled around the wireless," she said, "eagerly hoping to receive some coded message that meant, 'Invasion Begun.' We scanned the skies, looking for Allied planes. People walked along the dikes, hoping for ships on the horizon. We prayed. People in Holland were starving. The Jews were already gone. Could we endure another year of Nazi occupation?"

An old Dutch woman remembered the dark days of Christmas 1944 as Holland awaited redemption. What is it like to be a people captive, awaiting deliverance, dependent on someone, something to come from the outside to save?

Captivity, caughtness comes in different forms. How is it that A.A. puts it? Basically, "We are powerless to help ourselves. We have to reach out to a higher power." If you've never had debts you couldn't pay, a cancer that won't heal, a marriage that can't be fixed, a problem that defies solution, you won't understand this sermon.

Cicero, in his best book, *On the Nature of the Gods*, tells us of three religious options in classical Rome of the first century: You could be Stoic, a pantheist, believing that everything is impregnated with the divine, God in every rock and tree. You could be an Epicurean, believing that, if gods exist, they have better things to do than worry about us, so relax, don't whine, and get along as best you can. Or you can be as Cicero himself—an academic—smart enough to know that not much can be known on these matters anyhow so, even though you are skeptical, go to the temple once in a while and enjoy the sacred rituals that are mainly of value for holding the government together.

Sound familiar?

Nature worship. Stoic stiff upper lip. Intellectual scorn. These are among our deities. No wonder the world seems emptier than a college campus in late December. We are fairly much on our own now, left to our own devices. What care the gods for us and our vexations? Find what consolation you can in available therapy, or out of a bottle, relentlessly scan the information highway, scour the winter skies, or search the horizon at twilight. People are starving. Another winter of occupation may do us in, but where is deliverance?

I commend to you a movie, if you can take it: *The Ice Storm*. It's a cold night in post-Christian Connecticut 1971, and the beautiful people with mod houses and big cars and bell-bottom leisure suits are having a party. Upstairs, Mom and Dad delve into a little spouse swapping, and downstairs the kids are belting vodka and experimenting with sex, and it is an unrelieved, cold, empty world. *The Ice Storm*. The movie ends with the family in the cold car frozen, with Dad crying like a baby because that's all you can do in a world where deliverance is inconceivable.

"In those days Caesar Augustus declared that everyone throughout the empire should be enrolled in the tax lists" (Luke 2:1). Caesar calls the shots. What hope is there for Jews languishing under the heavy heel of the empire?

Nobodies named Mary and Joseph search in vain for a warm place to spend a cold night. There's no room at the inn. When is there ever room for the poor?

Caesar calls it "the end of welfare as we know it." People on the bottom, such as unwed moms like Mary, know it as no place to spend a dark night.

Bethlehem—an occupied town, full of refugees, caught, powerless, and what then? Stoic stiff upper lips? Epicurean accommodation? Keep up appearances, go through the motions even if you no longer believe it? What hope for deliverance?

Then, a flutter of wings. Songs flung into the silence. Light. All creation flooded with presence. A virgin conceives. A child cries out in the night. Passionate, risky intrusion. There is traffic between God and humanity; and tonight, it's one way. God with us, Emmanuel.

The invasion has begun.

Relating the text

"As C. S. Lewis said, if you are not going to be a Christian, the next best thing is to be a Stoic. I think he's quite right. Those are the only real options. Everything else strikes me as being whiney."

—W. Dale Brown, *Of Fiction and Faith: Twelve American Writers Talk about Their Vision and Work* (Grand Rapids: William B. Eerdmans Publishing Company, 1997), 9

Stoicism is that noble pagan teaching that God, if there is one, is mostly inactive, has left us to our own devices. Then the best we can do in life is to go on as best we can, not to complain against the outrages that come our way but to bear them with noble, stoic resignation.

This is about the best that can be expected from a religion that doesn't believe in incarnation.

In today's "Proclaiming the text," I refer to the rather bleak and depressing movie *The Ice Storm*. I saw the movie when I was in Stockholm giving a series of lectures there. On a dark, cold night in December, I saw this dark and depressing movie.

The next day, after my lecture, one of the seminarians asked me, "Do you really think that people must be saved by Jesus Christ or they have no hope?"

I expected that she wanted me to say something that seemed more "inclusive" or "pluralistic" than she had heard.

"Well," I replied, "yesterday I might have been willing to consider other possibilities for our redemption. But last night I saw the movie *The Ice Storm*, and I would have to say, especially if you live in Connecticut in an affluent neighborhood, that without Jesus Christ—his grace, forgiveness, and power—you are damned. No, I can't really imagine any other way that people like us could be saved except for a God who is willing to suffer for us, with us, to bleed, even to die. People like us couldn't be saved by any less of a God than that."

The seventeenth-century poet George Herbert noted that the letters with which we spell the name *Mary*, the mother of Jesus, can also spell the word *army*. Is there some kind of connection being made here between the name of Mary and the forces of death and violence? Does this lowly maiden also hold within her a confrontation with the forces of death?

Take this as a parable, not only about the way we ought to respond to life (you have to engage, throw yourself in), but also as a parable of the incarnation, the God Almighty deals with us in the nativity at Bethlehem. Our God did not remain aloof from human trouble but, in the incarnation, threw himself in.

How odd of the great, almighty God to invade our world as a baby. Do you recall Bret Harte's short story "The Luck of Roaring Camp"?

In a tough, lawless mining camp out west in the late 1880s, a miner discovers a little baby who has been abandoned by his parents. The baby is brought back into camp. Here are a group of rough-and-tumble miners who have, of all things, a baby. As soon as the baby is brought into camp, the transformation begins. One by one, each of the miners becomes a different person. There are clothes to be made, meals to be prepared, washing and tending to be done, all for the little foundling of Roaring Camp. Not only are the individual miners transformed, but the whole camp as well. Swearing and cursing, fighting and feuding, once typical of Roaring Camp, now cease. Each man tries to be on his best behavior because of the baby.

Take this as a parable of the "invasion" that happens among us at Christmas.

"Glory to God in the Highest, and on earth peace among those whom he favors" (Luke 2:14). That was the song the angels sang when Jesus was born. The words of the angels are almost an exact quote from the decrees of Augustus Caesar, one of the greatest rulers (dictators) the world has ever known. When Augustus became emperor, he had himself declared one of the gods. He erected a huge statue in the Roman forum, eleven times bigger than a normal man. At one point, through the Roman army, Augustus controlled every inch of the Western world.

Do you see what is happening in the Gospel account of Jesus's birth? "Glory to God in the Highest, and on earth, peace..." This was the decree of the angelic messengers at Jesus's birth. They are announcing a new king, a new emperor, one greater than Augustus.

The story of Christmas and the incarnation is politically charged. It is the story, not simply of a baby born to Mary and Joseph, but of a new king. Neither Augustus nor all of his army will be able to stop the progress of this infant king and his people. The invasion has begun.

Christmas Day

Isaiah 52:7-10
Psalm 98
Hebrews 1:1-4, (5-12)
John 1:1-14

Hoping for Christmas

Selected reading

John 1:1-14

Theme

Jesus, the Word made flesh, is the fulfillment of our deepest hopes. He is light into our darkness, the embodiment of all of God's glory, full of grace and truth.

Introduction to the readings

Isaiah 52:7-10
Isaiah speaks of the messenger who proclaims to suffering Israel that all will "have seen our God's victory."

Hebrews 1:1-4, (5-12)
The letter to the Hebrews speaks of the advent of the one who is "the light of God's glory."

John 1:1-14
The Gospel of John begins with the stirring cadences of the proclamation, "The Word became flesh and made his home among us. . . . We have seen his glory."

Prayer

Lord God, on this high, happy, holy day, we celebrate the birth of your dear Son, our savior, Jesus Christ. The Word has been made flesh and dwelt among us. And we have beheld his glory.

We praise your name, Lord God, that you did not leave us in the dark. You came to us as light and life. Your Holy Spirit has shown into our world in a way that nothing, no darkness that we create or in which we dwell, has overcome it. Amen.

Encountering the text

Even though we have arrived at Christmas, the Feast of the Incarnation, we are not yet done with John the Baptist. The John we are to meet is the John of the Fourth Gospel, the one who is here as "a witness to testify concerning the light."

We are not, on this Sunday, just meeting John the Baptist. We are meeting him as he is presented in John's Gospel. Unlike some of the other Gospels—and John the Baptist appears in all them—the Fourth Gospel cares nothing for how John was dressed. Luke says that John had a very peculiar diet and lived out in the wilderness. John tells us nothing of this. Luke also says that John called people to repent of their sins, to set their lives right. When people asked John what they ought to do, John told them to straighten up and live right.

But not in the Gospel of John. In John's Gospel, John is not even called John the Baptist. He is a "witness," a witness to the light.

John the Baptist may be the church's way of saying that, whatever we hope for, as we are hoping for Christmas, what we actually get in the arrival of Jesus is at some distance from that for which we were hoping.

At this time of year, one of the aspects of our pre-Christmas celebration is the stringing of lights all over town. We string lights in trees, up lampposts, over our streets, framing our windows, twirling around our trees. But you can hear John telling us that when he speaks of the light that is coming into the world, the true light that is lighting our darkness, it is a very different light from that which is an expected part of our Christmas spirit.

When John began preaching, he did not stand on a city street corner and preach to people. He went out into the wilderness. He called people out into the desert.

There, according to today's Gospel, the religious establishment of Jerusalem, the University Department of Religion, came out to examine John. Frankly, they didn't know what to make of him. These religious experts shined a bright flashlight into the face of John and demanded, "Who are you?" He certainly did not act or dress or eat like anyone religious whom they had encountered before. "Who are you?" (John 1:19), they demand. What is your denomination? Are you Calvinist? Pre-Millennialist, Arminian, Baptist, Methodist, Episcopalian? Are you high church or low?

Interestingly, John answers them, by not really saying who he is, but by telling him whom he is not: "I'm not the Christ" (v. 20). John's popular answer is curious because that isn't what his questioners asked him.

His interrogators regroup and ask, "Then who are you? Are you Elijah?"

"I am not."

"Are you the prophet?"

"No" (v. 21).

They want to pigeonhole him. They are determined to place John within their preconception of what religion ought to be and how a religious person ought to act. Furthermore, they want to place John within the context of their conventional expectation. They want to see John as either fitting into, or greatly disappointing, their hopes for the future of Israel.

But no matter what they suggest, John says no.

Some of them were hoping that he might be the great prophet Elijah come back from the dead. When Elijah was on the earth, God showed great power to do good through Elijah. Others hoped that while he might not be a prophet so great as Elijah, he might be one of the minor prophets. Maybe somebody like Micah or Obadiah. These people didn't do all that many powerful works, but they certainly had powerful words, and who needed powerful works and words more than Israel? An occupied people, with the heel of Rome on their necks? What hope had they other than for some sort of divine deliverance?

"Who are you?" They attempt again. "We need to give an answer to those who sent us. What do you say about yourself?" (v. 22).

John refuses to say anything concerning himself. He is Dr. No. We're given no details, nothing about his dress, nothing about his message, other than his message as one of negation. John says no.

The only positive thing John says about himself is that he is "the voice." That is all that he calls himself: "I am a voice crying out in the wilderness, Make the Lord's path straight" (v. 23). I am God's megaphone. I am the smell of the coffee that wakes you up in the morning; I am that alarm clock that jerks you out of your sleep. It's time to wake up.

We will attempt to honor the peculiarities of the Fourth Gospel's presentation of John the Baptist as we preach a joyous gospel on this joyous day.

Proclaiming the text

I can't stand it when people ask that favorite pre-Christmas question, usually addressed to a child, "What do you hope to get for Christmas?" Such a question plays right into the hands of the commercialism and materialism that mar the Christmas season. As Christians, we know that Christmas is more than greed or gifts. Christmas is about the birth of the Christ child.

- 36 -

And yet one could learn a great deal from the question, "What do you hope to get for Christmas?" For if you know our hopes, you know us fairly well. If you want to know who a person really is, and plans to be, inquire into what that person is hoping for.

What are you hoping for?

I expect that is what most of us think religion is about, the fulfillment of our hopes. We hope to find peace in our anxious lives. So we come to church on Sunday morning hoping that the music of the hymns and the words of scripture and preaching may fill us with a sense of peace.

We hope for thoughtful, reflective lives. So we come to church on Sunday morning hoping for an interesting sermon, something that will help us use our minds, something that will test our intellects, make us think about things in a way we haven't thought before.

Or maybe we hope for beauty. There is much ugliness in this world. Sunday therefore becomes a haven, an island of beauty amid a great deal of unloveliness.

What are you hoping for? Church is where we get our hopes met, where our yearning is fulfilled. I dare say that is the major reason why people keep coming to church. Though their hopes are often disappointed by what we do here on Sunday morning, there are enough Sundays where you are able to emerge from the service saying, "Why, that service really did something for me." What you are saying is that that service fulfilled some of your expectations for what "good" worship ought to be. Your hopes were met.

And surely all of that is as it should be. So maybe I ought to prepare my sermon, perhaps we ought to plan any service of worship by first conducting a poll, by meeting you at the door with a questionnaire, by asking you, "What is your hope for this service?" That seems to be the major point of religion—that our hopes are fulfilled.

The trouble is that the Gospels seem to engage in a continual debate with people's hopes and expectations. Jesus came, light into our darkness. But the problem with Jesus was he was not the sort of light that we expected. That is where the trouble started. Jesus was the hope of the world, but he was not the hope for which the world was hoping!

And thus the church in its wisdom confronts us with John the Baptist here on this Sunday in Advent. We are here, just a couple of weeks before Christmas, hoping for Christmas. But here comes John the Baptist, a rather strange figure, an odd preacher, who doesn't really match up with anybody's hope. And what does that tell us?

John intrudes into our messianic, religious expectations. He is an unexpected, annoying voice that you can't get away from no matter how far away you move.

Furthermore, John is the voice that has only one thing to say, "the light is coming." John did not say of Jesus, he is the one who is coming to take away your sins, to preach righteousness, to tell you what you ought to do. Jesus would do some of that. But right now, at Christmas, John calls Jesus "Mr. Light."

If we do not know what to make of somebody who says that he is nothing but a voice, what do we make of someone who is nothing but light?

Light. It is so difficult to define, to limit, to keep out. In the mornings about this time of year, when all the leaves are off the trees in our yards, the light comes streaming in at too early an hour. We pull our curtains as closed as we can, but still, there is light, streaming in to the bedroom at the most inopportune time.

John said he is not the light. He is a witness to the light. He is someone who receives the light, someone who points to the light, but who isn't the light.

To those religious experts, who wanted to define and classify and characterize and pigeonhole and know, John simply says, "Someone greater stands among you, whom you don't recognize" (v. 26).

Out in the wilderness, at some distance from Western civilization, and the places of power, the city with its walls and boundaries, John tells them, tells us, that we do not understand, we do not define, we do not know the light that is coming into our darkness. All he has to say is to negate our present definitions and expectations. At this point, we are given no substance, no defining content. Rather, we are told that our hopes are not necessarily going to be fulfilled as we expected by the one who comes among us. Our expectations may not be met. The light dawns upon us.

John does not tell his questioners that he does not know who the light is. He tells us simply that we do not know the light.

For now, they are not to define or to characterize. They are simply to do what the human being naturally does when light streams into our darkness. We are to open our eyes to the light. We are to allow our eyes to become adjusted to the light that dawns among us.

It's enough to make each of us ask, "What am I hoping for this Christmas?" It is an important question because like some of those people who questioned John, we are apt to miss something so fragile and miraculous as Mr. Light if we are too full of our explanations and definitions and expectations.

What are you hoping for today? If you are like many people around here, maybe you are not sure. What brought you to church this morning, this Christmas Day? You may have been called here by some strange, indefinable pull, some tug on your heart, that you would find difficult to describe. And maybe John is saying that's all right. An open heart may be better than one that is filled with definitions and preconceptions and preconditions.

Later, in this Gospel, Jesus makes many statements, "I am . . ." and then "I am . . ." I am the light, and the vine. I am bread. I am the way, the truth, the light.

But right now, here at the beginning, before we meet Jesus, John simply introduces him as light. John says, "I am not the light. I am only a witness to the light."

At times you may have heard me say that I am bothered by some of the spiritual renaissance that is going on in our country. There seems to be a great resurgence of interest in something called "spirituality." Most of this strikes me as rather thin stuff, a kind of free-floating, vague openness to something or someone who is infinite, spiritual. "Spirituality" becomes simply a great basket into which we toss all of our expectations and desires, calling that "Spirit."

But this Sunday, listening to the denials of John, I am wondering if maybe this is not a bad place to begin. Later, during the course of the church year, there will be occasions for us to find out more about Jesus. There will be opportunity for us to give more substance to the shining of the light. But this Sunday, let us attempt simply to lay aside our hopes and expectations, and let the light dawn upon us. Let's allow the light to enter into our darkness. Let's simply admit that we are in the dark, that there is much that we don't know.

One of Jesus's great problems, when his ministry got going, after this encounter between the authorities and John, was people who thought they knew exactly how the Messiah was supposed to act, how a messiah was supposed to look. The people decided that what they needed was a good general to raise an army and run out the Romans. And when Jesus didn't do that, they rejected him. They decided that they needed someone who spoke cool, soothing words of conventionality. And when Jesus didn't do that, they turned against him with murderous intensity.

Thus, John says that sometimes Jesus will be known by knowing that which he is not before we know that which he is. Therefore, we must be receptive for surprise, and wonder, and the shock of a God who is not the God we thought we knew.

That is the light coming into our darkness. Today I stand among you as witness to that light, the light coming into the world, the light that the darkness of the world has, over a couple thousand years later, thank God, not overcome. In him was light, and the light was the light of all. Amen.

Relating the text

When we were in Sweden a couple of years ago, about this time of year, we noted that it had become popular in many churches to build an area, often a large box filled with sand, in which dozens of candles were placed. People, upon entering the church, would light one of these candles.

We asked our Swedish host what was going on. He confessed, "I don't really know what is going on. Part of it may be attributed to the fact that Sweden, in our Northern Hemisphere, is dark so much of the day during this time of the year. I often wonder what modern, secular Swedish people think they are doing by lighting candles. When they light the candle and stand for a moment of silence, what's going through their heads? Many of them no longer know the Bible. Many of them are not at all well-schooled in the Christian faith. What is going through their heads when they light these lights?"

I certainly share some of the same questions. And yet, perhaps the light speaks to a yearning that modern people have, a yearning for some light beyond our present darkness, for something that comes into our world and enlightens us, something not of our own devising. They call it spirituality, something vague like that.

Perhaps today's Gospel, speaking of John, preparing the way for Jesus, by sweeping away our expectations, has something to say to us. We can work with contemporary humanity's vague religious inclinations and expectations. We can begin and work from there and tell them who the Messiah really is and is not.

Perhaps the present age, filled with such vague religious inclinations, lacking much definitive biblical substance, can be a great place to begin.

A number of years ago, a friend of mine who was a pastor said, "It used to be when you spoke to people about church, they would say things like, 'Well, even though I don't go to church, I do consider myself very religious.'"

At some point in our history, even that became too specific. Now, in speaking about church, they will say, "Well, even though I am not very religious, I do consider myself very spiritual."

Our religion has become the nonreligion of spiritual vagueness. But not to-day. The testimony of John's Gospel is that the eternal Word, the divine Lo-gos, has become flesh and has dwelt among us, flesh. Our God has a name, a face, a place, specificity, and definition that we name as Jesus, Bethlehem, and the incarnation.

Christmas Day
Isaiah 52:7-10
Psalm 98
Hebrews 1:1-4, (5-12)
John 1:1-14

Light into Our Darkness

Selected reading
John 1:1-14

Theme
Christ is the light of the world. He shines into all the dark places of our lives. His brightness, in his incarnation, dawns among us. His nativity is a grand fulfillment of our hopes and expectation for God with us. And thus we sing on Christmas.

Introduction to the readings
Isaiah 52:7-10
Isaiah prophesies of the beauty of the messenger who speaks the good news of God's redemption.

Hebrews 1:1-4, (5-12)
God has communicated with God's creation down through the ages in many various ways through the prophets. But now, on this day, God has spoken to us "through a Son."

- 43 -

John 1:1-14
John introduces the incarnation as light coming into darkness. The light shines in the darkness and the darkness has not overcome the light.

Prayer

Lord Jesus, in your nativity among us you came to show us the fullness of God's glory. Into our drab darkness, light has dawned. Into our unfulfilled lives, joy has come. Into our silence, a word has been spoken and that word is joy, that word is love. We praise you for making your home among mortals like us. Amen.

Encountering the text

John introduces Jesus in much the same way as Genesis 1 introduces God the creator. Into the primal darkness, God says *light* and a benighted chaos comes alive (Genesis 1). John's Gospel begins with that word *genesis*, "in the beginning." We are surely meant to read, in the first five verses of John, the coming of Christ as light coming into our darkness. Today, on Christmas Day, we gather to celebrate the full advent of light, Jesus the light of the world. Jesus says in this Gospel that he is the "light of the world" (John 8:12).

And yet John's Gospel does more than simply announce the advent of light. John also says that "the light shines in the darkness, and the darkness doesn't extinguish the light" (1:5). This contrast of light and darkness is typical of the Fourth Gospel. Therefore, *darkness* can be taken here in verse 5 to mean more than simply the light of God shining into the world; it can also mean that Jesus intrudes into the world amid all of the world's enslavement in chaos and evil. I expect specifically that this claim of the darkness not overcoming the light is an allusion to Jesus's resurrection.

The NRSV notes that the darkness "did not overcome" the light, which is a good rendering of the Greek *katalambano*. This reflects the Greek aorist tense—past action that continues to have significance into the present—

rather than the RSV's "has not overcome it." The KJV rendered *katalam-bano* as "the darkness comprehended it not," and the CEB says, "the darkness doesn't extinguish the light," both of which are also legitimate.

As you know, John delights in the use of double entendre. Therefore, we are justified in thinking that it's appropriate to render *katalambano* as either "overcome" or as "comprehend" or as "extinguish." The darkness, thank God, has not been able to comprehend, overcome, or extinguish the light of the world.

Thus, as we move into our yearly celebration of the incarnation, we are able to stand and proclaim that light shines in the world, and all adversaries to the light have, throughout the ages, been unable to extinguish it. The adversaries can't even grasp its significance.

Our service today is therefore particularly joyful as we gather as those who, by God's grace, have been enabled not only to see the light of Christ coming into our world but also to celebrate the light of Christ's ultimate victory over everything that might endanger or extinguish the light. Thus we sing.

Proclaiming the text

We gather this joyous day to celebrate, singing the beloved music of Christmas that proclaims a grand article of faith: the light shines in the darkness. We have read the majestic opening cadence of the Gospel of John—in the babe of Bethlehem is light, the light of the world, and the light shines into the darkness, our darkness, with a radiance that is inextinguishable.

Each one of you is here this morning because in some way or another, the light that is Christ has shined in each of your lives. Some of you, had we the time for you to tell it, were stumbling about in the dark, clueless and lost, and then you were unexpectedly blinded by his light. For others of you, Christ coming into your life was more like a light coming on in your heart, as if someone flipped a switch and you came to your senses as Christ became real and present to you. And I know that there are some of you for whom that light was lit when you were very young, perhaps by a parent or a wise older friend. Sure, that light has at times flickered, has burned brighter at one time than at another. Still, through it all, the light of Christ has continued to shine and that's why you sing today: "In him was light . . . and the light shines in the darkness." Amen and amen.

And yet you will note that John proclaims even more for Christ, the light of the world. John says not only "the light shines in the darkness" but also "and the darkness did not overcome it." The word that NRSV Bibles render as "overcome" is the Greek word *katalambano*.

I think of floodwaters rising after a torrential spring rain. The water in the river rises gradually at first, then rises more and gathers force until it crashes down through the canyon sweeping everything away. The nightly news tells of the tragedy of the little mountain village that was "overcome" by the raging flood.

The psalmist speaks about tragedy in life when "waves surged over me" (Ps 42:7).

Some of you know what it feels like to have the waves crashing around you and the waters rising, and you fear that you are going to be overcome with sadness.

"When it rains it pours," we say. There are times when it's one struggle after another and the good news seems to be in danger of being overcome by the bad.

But John rejoices because "the light" (the light who is Jesus Christ come into world) shines forth "and the darkness doesn't extinguish the light."

This Greek word *katalambano* can also be rendered as the old King James Version does it: "And the darkness comprehended it not." I like that, too.

We've got a nice crowd here this Sunday, but still only a minority of folks in our town join us to sing our Christmas carols. For most of those who are not here it's not that they are opposed to the Christian faith, not that they are hostile to us. They just don't get it. For them, Christmas is a holiday, a grand time to eat and to drink too much, to spend too much, and to travel too far. That a minority of people would gather to sing "Joy to the world, the Lord has come!" strikes most of those who don't get it as odd. They "comprehend it not."

Some of you have had the experience of a dramatic, life-changing spiritual event when God seemed particularly present and real to you. Then you went out to share this grand experience with your friends or family. You excitedly narrated to them what happened to you, only to have them listen politely and respond, in effect, "Sorry, I just don't get it." That which was undeniably life-changing for you was incomprehensible to them.

Our Epistle lesson this day says that God, having tried to speak to us down through the ages, has in the incarnation at last spoken to us "through a Son." We look at Jesus of Nazareth and see God speaking, revealing himself to us, here, now. But most people look at Jesus and see only a historical figure from the past who said a few interesting things and then faded into obscurity. They don't see a light shining in the darkness; they see that which they "comprehend not."

And yet the amazing thing is that you have comprehended Jesus. You "get it." Your presence here this morning is testimony that you—despite any intellectual or cognitive limitations—comprehend the deep, cosmic, world-shaking significance of this peasant baby born in Bethlehem. You think of all the things in the world you don't understand and yet, you understand this. Of course, your understanding of the gift of God in Christ is, itself, also a gift of God in Christ. Still, when you consider all the factors working against your ability to stand this day and truly to sing, "Hark the herald angel sing, Glory to the new born king," it's rather amazing.

See? John was right. The "light shines in the darkness" and though the darkness did not comprehend it, still the darkness has not been able to "overcome" the light.

But this Greek word *katalambano* can also be rendered in yet one more way than "comprehend" or "overcome." It could also be rendered, "The darkness has not overtaken it." The darkness doesn't "get it" in more than one sense. The darkness doesn't comprehend it and the darkness doesn't "get it" in the sense that the darkness doesn't catch the light, doesn't grasp or capture the light. In John 12:35, Jesus warns his disciples to walk in the light lest the darkness "overtake you." Same verb, *katalambano*.

The Gospels depict Jesus on a perpetual road trip, on a constant journey. Jesus is always in motion in the Gospels. I remember asking a college class why the Gospel writers presented Jesus constantly on the road and one answered, "Because from the first he knew that people were out to get him so he had to hightail it out of town as quickly as possible."

There is something to be said about that. Jesus's whole ministry was a race against time. His critics are always on the prowl and threaten to overtake him.

I don't mean to be overly dramatic about our own trials and tribulations as followers of Jesus, but some of you here can identify with this rendering of *katalambano* as pursuit and capture, the darkness threatening to "overtake" the light.

When I asked a director of our town's ministry to the homeless what her greatest challenge was, she answered, "We are always on the brink of financial disaster, no more than a couple of weeks between us and bankruptcy. We've got to race just to keep up with this week's bills."

And yet, that same person who is constantly under threat of being overtaken by the darkness this year celebrates her tenth year as director of this ministry to the homeless. The darkness has not overtaken the light.

I was in a meeting in which a number of us church officials were lamenting the church's difficulty in keeping up with the times. We castigated the church for being so backward, so old-fashioned and enslaved to the past. There was a woman present who had been an executive with one of this country's most prosperous computer companies. She said, "As a business person, I'm amazed by the church's ability to adjust, adapt, and to compete in every age, in every culture."

She pointed out to us that the church had never met a society so closed and antagonistic to the church that the church couldn't find a way to make converts in that society. For seventy years the Soviets tried every way they knew how to extinguish the light of the gospel and miserably failed to "overtake" the light. They got overtaken by the light, the way I see it.

This congregation has had many challenges. There have been times in our history when it seemed as if the bill collectors, the naysayers, the critics, and the culture would overtake us and we would be forced to close our doors and be transformed into a restaurant or a warehouse. But we weren't overtaken. We're still here, not only surviving but even prospering.

I've seen the world try to turn a child into a grasping, materialistic, self-centered dolt, the embodiment of some people's "American Dream," only to watch God work through you to transform that child into a caring, compassionate Christian. The world tried to overtake the light of the world and, through you, the world got overtaken!

And that's a long way of saying, musing on the ancient Greek word *katalambano*, why we sing this glorious day not only with joy but also with hope. Sure, we've got our challenges in the days ahead. Sure, there are perils and evils before us. And yet I've got some good news for you: the light of the world shines in the darkness, and the darkness did not overcome it, extinguish it, comprehend it, or overtake it!

Relating the text

Paul says in Romans 12, "Don't be defeated by evil, but defeat evil with good." In other words, we are to respond to evil in the world as God has responded in Christ. We are to let light shine. We don't overcome evil with the ways of the world—through force, violence, retribution, or lying. We overcome evil as Christ has overcome evil—through his love shining into our darkness.

That Greek word *katalambano* is rendered, in various places in the English New Testament as: make one's own, catch, attain, comprehend, find, overcome, overtake, realize, seize, surprise, understand, extinguish, and win.

In today's proclamation of John 1:5 the preacher could do an extended meditation by substituting any of these meanings of *katalambano* within the sermon:

"The light shines in the darkness and the darkness has not won."

"The light shines in the darkness and the darkness has not seized it."

"The light shines in the darkness and the darkness has not realized it." And on and on.

While we might question the incipient dualism of the Fourth Gospel's division of the world into the realm of "darkness" and the realm of "light," many have accused mainline, liberal Protestantism of a too-sanguine view of evil in the world. We tend to be overly positive about the cosmos. When it comes to our views of human nature, we tend to think of ourselves as basically nice people who are making progress.

We can only assert that the world as we have it is "good" by denying the evil that runs rampant in the world, the suffering that the innocent suffer, and the injustice that afflicts so many. John joyously proclaims the triumph of the light of the world. But he is also honest about the power of darkness to resist the light. The light will overcome all the forces set against it, but it will not be pretty. There will be suffering and blood before the full story of the babe of Bethlehem ends.

Therefore, as the church sings its songs of joy, it must take care always to admit to the sadness that still occurs among us. Jesus is light, but he is the light that shines into real, serious darkness. When the church exclusively celebrates the light, the joy, and the victory, without also being honest about the struggle, the sadness, and the defeat, we do the gospel an injustice and we alienate our proclamation of Christ from some of the very people Christ means to love.

The light of the world does not avoid or deny the reality of the darkness; the light enters into the realm of darkness, works within the realm of darkness, and ultimately triumphs. That is one reason why we call the message of Jesus the gospel.

First Sunday after Christmas
Nativity of Our Lord

Isaiah 9:2-7

Psalm 96

Titus 2:11-14

Luke 2:1-14, (15-20)

Reckless Love

Selected reading

Luke 2:1-14, (15-20)

Theme

In the nativity of Jesus, we have experienced the extreme lengths to which the love of God will go in order to be with us. The love of God is not that of an aloof, distant deity. The love of God that meets us in the babe of Bethlehem is a dramatic, passionate incarnation of the divine love that seeks, saves, reaches, rescues, and embraces. This message of incarnate love is at the heart of the good news that is Jesus Christ.

Introduction to the readings

Isaiah 9:2-7

For the people of Israel, who once "walked in darkness," a great light has shined, a day has dawned, and they are given hope. In God's advents among us, it is as if poetry is demanded in order to bring to speech the great miracle that has been worked among us as God with us.

Titus 2:11-14
Now, at long last, the sweeping, hope-filled "grace of God has appeared" for all, says the letter of Paul to Titus in this, a traditional Christmas reading.

Luke 2:1-14, (15-20)
Luke tells the beloved story of the birth of Jesus in Bethlehem.

Prayer

Jesus, in your incarnation, you came near to us. You were not content to be God alone. You ventured out into our world so that we might come to you.

We give you thanks for your presence among us, standing beside us, standing with us. You took on our flesh, our humanity so that we might partake of your divinity.

Praise, praise, praise for your incarnation. Amen.

Encountering the text

The story that Luke tells is so beloved, so utterly familiar that we are apt to be in danger of losing its shocking power. To say that God, the creator of the universe, the one who set the stars in their courses, that this one is somehow fully present, birthed in a cow stable—well, it's a thought not found in any other religion.

Of all the shocking, demanding things that Christianity affirms, the nativity of Christ may be the most shocking. Most deities are known for their distance from humanity. This God—who is fully present in the babe at Bethlehem—is distinguished by God's propensity for closeness.

We will interpret this closeness, this nearness, as an aspect of the "passion" of God. This God is passionately engaged with us, so much so that this God is willing to suffer for us and with us. In a few months, as we contemplate the passion of Christ on the cross, we shall see to what extreme lengths a passionately engaged God will go to be with us.

Let us therefore see Luke's story of the nativity as a grand occasion for the church to stand before the wonder of a passionate God.

Proclaiming the text

A few years ago I was on a panel with the dean of a divinity school. During the course of the discussion, someone asked the dean, "What do you think is the most important virtue that you would like to instill in your seminarians; what is that main thing that will help them in their future ministry?"

Dean Jones replied, "Passion. I would like to see among our students passion, passion for God, a passion for people."

Wait a minute. I thought we were against passion! I know a popular preacher in the Midwest who was removed from ministry due to an inappropriate exercise of passion!

I thought that the virtue to be cultivated among professionals like doctors, lawyers, and others was distance, professional detachment, and objectivity, not passion.

It is important to care for people. It is also important to be careful in our caring. I was visiting a college campus where a student excitedly told me about the president of the college. This president really believes in being accessible to the students. On more than one evening a week, the president is known to be hanging out in the coffee shop, visiting the students, or sitting in the lounge of a dormitory, just hanging out. The student had been in the president's home a number of occasions.

And yet when I praised the actions and accessibility of this president, a faculty member told me that he thought the president's accessibility and availability were inappropriate. Why?

"He is supposed to be the president of the college, not the students' best buddy. There are times when the president must stand against the students, discipline the students, in order to lead the college. What happens then? After he has become such a buddy to the students, how can he be their leader?"

And I could see his point.

As a parent I learned that children don't want us to be their buddy, their best friend; they want us to be parents. It is important to be a caring parent, but a parent learns to be careful in the caring. A certain amount of parental distance is appropriate. You must be interested in the lives of your children, but you cannot allow yourself to become overly involved. You can't micromanage your children's lives. You can't always be standing next to them, with your arm around them. Sometimes you have to push against them.

And if this is true for a doctor, or a college president, or a parent, how much more so must this be true for God? Centuries before the birth of Jesus, the philosopher Aristotle insisted that God was immutable, that is "unchanging," untouched by the movements of the world. God cared but not overly cared. If God became a micromanager, if God got God's hands dirty every time the world shifted, then God wouldn't be God. God would be a being, much like us, tugged to and fro by various events. To be God is to be above all of that—immutable.

If God had feelings, argued Aristotle, then the perfection of God would be cheapened. God would be jerked around by every joy and pain of this world. This would be less than God.

There have been Christians who have accepted Aristotle's thoughts about the nature of divinity. But I don't see how. Not after what we have experienced this week. On this week, this holy night, this joyful nativity, this joyful time of incarnation, we see the lengths to which God will stoop in order to stand with us. We are at the "feast of the incarnation." Christmas. The Word has become flesh and dwells among us. Flesh. Among us.

This, in the words of the great theologian Karl Barth, is the time of God's supreme "condescension." God became a baby in a manger at Bethlehem.

And yet, Christians believe that the stooping, the enfleshment, the incarnation is a sign of God's greatest strength and is far from being a sign of God's weakness.

The fourth-century theologian Gregory of Nyssa said that the incarnation, God's intimate involvement with the world, was the supreme sign of God's "transcendent power."

That is a bit strange because the word *transcendent* means "distant, apart." And yet Gregory wrote that God's transcendent power is not so much displayed in the vastness of the heavens or the luster of the stars or the orderly arrangement of the universe or his perpetual oversight of it, as in his condescension to our weak nature.

The greatest power of God is in God's stooping to our weakness.

It takes a strong, secure love to stoop. If you have ever been in love, you know that one of the great challenges of love is just how much you ought to get involved. During a time of courtship, this is often the great challenge. Should we take the next step? How far should we go? Are we ready for this level of commitment? Will the other person return our love or reject it?

If you have ever reached out to someone in love, made yourself vulnerable, only to have that person reject your love, you know, it hurts.

You will be more careful the next time.

And yet it is of the nature of love—passionate, committed, real love—to risk. It takes great strength and great courage, too, to risk rejection. As you love, and lose, and love again, you learn to be more careful, more cautious.

We mere mortals dare not love with utter recklessness. I cannot care about every needy person I meet on the street asking for a handout. How do I know that this person will not take advantage of me? When a friend or child or spouse falls into addiction or crime, I cannot commit myself to them utterly without the risk of destroying myself in trying to help. Sometimes "tough love" is required, that is, loving at a distance.

I think that is what they taught us in the Boy Scouts' life-saving courses: "Drowning people tend to drown their saviors." Therefore, if you see someone in difficulty in the water, throw something to them, reach to them, but never jump in with them because drowning people tend to drown those who would help them. Drowning people are desperate.

As a pastor, I've often had the opportunity to think about that advice given during life-saving classes. You wade into the mysteries of someone else's life, particularly someone who is in great confusion, doubt, or pain, and it is easy to get hurt. Desperate people can be hard on their saviors.

Which makes all the more amazing what God has done this day, this night of nights, this Feast of the Nativity. God has become flesh and dwelt among us. God has become one of us. God, being so great, did not have to hold back. No risk is too great for this God, this God who loves without limits. In Christ's nativity we learn that none of us can ever sink to such depth that God's love will not reach down and stoop to save us. What sort of God would stoop so low as to be born to a poor family in a dirty stable, as our God?

As the theologian Karl Barth said, "God does not forfeit anything by doing this," but rather, enjoying a readiness to risk, for this "condescension, this act of extravagance, this far journey," God is different from us. What reckless love. Our God is a passionate, intensely involved God. Our word *passion* comes almost directly from the Latin word meaning "to suffer." Later in the church year, during Holy Week, the week of the crucifixion, we will focus on what has been called "Jesus's passion," that is, the time when Jesus suffered, the time leading up to the cross and on the cross. This was his passion, his time of suffering.

And yet, his passion did not have to wait until Good Friday when he hung on the cross. His passion, his risky, reckless willingness to suffer with us, even to suffer for us and to suffer because of us, is known from the first, in his beginning. This great God is so secure in God's greatness that God is willing to be jerked around by our needs, is willing to wade into the struggles of our human life, dares to stand beside us, dares to be there for us. True love, real love, deep love, is willing to take such a risk. "He was despised and avoided by others; a man who suffered, who knew sickness well. . . . He was despised, and we didn't think about him" (Isa 53:3).

His willingness to risk, his recklessness, and his willingness to suffer does not negate his divinity but proves his divinity. Only a limitless God could love in such a limitless way.

If you want a one-sentence definition of the meaning of Christmas, here it is—God is going to get back what belongs to God and will stoop to almost any level in order to get it.

And that's why we so passionately sing.

Relating the text

"The hardest lesson to learn, as a social worker, is not to get too deeply involved," said the young new social worker.

"My supervisor told me that, in dealing with people who have severe, chronic problems, if you get too involved, if you develop relationships with these people, you can take their troubles home with you. It will get to you. Before long, you won't be a social worker."

What the supervisor told her may be true, but I still find it sad, and whether or not it's true of social workers, the greatness of our God is that this God did not let it be true in God's dealings with humanity. The Word became flesh and dwelt among us.

In our proclamation of the word today we speak of the "passion," the suffering of Christ. One of the earliest heresies of the church was that theology that taught the "impassability" of Jesus—that Jesus did not suffer, that Jesus only appeared to suffer. Part of the argument was that, if Jesus were truly God's Son, then, being like God, Jesus could not be moved, could not be jerked around by the same struggles that afflict ordinary human beings. Jesus could not suffer.

The church rather strongly, and universally, condemned the notion of impassability, citing not only the stories about the suffering of Jesus on the cross, but also the incarnation. If God has indeed come among us in the flesh, then God must be able and willing to suffer or God would not be God in the flesh, our flesh.

A God whose love is less than this is no loving God at all, Christians have dared to believe.

A few years ago, I reread Dietrich Bonhoeffer's *Letters and Papers from Prison* and was thunderstruck by a letter I'd never noticed before. Bonhoeffer, who sat alone in an empty stone cell on Christmas Eve in 1943, was reflecting upon family that he had loved and lost, on his own fate, and on his separation from his family. He wrote these jarring, eloquent words:

"Nothing can make up for the absence of someone whom we love, and it would be wrong to try to find a substitute; we must simply hold out and see it through. That sounds very hard at first, but at the same time it is a great consolation, for the gap, as long as it remains unfilled, preserves the bonds between us. It is nonsense to say God fills the gap; he doesn't fill it, but on the contrary, he keeps it empty and so helps us to keep alive our former communion with each other, even at the cost of pain. . . . The clearer and richer our memories, the more difficult the separation. But gratitude changes the pangs of memory into tranquil joy. The beauties of the past are borne, not as a thorn in the flesh, but as a precious gift in themselves."

—Dietrich Bonhoeffer, *Letters and Papers from Prison* (New York: Simon and Schuster, 1997)

"What do I want for Christmas? How about a little brokenness? An empty place I dare not rush to fill? What about a sermon I'd better hear before I preach again—that God keeps the gap empty? Will the multitudes flock in to buy this message? I do not know, but at least the cruciform beauty of the gospel will be spoken truly, and perhaps more helpfully."

—James Howell, "What I Want for Christmas," *The Christian Century*, December 14, 2004

Christianity is a faith that transforms us, makes us better than we would be if we had not been gripped by this faith. Every Christian is, in a way, a "Christopher," literally a "Christ bearer," someone who is formed into the image of Christ. In my part of the world, the American South, sometimes we say of someone, "She is the spittin' image of her mother."

Some linguists say that the phrase *spittin' image* derives from the Southern dialect where spirit and image were contracted (some say corrupted) into one. To say that you are the spittin' image of your father is to say that you bear both his spirit and image. You bear the visible imprint of your parent.

Well, we actually believe that Jesus, in his incarnation, enables us to be his spittin' image.

.

Second Sunday after Christmas

Jeremiah 31:7-14 or Sirach 24:1-12

Psalm 147:12-20 or Wisdom of Solomon 10:15-21

Ephesians 1:3-14

John 1:(1-9), 10-18

The Real Meaning of Christmas

Selected reading

John 1:(1-9), 10-18

Theme

The incarnation means God in the flesh, God with us. The truth of the nativity is that though we could not come to God, God came to us, embraced us, and saved us in Christ. We don't have to work hard to attempt to climb up to God; God has in Jesus Christ climbed down to us.

Introduction to the readings

Jeremiah 31:7-14

Jeremiah calls Israel to celebrate Israel's deliverance by a gracious God.

Ephesians 1:3-14

God "chose us in Christ to be holy and blameless in God's presense before the creation of the world," claims the writer to the Ephesians, in order that we might praise "his glorious grace."

John 1:(1-9), 10-18
John's Gospel opens with the affirmation that though "no one has ever seen God . . . the only Son . . . has made him known."

Prayer

Almighty God, though we knew not how to come to you, you have come to us. You became incarnate and entered our world. Therefore, we gather in your name, coming into your presence because you came to us.

Enable us, in this time of worship, to renew our faith in you. Give us eyes to see you when you come near to us in worship so that we might see you in our everyday lives. Amen.

Encountering the text

Because this is Year C, the year of Luke's Gospel, we have been treated to a great deal of talk about the baby Jesus, the shepherds, and the infancy stories. This is the most beloved, most familiar of the Christmas narratives.

But what is the significance of these beloved stories? Is there meaning here beyond the beloved and the sentimental? Therefore, the common lectionary, with great insight, gives us John 1 for the Second Sunday after Christmas as an opportunity to go deeper than the sentimental and to engage in some serious theological reflection upon the meaning of the incarnation. The lectionary makes the first nine verses of John 1 optional, but we will want to include them because they are necessary for an understanding of some of the most important messages that are reiterated in John's Gospel.

Jesus existed "in the beginning." Of course, we are meant to hear an echo of an earlier text, Genesis 1:1. This is the "genesis" of the story of Jesus, but it is a beginning that begins, not with the birth of Jesus, but rather with the foundation of the world. Back before creation, when only God existed, Jesus existed.

John does not name the Christ "Jesus" until after he names him as "the Word." God's word is God's action and power. All God must do is to speak and there is a world (Gen 1:3, 6, 9). Moreover, in John's hands, the Word is not only from "the beginning" but also personally "with God." Literally John says that the Word was "with the God" and then intensifies the statement to say the Word "was [with no article] God." This is what has become "flesh and made his home among us."

Of course, a bold claim is being made here, a claim that goes against just about everything the classical Greco-Roman world believed in. Dualism— separation of "spirit" from "world" or "soul" from "body"—permeated everything that classical pagans believed about reality. Things were more real, Plato said, the higher one ascended, the further one got from the material and the fleshly. Matter was decadent, mortal, and finite; spirit was immortal, pure, and ideal. Therefore, the goal of Greek philosophy (which can also be thought of as Greek religion) was somehow to ascend out of the grubbiness of the fleshly and the material and rise into the spiritual and the immaterial.

John shows a linkage more with Hebrew thought than Greek thought on this issue of material and flesh. The Word, the Eternal Logos, has become flesh, stands before us, speaks to us, and reveals the deepest truth of God to us. This is the real meaning of Christmas.

Using the thought of Kierkegaard, I propose that our sermon this Sunday be a theological reflection of the significance of the incarnation: God with Us.

Proclaiming the text

We have gathered this Sunday after Christmas, this season of the incarnation, to come close to God. That's what Sunday is all about—coming close to God. That's what religion is all about—getting close to God—right?

But for us humans to get close to God is no easy task. The nineteenth-century Danish philosopher Søren Kierkegaard stressed that there was an "absolute qualitative distinction between humanity and God." By this he meant that

God is so much unlike humanity that there is little humanity can do to get close to God. In fact, Kierkegaard said that humanity, despite its declarations to the contrary, will do almost anything to avoid God.

Kierkegaard saw himself as a missionary to a non-Christian land that thought it was Christian—a land much like our land. Whenever Christianity was mentioned, the typical Dane replied, "Oh, Christianity, yes, yes, we know all about that. This is a Christian country." Christianity was synonymous with being born a Dane.

Kierkegaard felt that the average Dane of his day thought that Christianity was mainly about more information—information about the secret to a happier life, about the nature of God, or about a technique that would lead to greater happiness.

"Being a Christian," Kierkegaard said, "is much more than helpful information that enables us to get whatever it is we want out of life. Christianity is not a matter of discovering the correct answer and then repeating this answer back on a test. To do so was to cheat, to offer the answer without working it out for yourself."

More important, the "answer" that Christianity supplied to all of life's great questions was not more information but a person, Jesus Christ. And Jesus Christ came not to give us an exam about what information we know. Jesus came seeking disciples, saying, "Follow me," rather than simply, "Know all about me." What is needed is what Kierkegaard called "appropriation." Not intellectual assent but an engaged relationship.

Kierkegaard said that lots of people think that they are "religious" when their religion is actually a rather complex way of avoiding discipleship. That is, avoiding appropriation of the way of Jesus, avoiding relationship with the person of Jesus Christ.

Kierkegaard said that we have three main ways of avoiding the Christian life: the aesthetic, the ethical, and the religious.

The aesthetic stage of avoiding discipleship is the life of the romantic, the realm of feeling. The aesthete flits from flower to flower, sipping sweet nectar here and there, having various sorts of experiences but never actually committing. The aesthete enjoys the passion of the moment but not settling down anywhere, not having any continuity. The aesthetic is what being infatuated with someone is to being married to someone, the difference between momentary lust and committed marriage.

Today we live in an entertainment culture in which people would rather watch a sport from the bleachers—or better, from the living room sofa on television—than to actually play the sport themselves. We seek ever higher thresholds of emotional stimulation. The drug culture promises instant gratification now, being entertained and amused and savoring the joy of the transitory moment, rather than patiently waiting for something that endures. This is the aesthetic.

Another way of avoiding discipleship, according to Kierkegaard, is the ethical. This is the person who moves beyond the transitory thrill of the aesthetic with its momentary fulfillments. The ethical is the arena of human action, of good actions and bad actions, or people who become heroes, heroically launching out to do the right thing. I watch commercials for the US Army on television and I see the appeal of the ethical. You can step up and become somebody; you can contribute something to the larger good; you have it within your power heroically to create something good that endures. "An Army of one!" proclaim the commercials.

But the person who seeks more than momentary stimulation (the aesthetic) and who feels strangely unfulfilled by strenuous striving and moral effort (the ethical) may sometimes move to a third option—what Kierkegaard called "religiousness." This is the person who longs to move into the realm of the transcendent, the spiritual. But don't think that Kierkegaard considers the designation "religious" to be a compliment!

Lots of Americans today say that they are "spiritual" but not "religious." They seek to develop their spiritual nature, devising spiritual goals and spiritual methods, which are in reality a way of satisfying their own self-centered desire. They imagine a God who is the idealized image of their highest aspirations and wishes. They delve deeper and deeper into themselves, thinking that they are climbing up higher toward the divine. The "God" that they are imagining is but a creature of their own imaginations, something that is projected out there to reinforce their desires in here, something that gives importance to their own sense of importance and virtue.

Kierkegaard says that all three of these approaches conflict with Christianity. Christianity is the story of a God who came to us. Christianity is not the final stage of human aesthetic, ethical, or religious development. Rather Christianity involves the story of a God who became a human being and brought about our salvation, working out our salvation in great part by demolishing our idolatries.

Rummaging about in our own desires, focusing ever more deeply on our highest aspirations feels like a means of getting us closer to God. In reality, this is simply our subjectivity written large, "religiousness," which is a projection of ourselves.

If God is to be truly there for us, it will not be because of our wise choices, our heroic striving. It will be because of God. God must come to us, must take the initiative, and must be something qualitatively different than human wishes writ large.

And that's what John's Gospel says has happened to us at Christmas, the incarnation. God has come in the flesh, has come to us because we could not come to God.

To meet this God who comes to us in the flesh, to encounter the God who has taken the initiative to move toward us, presents us with a God who appears to have little to do with the fulfillment of our greatest desires. It is not so much the feelings engendered by the Christian faith that are different, but its content. We are face-to-face with a paradox—a peripatetic rabbi who is killed on a cross, God with us.

Christianity cannot prove itself on the basis of our expectations and our reason. It has a sort of improbability in which we discover that the truth about God is beyond our thoughts and desires, sometimes a defeat of our thoughts and desires.

Thus, we are confronted in the incarnation not by an idea, not by a philosophical system or a set of principles, but rather by an historical person. This is "good news": though we don't always feel godly or act in a godly way, God comes to us.

And this, my friends, is why these twelve days of Christmas are the very highlight of the Christian Year.

Good news: God is with us!

Relating the text

A distinguished businessperson told me that her first principle for running a successful business is hands-on management.

"You have got to be there," she said. "You must have your feet on the ground. The employees have got to trust that you really know for sure what's going on."

Think of Christmas, our yearly celebration of the incarnation, the feast of the nativity, as our celebration of the Trinity's hands-on management. We're in the "twelve days of Christmas," that time when the church attempts to come to terms with the God who, in the babe at Bethlehem, has come to terms with us. The nativity of the Christ is when God Almighty practiced the ultimate in hands-on management.

The management book by Marcus Buckingham, *First Break All the Rules*, is the result of a nationwide study of middle-level management. What qualities make for good managers? Buckingham and the Gallup Organization studied hundreds of managers, asking that question. Among the chief qualities of a good manager is presence. The book says that a major quality needed in good managers is being there. Hands-on management is essential.

Perhaps more interesting is that *First Break All the Rules* says that any manager who would change an organization must be there even more, even more actively present in the organization than if mere management of the status quo was the challenge. Change requires trust, and there can be no trust without presence.

So if God wants to change, to transform, to rebirth us, then it is necessary for that God to be with us, beside us, for us.

"And the Word became flesh and . . ."

Lovett H. Weems Jr. has written a book on what it takes for a pastor to be a leader of change in the congregation: *Take the Next Step.*

What does it take to have lasting change in a congregation? The first thing that leaders must create is trust. People give out of trust. People risk out of trust. They must have leaders who are creditable to them. "A leader wins trust slowly, but can lose it quickly," says Weems.

"Relationships are the first imperative for trust." Working on a fulfilling, common purpose, with all the struggle that entails, we can build strong relationships. And yet, Weems says that a recent study of pastors and clergy leadership shows that "the single most common source of difficulty for pastors was in their struggles around interpersonal relationships within the congregation." Building trust takes time and patience.

And here is a statement that is relevant to today's sermon theme: Weems says, "I am coming to believe that all leadership is local. There is a sheer presence required for effective leadership. Leaders must stay close to the people with whom they work and close to the details of what is happening in their setting of leadership. When too much time and emotional energy are being given to endeavors outside that setting of leadership, there is almost always the deterioration of the quality of relationship and leadership."

Weems says, "I have noticed how closely great leaders stay connected to their local settings of leadership." Credibility is built on relationships and relationships are built on presence. "Whom you would change," Martin Luther King, Jr. said, "you must first love."

—Lovett H. Weems Jr., *Take the Next Step: Leading Lasting Change in the Church* (Nashville: Abingdon Press, 2003), 29, 31

Dorothy L. Sayers offered a penetrating analysis of the relation of the divinity and humanity of Christ in a lecture delivered in England in 1940, later published in a collection entitled *Creed or Chaos?* (Sophia Institute Press, 1947). Using the rise of Nazism in Germany under Adolf Hitler during the 1930s as an example, she argues that claims to moral or cultural authority must be grounded in something more than in human notions of righteousness. They must be grounded in the intrinsic qualities of the person of Christ. Otherwise, Christ will be judged by our merely human moral and cultural principles instead of acting as their foundation and criterion. Sayers argued: "The question, 'What think ye of Christ?' lands the average man at once in the very knottiest kind of dogmatic riddle. It is quite useless to say that it doesn't matter particularly who or what Christ was or by what authority He did those things, and that even if He was only a man, He was a very nice man and we ought to live by His principles: for that is merely Humanism, and if the 'average man' in Germany chooses to think that Hitler is a nicer sort of man with still more attractive principles, the Christian Humanist has no answer to make.

"It is not true at all that dogma is 'hopelessly irrelevant' to the life and thought of the average man. . . . The central dogma of the Incarnation is that by which relevance stands or falls. If Christ was only man, then He is entirely irrelevant to any thought about God; If He is only God, then He is entirely irrelevant to any experience of human life. It is, in the strictest sense, necessary to the salvation and of relevance that a man should believe rightly the Incarnation of Our Lord Jesus Christ."

—Dorothy L. Sayers, *Creed or Chaos?* (Bedford, NH: Sophia Institute Press, 1947), 31

New Year's Day

Ecclesiastes 3:1-13
Psalm 8
Revelation 21:1-6a
Matthew 25:31-46

The Right Time

Selected reading
Ecclesiastes 3:1-13

Theme

How, then, ought we to live in the present time? Part of the difficulty in making decisions in the present is that we do not really know the significance of the time. Is this the right time or the wrong time, a time to move forward, or a time to stay where we are? We are finite, limited creatures who cannot always know everything, particularly everything about time. Therefore, we must trust God to care for us, even when the time is not right.

Introduction to the readings

Ecclesiastes 3:1-13
The writer of Ecclesiastes ponders time and its passage.

Revelation 21:1-6a
In a stunning vision, John sees a new heaven and a new earth.

Matthew 25:31-46
Jesus tells the parable of the last judgment.

Prayer

Lord, creator of night and day, author of the seasons of the year and their passage, Alpha and Omega, beginning and end: all the seasons of our lives are in the palm of your hand.

A generation comes, a generation passes, and you remain forever.

Lord, as we stand on this threshold of a new year, a new century, be with us. Preserve us in the days ahead as you have cared for us in days past. Calm our fears about the future, instill us with a quiet confidence in the present, with hope for what lies ahead.

Lord, we do not know what the future may hold for us, but we do know from your past faithfulness to us, that you hold the future. Amen.

Encountering the text

The lessons appointed for New Year's Day are about the only time that the church encounters this portion of Ecclesiastes. Today's beautiful cadences from Ecclesiastes give us an occasion to ponder time, more specifically the "right time."

Proclaiming the text

We have just lived through one of the happiest times of the year, Christmastide. And we are entering, what is for me, one of the most melancholy times of the year, New Year's.

At Christmas, all things brighten, glow with hope and cheer. Ebenezer Scrooge, who had spent his whole life in miserliness, is transformed at Yuletide. Aren't we all transformed?

Shakespeare recalls (in *Hamlet* act 1, scene 1) the tradition that at Christmas, time is transformed; for one glorious night, all time is redeemed by Christ's birth:

Some say that ever 'gainst that season comes
Wherein our Savior's birth is celebrated
The bird of dawning singeth all night long;
And then, they say, no spirit can walk abroad;
The nights are wholesome; then no planets strike,
No fairy takes, nor witch hath power to charm,
So hallow'd and so gracious is the time.

Christmas carols speak of a "holy night" when, at Bethlehem "the hopes and fears of all the years are met in thee tonight."

How different the time of New Year's. I find New Year's depressing, a non-event, dreamed up by restaurants and makers of Cold Duck. Another year has ended, and another has begun. You are one year older, one year closer to your end. Happy New Year.

New Year's Eve parties reveal the sadness of the season. Why do so many celebrate New Year's Eve by inebriation, unless to mask New Year's depression? Flip a page on the calendar. Whoopie!

And though we rarely have church on New Year's, we do this year. Our scripture is appropriately depressing, but perhaps instructive, poetry from the biblical book of Ecclesiastes: "There's a season for everything and a time for every matter under the heavens: a time for giving birth and a time for dying, a time for planting and a time for uprooting what was planted, a time for killing and a time for healing."

There was a time when I thought those words beautiful, sung in the sixties by the Byrds, "For everything, turn, turn, turn, there is a season, turn, turn, turn."

I thought these words beautiful, until I read them in context; and beautiful though they may be, they suddenly revealed themselves to be terribly dark.

"A time for crying and a time for laughing, a time for mourning and a time for dancing, . . . a time for embracing and a time for avoiding embraces, . . . a time for keeping silent and a time for speaking, a time for loving and a time for hating, a time for war and a time for peace."

See? Everything has its time, as the swift seasons roll along. After the flood in Genesis, God promised, "As long as the earth exists, seedtime and harvest, cold and hot, summer and autumn, day and night, will not cease" (Gen 8:22).

But such is not the conclusion of Ecclesiastes. If the scripture stopped here, all might be well. Time passes, the seasons roll along, a time for this, then a time for that. Nice.

After considering the passing of time, Ecclesiastes asks, "What do workers gain from all their hard work? I have observed the task that God has given human beings." Where does it all lead? And what good comes of it?

Look back on last year. You made twelve car payments. You painted the bedroom and the bathroom. You shampooed the downstairs carpet. But what gain had you from your toil? There is a time to live, yes. A time to write checks, a time to paint bedrooms, a time to care for the carpet, a time for Democrats, a time for Republicans, and a time to die.

And with that time, a January wind blows through this ancient poem. We're not in the time of the Hebrews, a time that begins somewhere and moves, steadily moves somewhere to its gracious fulfillment. This is Greek time, circular, without beginning, without end. A time to plant, a time to pull up what is planted, a time to laugh, a time to weep, a time to be born, a time to die. We are, in this circular, ceaseless ticking of time, not moving forward, onward, upward. We are the rat in the cage, breathlessly running, turning the treadwheel to nowhere. A time to plant, a time to pull up what is planted, a time to be born, a time to die, and what gain have the workers from their toil?

How old was the man who wrote these words? A youthful cynic, sitting alone in his dorm room, making sarcastic comments about the capitalist rat race. I heard one twenty-year-old say: "My old man gave his life for GM, sacrificed his health, his marriage, his happiness—and what good did it do him when GM laid him off?"

Are these the words of an embittered, resentful older person, cast aside by the company, sitting alone in an apartment where the telephone no longer rings? What gain have the workers from their toil?

Depressing? It's about to become more so.

"I have observed the task that God has given human beings. God has made everything fitting in its time, but has also placed eternity in their hearts, without enabling them to discover what God has done from beginning to end."

See? The writer isn't just talking about how time passes, boringly trudges, each season followed by another, a time for this and a time for that. The writer says there is a right time for every matter under heaven. There is a right time to speak and a right time to keep silent. It's a passage that ponders the problem of the right time.

One of Aesop's fables says, "It is a great thing to do the right thing at the right seasons."

The philosophers, particularly the Stoics, taught that there is a right time and wrong time for everything. Philosophy devoted itself to discerning the proper time. Isn't that what education is all about, whether you are a philosophy major or not? Training in discernment of the right time.

Everything, when you think about it, is a matter of proper timing. What am I seeking when I ask the advice of a stockbroker? Is this the time to buy, or is this the time to sell? A doctor told me that timing is everything in diagnosis. If the patient comes too early to the physician, the complaint is unspecific, difficult to pinpoint, vague. But if the patient waits too long, the illness has progressed too far, and it is too late for treatment.

Mark Twain said the difference between the right word and almost the right word "is the difference between lightning and a lightning bug." The same could be said about the difference between the right time and almost the right time.

Recently, I read Garry Wills's book on leaders (*Certain Trumpets: The Nature of Leadership*). It really impresses on you how a leader is not only someone who has great talents, but also someone who has great talents at the right time. Winston Churchill was the right man for England in the time of war, but he was the wrong leader in the time of peace. So we speak of the "man of the hour," or "an idea whose time has come."

There is a time to make peace, but Neville Chamberlain, earnestly desiring to make "peace in our time," even a time in which Hitler roamed, demonstrated that there is a time to make war. Chamberlain was the right man at the wrong time.

> There comes a tide in the affairs of men,
> Which, taken at the flood, leads on to fortune;
> Omitted all the voyage of their life,
> Is bound in shallows and in miseries.
> (William Shakespeare, *Julius Caesar*, act 4, scene 3)

In all things—birth, death, love, war, planting, and harvesting—there is the right time.

So, the philosophers sought those sensibilities whereby we might know the right time. Aristotle advises moderation as a key to knowing when the right time for action is. Today, we build computer models. We erect the Institute of Public Policy, hire economists, and consult astrologers. A whole pseudo-science has arisen—futurism—to predict and prognosticate, to know the right time. Is this the right time? So we work to figure out, to predict the right time.

Ecclesiastes believes that this is a lie—"vanity of vanities" (1:2 NRSV).

Ecclesiastes, while agreeing that there is a right time for everything, believes that only God can know it (3:11).

How is it possible to know the right time? This is the question of Ecclesiastes 3. Only God knows. It is beyond us to fully know the appropriate time for anything. God is God and we are not. We normally think of God's distance from us in terms of knowledge or power. Today, New Year's, Ecclesiastes bids us to think of the difference between us and God in terms of time.

As a teacher, I have learned that there is a "teachable moment," that sacred, unknown moment when the listener becomes a learner, the eyes light up— you can see it in the eyes—the heartbeat quickens, and it is the right time.

The way I figure it, about 80 percent of what I teach is the right information at the wrong time. Oh, to be granted the wisdom to know the right time, when the student is at last receptive, ready to learn that which I am longing to teach. But after two decades of teaching, I know as little how to predict or prepare for that time as I did when I first tiptoed into a classroom as a first-year student.

The older you get, the more you see how often you have done something right but at the wrong time. Either you pushed your children too soon or you missed a golden opportunity or you jumped forward prematurely when you should have stood still.

It would be wisdom to know the right time. But you can't. You are not God.

It would be great wisdom to always know the right time. But Ecclesiastes says that it is greater wisdom to face the facts, to accept our finite, creaturely status. Too much is outside our ability to control and therefore to predict. Time—the right time—is in God's hands, rather than in ours.

Thus, the New Testament writers often speak of Jesus as God's gift to us at the right time: "For while we were still weak, at the right time Christ died for the ungodly" (Rom 5:6; see also 1 Tim 2:6; 6:15).

Paul speaks of the fullness of time: "When the fullness of time had come, God sent his Son . . . in order to redeem . . . so that we might receive adoption as children" (Gal 4:4-5).

Jesus came at the right time, time that only God knows. In graciousness, God makes our feeble, fumbling time, about 80 percent of which is the wrong time, into his time. In certain, wonderful, gifted moments, God catches up our untimely actions into the right time.

Christmas is such a time—the right time. Mary and Joseph didn't know it as they went about paying taxes, visiting relatives, getting engaged, having babies, that it was the right time. God knew.

When a young couple comes to me, thinking about marriage, they often say, "We're waiting to be married until we're sure it's the right time." And I say, "Forget it. It's always the wrong time for marriage. You never have enough money, or security, or certainty. So it's best just to join hands, close your eyes, and take the plunge."

Poor things, many of them have so planned and programmed their lives that they expect all life to be a series of right actions at the right time. Even though they scored 1350 on the SAT, they can't know the right time.

But many who get married at the "wrong time" today can confess that, in God's great grace, their bad timing was transformed into God's right time. You go on about your life, as Ecclesiastes says, eating and drinking and taking pleasure in what time you have (3:12-13), and one day you look back and, wonder of wonders, it is the right time.

The truth I have to tell this New Year's is not one that modern people want to hear: you and I are not gods unto ourselves; we cannot know the right time. Yet, here is the good news: wherever life takes you in the coming year, the seasons of your life are held in God's hand; and by God's grace, it will be well.

Relating the text

At this time of the year, as the calendar changes, the Romans often paid special attention to their god Saturn, or, as the Greeks knew him, Cronos (Time). On the whole, they pictured Time as a rather benevolent deity except for one terrible, horrible trait. He devoured his own children!

Time is always and forever devouring his offspring, each day diminishing the very ones to whom he gave birth.

The Epiphany of Our Lord

Isaiah 60:1-6
Psalm 72:1-7, 10-14
Ephesians 3:1-12
Matthew 2:1-12

Epiphany

Selected reading
Ephesians 3:1-12

Theme

Christianity is a revealed religion. Our ideas about God are linked to God's self-revelation in Jesus Christ, through the power of the Holy Spirit. God is more than a projection of our collective human imagination. God has self-disclosed. Our faith rests upon Epiphany, upon God's loving willingness to reveal to us the nature and the ways of God.

Introduction to the readings

Isaiah 60:1-6

"Arise, shine, for your light has come, and the glory of the LORD has risen upon you," announces Isaiah the prophet to suffering Israel.

Ephesians 3:1-12

Paul speaks of the glory of the grace of God, and of Jesus Christ "in whom we have access to God in boldness and confidence through faith in him."

Matthew 2:1-12

Matthew tells the story of the journey of the magi to worship the baby Jesus.

Prayer

Show yourself to us, Lord. Surprise us with your true nature. Speak to us in today's sermon. Show us something in the reading of today's scriptures. Upset our settled experience. Challenge our preconceptions. Go ahead; show up to us when we least expect you. Manifest to us, in love, so that we might come to you. Epiphany to us. Amen.

Encountering the text

It's a rare occurrence to have Epiphany fall upon a Sunday. All of our assigned texts speak to some of the ways in which God self-reveals to us. The magi come to worship the babe at Bethlehem because they have seen a star that reveals to them that something wonderful has occurred in their world. They have been the recipients of an epiphany.

Paul writes to the church at Ephesus because he has seen something. He witnesses to an event that was not self-generated. He has been the recipient of revelation. Through Jesus Christ, we now have "access" to an otherwise inaccessible God. That access is a gift of God, not a result of our intellectual or spiritual achievement. Any "boldness and confidence" that we feel is based upon our faith in the trustworthiness of the gift of revelation that we have received.

Today we shall speak of a faith that is initiated by and rests upon Epiphany.

Proclaiming the text

No one in the congregation today has come to this faith on his or her own. There is no one here who is a "self-made Christian." You can't really discover the Christian faith; it is given to you, revealed to you as gift of God.

Today is Epiphany, January 6. It's a rare gift for Epiphany to occur on a Sunday. Let us take this as an invitation to explore our Christian faith as an epiphany from God. Christianity is a faith that you can't embrace on your own. We don't actually find this faith; it finds us. *Epiphany* means "revelation," and revelation is a gift.

Sometimes you hear people explain their presence in this faith community by saying, "Since I took Jesus into my heart," or, "When I decided that the Christian faith is the most helpful and meaningful of the world's religions." Whether they mean it this way or not, it makes faith sound like our achievement, our discovery, something that we attained through thoughtful thinking—our way into belief.

But Paul is clear; faith is a gift. Our appropriation of the Christian faith is more akin to the work of the star in shining upon the magi. In a great sense, they didn't come toward the star; it shined toward them. I think that's a good way to think about how we come to Christ: we come to him only because he came to us.

I'll admit that's not how we are accustomed to think about thinking. Most of us think by using some variation of the scientific method. We collect the facts, assemble the data, and then make a judgment on the basis of our experience.

But how do you think when you are thinking about something that is deeper, more conflicted than mere hard and cold facts? Above all, what if you are thinking about a subject (God) that is completely outside of and beyond your human experience? God is, by definition, outside of our human powers of comprehension. God isn't the sum of all the human experiences that we have had; God is an experience above and beyond our human experiences.

Many modern people, if the subject of God ever comes up in conversation, respond, "God? Oh, God is large, distant. Can't say anything for sure about God." It makes a person sound somewhat arrogant and dogmatic to say anything definitive about God. God is large, inaccessible, indescribable.

I heard a podcast of a famous liberal preacher. He began by ridiculing some of the theological controversies that have rocked the church in the past. He sarcastically described the christological debates of the fourth century, ridiculing all the fuss the church made over the two natures of Christ.

"How do they know?" he asked rhetorically.

His implication was that it was absurd for people to argue about matters that no one can possibly know. God is a subject beyond our human comprehension. Therefore, implied the preacher, it is ridiculous to debate ideas about God. One idea about God is about as valuable as another idea about God because all of our ideas about God are limited, false, and inadequate because of who we are and who God is. Only an incredibly arrogant, incredibly small-minded person could hope to say anything for sure about God.

Of course, we humans have limits in our thinking about these matters. Of course, God is greater than our puny human conceptions about God. Even after our best thinking about God, there is always more to be said about God, more to be known.

And yet the Christian faith is bold to assert that in Jesus Christ, God has graciously overcome our cognitive limits in regard to God. It is the nature of God, we are bold to proclaim, not only to be loving, powerful, and righteous, but also to be revealing. It is of the nature of God to do epiphany.

The Bible has all sorts of contradictory and conflicting ideas about many matters, including God. But the Bible is sure about one thing: this God reveals. From the first chapters of Genesis, we see that our God wants not only to create but also to communicate. All biblical material, everything that scripture has to say about the world and us begins with those fruitful words, "And God said . . ."

It's a somewhat hackneyed truism, but it's still true: a good marriage is a relationship that is characterized by frequent, meaningful, sometimes intense communication. I've heard couples criticize marriage counselors for having only one prescription for every marital problem—communicate! And yet all of us know that every human relationship, including marriage, thrives on communication. Friendship is utterly dependent upon people willing to reveal themselves to other people.

And what is true of human relationships is even more true of divine-human relationships. For there to be a relationship between God and us, then God must communicate. God must reveal. And Christians believe that in Jesus Christ, in his life, work, death, and resurrection, we have seen as much of God as we ever hope to see.

I'm not describing some strange phenomenon when I speak of God's propensity to epiphany. I think your presence here this morning proves my Epiphany Sunday point. Despite any of your modern limitations, despite the limitations in your religious instruction or your knowledge of the Bible or your personal defenses, God has gotten through to you.

So often we talk about our faith as if faith were our means of getting to God. We say, "I'm searching for something more in my life." Or, "Since I found Jesus, I . . . " Trouble is, that puts the entire burden of divine-to-human communication on us, and, as we've said, we are limited in our ability to conceive of God.

No. As today's scripture shows, Christ is our "access to God." We can't climb up to God; God climbs down to us. Somehow, someway, God got to you. Call it a strange coincidence, call it a mystical experience or a still small voice, call it "Epiphany."

One evening we were discussing why people believe or don't believe as Christians. Some in the group cited some theological assertion of the Christian faith that they found to be particularly compelling. Others said they were raised in a Christian home where the Christian faith just seemed natural.

Then someone said simply, "God showed up." She explained, "I wasn't looking for God, but, to my surprise, God was looking for me." Even though I didn't ask, God showed up.

I thought she got it just right. Our faith, our relationship to God is God's self-assigned task. God shows up. Epiphany.

Relating the text

The Long Search was the title of a TV series a number of years ago, a sort of documentary, as I recall, that was designed to look at the role of religious faith in human life. Thinking about it, I noted that they didn't call the program *The Great Discovery* or *How God Gets to Us*.

We enjoy thinking of ourselves as perpetual searches, seekers, and travelers. We like to think that we are curious seekers.

But what if Epiphany is true: God is searching, seeking us?

As a young pastor in Switzerland, theologian Karl Barth said that we limited, earth-bound, sinful mortals were unable to speak of God. This posed a terrible dilemma for him as a preacher! After all, preachers are supposed to stand up on a weekly basis and say something about God. Barth thus categorized the poor preacher's weekly dilemma: "O little man, how dare you presume to have the word 'God' on your lips?"

Barth said that to preachers! Then the great theologian said, "Only God can speak of God."

We can't speak of God and yet we must speak of God. It's an insoluble dilemma.

And the grand Epiphany claim is that in Jesus Christ, God has indeed dramatically, specifically spoken to us. God took the first step toward us. We have not the means to know what to say to God, so God said something decisive to us: Jesus Christ.

It's so easy for us preachers to think of preaching as an activity that we do. We preachers go to school for years in order to be able to construct a sermon. We learn skills of biblical interpretation and rhetorical strategies because preaching is what we are called to do.

But what if preaching is something that God does? What if it's not really a sermon until God uses the sermon to speak God's word to God's people?

We preachers frequently stress that Christians ought to be givers. In our worship we always have a time of offering, a time to give, and well we should. "It is more blessed to give than to receive," as we often say.

And yet, on Epiphany, perhaps we ought to recover a sense that Christians ought to be good receivers. It is blessed to give; it is also blessed to be open enough and willing enough to be surprised in order to receive. All that we have of our faith has been that which was received. None of us were born Christian. Someone had to tell this faith to us, had to live it before us. Someone had to give the faith to us.

And yet, we also had to receive the faith, to be receptive to the notion that God might be other than the God we had previously conceived. Anyone who attempts to be open to a living God must be open to surprise, willing to be shocked by what a free, sovereign, and living God might have to say to us. We must be free, not only to hear the word of God but also to obey what we hear. In other words, we must be free to be receivers as much as givers.

This is one of the great challenges of practicing a revealed religion.

Today's Epistle speaks of the "confidence" and the "boldness" that we have through Christ. In the context of revelation I think that Paul would say because of the epiphanic nature of God, we preachers may be bold in what we preach, confident that what we preach is not only sometimes helpful, encouraging, and compassionate but also true. We talk about reality, the truth all the way down, the way things really are. That which God has shown us is true. Of course, there are many instances in the world that cause one to doubt the truth of what we proclaim. Yet we believe that God has actually revealed to us the truth, a truth that we could not have accessed on our own—not a fantasy or wish projection, but the truth.

We may not fully understand that which is revealed to us. We may spend the rest of our lives trying to make sense of what we have been shown of God by God, yet we have confidence that what we are being shown, whether we fully understand it or not, is true.

The late John Silber, former president of Boston University, told the story of how he, as a first-year student at Yale Divinity School, upon learning that Martin Buber, great Jewish philosopher, was to speak at Yale, got himself selected to take Dr. and Mrs. Buber back to the airport.

On the trip back, with Mrs. Buber sitting in the backseat, John Silber asked, "Dr. Buber, if I asked you to prove to me that God exists, could you do so?"

Buber asked Silber, "Are you asking this from a deep concern to know God, or only out of curiosity?"

Silber replied, "I guess out of curiosity."

Buber replied, "How bourgeois," and turned away and never spoke again.

John Calvin taught that we cannot truly know who we are before we know who God is. Calvin declared: "Without the knowledge of God there is no knowledge of self . . . it is certain that man never achieves a clear knowledge of himself unless he has first looked upon God's face, and then descends from contemplating him to scrutinize himself."

Calvin went on to illustrate:

"For it is in broad daylight we either look down upon the ground or survey whatever meets our view round about, we seem to ourselves endowed with the strongest and keenest sight; yet when we look up to the sun and gaze straight at it, that power of sight which was particularly strong on earth is at once blunted and confused by a great brilliance, and thus we are compelled to admit that our keenness in looking upon things earthly is sheer dullness when it comes to the sun. So it happens in estimating our spiritual goods. . . . Then, what masquerading earlier as righteousness was pleasing in us will soon grow filthy in its consummate wickedness. What wonderfully impressed us under the name of wisdom will sink in its very foolishness. What wore the face of power will prove itself the most miserable weakness. That is, what in us seems perfection itself corresponds ill to the purity of God." (*Institutes* 1.1.2)

"If there were no God, there would be no atheists."

—G. K. Chesterton

First Sunday after the Epiphany
The Baptism of Our Lord

Isaiah 43:1-7
Psalm 29
Acts 8:14-17
Luke 3:15-17, 21-22

Jesus: God and Humanity Meet

Selected reading
Luke 3:15-17, 21-22

Theme
John the Baptist introduces Jesus the Christ to the world. He gives a short preview of what Jesus does—transforms the world in the name of the reign of God. Jesus arrives to rock our world, to bring dramatic, personal, and cosmic change. To meet Jesus, says John, is to meet one who leaves nothing, and no one is the same as before.

Introduction to the readings
Isaiah 43:1-7
Isaiah proclaims God's love for Israel, God's great promise: "Don't fear, I am with you."

Acts 8:14-17
Peter and John pray for the Samaritan converts that they might receive the gift of the Holy Spirit.

Luke 3:15-17, 21-22
Luke tells the story of the baptism by John of Jesus in the Jordan. In his baptism, Jesus's unique identity is revealed.

Prayer

Lord Jesus, you come to us as one unknown. All of our expectations for who God is are being overturned by your appearance among us. All our images of humanity are also being overturned by you. Give us the grace, Lord Jesus, to receive you in your incarnation, to submit our notions of God to your definition, to follow you wherever you lead. Give us the courage to receive you, to have our cherished definitions of humanity and divinity dramatically rearranged. Reveal yourself to us as you are rather than as we would have you to be. Amen.

Encountering the text

All of the Gospels introduce the ministry of Jesus through John the Baptist. John the Baptist signifies what is important and world-changing about Jesus. In Luke's account of his baptism, in this brief narrative, everything important and deeply significant about Jesus is revealed upfront. John preaches to the expectant multitudes about the coming of a Messiah. But when the Messiah shows up as Jesus, expectations are overturned and people are forced to re-think their notions of messianic deliverance.

We see a tightly packed presentation by Luke, here at the beginning of Jesus's ministry, of the twofold identity of Jesus. Here is obviously a human being who stands in the Jordan water with his cousin, John the Baptist. Yet here is also the Lamb of God who takes away the sins of the world. Here is one whom John hails as one in the tradition of the prophets of the Hebrew scriptures. Here is the one who, in his baptism, is designated by a heavenly voice as God's very Son.

Here is the bifocal Epiphany—the manifestation, the revelation of Christ. His divine authorization and commendation, the peculiar quality of his reign—all of that is here along with his human presence.

Let us allow John to introduce Jesus to us this Sunday, the one whom his followers hail as both fully human and fully divine.

Proclaiming the text

John the Baptist is out in the wilderness preaching. We met John back in Advent. He reappears now, during Epiphany. And that is as it should be because John is our first epiphany, our first vivid manifestation of who Jesus is.

In linking John the Baptist and Jesus, Luke puts Jesus in the line of the prophets of old. The prophets also spoke fierce words of truth. The prophets also called upon Israel to repent and change its ways. John does that. In fact, John has always been thought of as the last of the prophets of the Hebrew scriptures.

But John says that though many people come out to the wilderness to hear him, and though he is renowned for his preaching, there is one coming after him who is "mightier" than John. John preaches judgment; the mighty one coming after him will be the judge. John baptizes with water; the one coming after him will baptize with fire.

Jesus stands in the Jordan River humbly submitting to John's baptism. Jesus is also praying, a gesture in which someone bows and humbly submits to God. Jesus is clearly a human being, showing the humility that is appropriate for human beings in the presence of God.

And yet when Jesus is baptized by John something happens that occurs in none of John's other baptisms: the "heaven was opened" and "the Holy Spirit came down on him" and there was "a voice" that came from heaven that proclaims, "You are my Son, whom I dearly love."

Luke is here saying, right at the very beginning of his Gospel, that Jesus is definitely a full human being, and Jesus is also the long-awaited Messiah. He is fully God and fully human.

When the first people encountered Jesus, they had two things to say about him: he is really a person, an obvious human being, and he is the fullness of God. His followers looked at him and, very early on, began using the most effusive, extravagant words to describe him. They told stories about him, just like the story Luke has told us this morning. In later years, some dear scholars (some of them members of the Jesus Seminar that worked a few years ago) may have called Jesus a "great man of history" or "a fine moral teacher," but nobody said that about him who met him.

What people said about Jesus from the earliest days was that Jesus was God. More even than an angel, he was God's Son, God's Beloved, the savior of the world.

The New Testament is a report on how Jesus's followers quickly moved to the acclamation that this Jesus from Nazareth, who lived briefly, died violently, and rose unexpectedly, was in complete union with God. God does what Jesus does. God is one with who Jesus says God is. Jesus is not just an aspect of God, a messenger of God. Jesus is the one whom we acclaimed him to be here on Christmas: God with us.

The modern idea that the followers of Jesus, after he was crucified, let their feelings get the best of them and got carried away by their grief into believing that Jesus was divine is absurd. You just can't get from *there* (Jesus was a great moral teacher, a deeply spiritual person, or some other exalted by completely human attribute) to *here* (the church spread out across every nation and race, Christians eager to die for Jesus in order to tell everyone about Jesus).

The only plausible explanation for the martyrs, for the church, for the Gospel of Luke, for the presence of this congregation gathered here two thousand years later is that Jesus was indeed a great moral teacher, a deeply spiritual person, and God's Son, the Beloved, the Messiah in whom the fullness of God was pleased to dwell, God not holding anything back. There is no lack of the man Jesus in God and no lack of divinity in the man Jesus.

Luke says that "the people were filled with expectation" wondering if John was the Messiah. Jesus clearly caused problems for the expectations of lots of people (you hear that story in the rest of Luke's Gospel) because in Jesus, people got a redefinition of God and a redefinition of humanity. Later, in John's Gospel when Jesus stoops and washes his disciples' feet (on his way to die for them and the world), God is being redefined as God, not just in power and glory but also in service and suffering weakness.

Thus when someone asked me recently, "How can you believe in God with all the suffering and heartache in the world?" I suspected that the questioner was working with a limited idea of "God." God is that "supreme being" who is always in control, whose essence is unconstrained power, rather than the God who was in Jesus Christ reconciling the world through service, suffering, sacrifice, and love—not the most appealing of messages in a culture that worships (not Jesus, but) self-sufficiency and potency.

The aggravating things about being a Christian are those times when someone says, "I don't believe in God," to try to find a nice way to respond, "Tell me who is the God you don't believe in because I bet we Christians also don't believe in that God."

Luke says that the one who stands knee deep in muddy Jordan water, being baptized by John, is none other than God's Son, the Beloved. And if you believe that, then you will have some rather odd (by much of the world's standards) views of God.

Beginning that day in the Jordan River Jesus redefined both "humanity" and "divinity" so that never again could people think "human being" or "God" without thinking of Jesus. Never again could anybody say that humanity was without hope, rotten, and of no account after God Almighty became present in this Jew from Nazareth. Never again could anybody say that God was distant, threatening, fierce, and overpowering after God was revealed to be who Jesus is.

The church eventually expended much effort to guard the mystery of the comingling of humanity and divinity in Jesus. You will note that Luke offers no explanation of Jesus's divinity/humanity. Rather Luke testifies to what everyone who followed Jesus eventually knew—Jesus Christ was fully God and fully human. God was in Christ (2 Cor 5:19). To see Jesus is to see God, the father of Jesus (John 14:9).

Sorry, if you prefer your God to be with you as a remarkably effective moral teacher or wise sage. When Jesus was baptized the heavens opened, the Holy Spirit descended, and there was an identifying voice. In Jesus, humanity/divinity met. A domesticated Jesus, whose strange, inexplicable mix of humanity and divinity has somehow been made simpler—either human or divine—a Jesus easier for us to handle, is no Jesus at all. At a minimum, intellectual humility is required, a willingness to let God be God incarnate, close to us, rather than the simpler God we thought up on our own. Sometimes the strange, rational impossibility just happens to be true; God was in Christ reconciling the world to Godself.

Sorry, if you prefer your God to come at you in an exclusively spiritual, inflated, pale blue, and fuzzy vagueness hermetically sealed from where you actually live. When Jesus was baptized, he stood in solidarity with all of us sinners, submitting to baptism as we must submit to baptism and to God if we are to be brought back to God. In Jesus, divinity/humanity embraced.

It's a lifelong task to think about God with all the complexity that God is present to us in Jesus, fully human and fully divine. Sometimes people ask, "Can I really trust the Bible, seeing that it is a thoroughly human product, full of all the errors and contradictions that characterize any human endeavor?" The implication is that if scripture has any human taint, shows any creaturely weakness, the Bible can't be trusted to talk about God. But what if Jesus is true? What if we don't know anything for sure about God except that which is shown to us by the God/human Jesus? What if Jesus really is fully human and fully divine? Then where on earth would we expect to know anything about God except through a medium that is human? God came to us as we are, met us where we live—in the human words of scripture that become the very voice of God—in the man Jesus who becomes the very presence of God.

And so this Sunday of the Baptism of Jesus is an epiphany. God is not exactly the God we presumed God to be; God is whoever speaks on behalf of, and who is fully represented to us in Jesus of Nazareth. And we are not exactly the lost, forlorn, irredeemably sinful ones we thought ourselves to be; God comes to us, stands with us, prays for us, speaks to us, holds nothing back from us in Jesus of Nazareth, God's Son, the Beloved.

So toward the beginning of another year, at the beginning of Luke's Gospel, in our first glimpse of Jesus, nothing is held back. We are told everything that is absolutely essential to know about Jesus. The curtain is pulled back; Jesus's full identity is made manifest to us. The greatest mystery at the heart of the Christian faith is exposed through a voice from heaven, so that we in our time might adore and worship: "You are my Son, whom I dearly love."

Relating the text

I think of two places in Luke/Acts where the crowds, when confronted with the claims of God, ask, "What then should we do?" One is here at Jesus's baptism and the other is in Acts 2 after Peter preaches on Pentecost.

Note that John the Baptist does not ask the tax collectors and soldiers to give up their occupations. The early church would demand that soldiers stop being soldiers in order to baptize them, but John the Baptist does not. In other words, they are not asked to quit what they are doing; they are rather asked to make a new beginning.

"What should we do?" This is the great beginning. They do not fully repent, they are not fully there, but they are on the way by asking this crucial, self-critical question, "What then should we do?"

Remember that Jesus never asks anybody to simply think about him or agree with him. He asks people to follow now, to do what he said. And that's what these crowds asked, "What should we do?"

I think this implies that the church makes a big mistake in presenting the Christian faith as a set of principles, a set of ideas to think about, or a set of convictions to be mastered. We ought to present the Christian faith as a set of practices, things that we do, a way of life, something that we take up and follow, a way of walking behind Jesus of Nazareth, the Lamb of God, who takes away the sin of the world.

"You brood of vipers!" John the Baptist said to them. "Who warned you to escape from the coming wrath? You'd better prove your repentance by bearing the right sort of fruit! And you needn't start thinking to yourselves, 'We have Abraham as our father.' Let me tell you, God is quite capable of raising up children for Abraham from these stones! The axe is already taking aim at the root of the tree. Every tree that doesn't produce good fruit is to be cut down and thrown into the fire."

The road, the water, the fire, and the axe. Four powerful symbols set the scene for where the story of Jesus really starts.

Think first of a police motorcade sweeping through a city street. First there appear motorcycles with flashing blue lights. People scurry to the side of the road as they approach. Everybody knows what's happening: the king has been away a long time and he's come back at last. There are two large black cars with a flag at the front, one of which contains the king himself. By this time the road is clear; no other cars are in sight; everyone is standing still and watching, waving flags, and celebrating.

Now take this scene back two thousand years into the hot dusty desert. The king has been away a long time, and word goes around that he's coming back at last. But how? There isn't even a road. Well, we'd better get one ready. So off goes the herald, shouting to the people of the desert: The king is coming! Make a road for him! Make it good and straight!

That message had echoed through the life of the Jewish people for hundreds of years by the time of John the Baptist, ever since it was first uttered in Isaiah 40. It was part of the great message of hope, of forgiveness, of healing for the nation after the horror of exile. God would at last come back, bringing comfort and rescue. Yes, John is saying, that's what's happening now. It's time to get ready! The king, God himself, is coming back! Get ready for God's reign! And John's striking message made everyone sit up and take notice. In today's language they saw the blue flashing lights and stopped what they were doing to get ready.

First impressions are everything. That's what I recall a management consultant saying to a group of us pastors. She stressed the crucial importance of a pastor's very first days in a new church.

"Take great care about what you say in your first few weeks," she warned. "First impressions tend to be much more powerful over people's imagination than second and third impressions."

Second Sunday after the Epiphany
RC/Pres: Second Sunday in Ordinary Time

Isaiah 62:1-5
Psalm 36:5-10
1 Corinthians 12:1-11
John 2:1-11

Some Saw Glory

Selected reading
John 2:1-11

Theme
We are forever in danger of trivializing the gospel, of reducing Jesus as a means to our ends. Yet, he is Lord. He will not be contained or managed by us. As glorious Lord, he intrudes among us, transforming our trivialized church into a sign of his glory, bringing us face-to-face with the living God.

Introduction to the readings

Isaiah 62:1-5
Israel's vindication by God will shine before the nations like the light of dawn.

1 Corinthians 12:1-11
Paul speaks to the church at Corinth about spiritual gifts.

John 2:1-11

Jesus attends a wedding at Cana and turns water to wine.

Prayer

Lord Christ, come among us in your glory. Forgive us all the ways we have trivialized and scaled down your glory. Forgive us the ways in which we have used you for our purposes rather than allow you to use us for your work.

We have come before you in worship, daring to ask you to stand before us in your glory.

Give us the grace to allow you to behold your glory, to allow you to rule, to speak, to be the very presence of God among us.

Lord, change our church from its predictable, staid, comfortable, merely human ways, into a place of your divine glory. Amen.

Encountering the text

What an odd way to begin a Gospel! John begins Jesus's ministry at, of all places, a wedding party. Luke takes Jesus (as we will see next week) to a synagogue to start things rolling. But here is Jesus at the most ordinary of locations—a wedding reception.

And what an odd thing to do at a wedding reception! Wouldn't a more appropriate "sign" have been a healing or some work of compassion? Not this water into wine. Yet behind the story is a claim. Jesus is Lord. He is Lord wherever he intrudes among us, bringing his glory into our ordinary places. Note that, in the story, Jesus is in command. He will not be jerked around, even by his mother. He speaks and glory breaks out, strange things happen—life.

Against our attempts to reduce Jesus to more manageable proportions, to scale down his good news to our size, John's Jesus strides in upon the scene in majesty and mystery. Whenever Jesus arrives, even at a wedding reception, glory breaks forth.

In Jesus, we are reconciled to God. Not because of what we do, but because of who he is. Glory.

Proclaiming the text

Let's say that we are here this morning in an attempt to "get right with God." Isn't that what the church is about? To bring us close to God? Yet John's Gospel opens the story of Jesus with a strange account of how Jesus comes close to us, coming to us at a wedding reception in Cana of Galilee. John says that after Jesus got through with them that day, some saw glory, many believed. What can we see in this story?

First of all, the amount of water is huge—about 120 to 130 gallons. What were they doing with all that water? The water is for the Jewish rites of purification. The Jews have many such rites for making oneself pure. Here, in this story, there are 120 to 180 gallons of water present for the ritual of purification.

The ritual of purification was strictly regulated within the Torah. This was not water for cleansing but rather water as a sign of preparation for worship. Worship is when we all come together to meet God, to get close to God, to be with God. And the Torah declared that one needed to get clean, by ritual cleansing, in order to get close to God in worship. In fact, in the Talmud, it is specified how much water is needed for the rites of purification. Only about a cup of water was necessary to purify a hundred men. But here, in this story, there is well over a hundred gallons of water! That is enough water to purify the entire world!

Get it? Jesus is that purifying water that is available in enough quantity for the whole world.

The water in the jars was water used for the rites of purification, so that people would be ready to worship. As people came into the wedding, into this time of worship, they would dip their hands into the water and purify themselves, making themselves ready for this sacred event. The meaning of the story is not that Jesus took plain drinking water and turned it into delightful wine. Rather, the issue here is purification, making oneself right with God.

Justification. How does one get close to God? Jesus has, in this story, transferred us from one means of getting close to God—the rituals of purification as specified in Torah—to himself. He has become, in this story, the new path to God.

The steward notes that, in most of these affairs, the good stuff is never saved until the last. Now John is making the same claim about Jesus. Throughout the history of Israel, God sent the great patriarchs and the prophets. But now, in Jesus, the best is being saved until the last. Earlier John claimed that John the Baptist was former; Jesus is later and greater. You get these comparisons throughout the Gospel of John. Moses was the former; Jesus is the latter and the greater.

In verse 10, the story seems to stop. The narrator steps in and says, "This is the first of his signs." In John's Gospel, a sign is not a miracle as we sometimes describe miracles. It is not just some reversal of natural processes. A sign is something that points beyond itself to something else. If you look in your rearview mirror and see a flashing blue light, and you say, "There is a police officer behind me," you do not really mean that. What you mean is that this is a sign that a police officer is on the way. The sign precedes the thing itself, points beyond itself to the real thing.

This, Jesus's miracle at Cana, is said to be the first of his signs, a sign pointing to his glory. When they saw the sign, they saw glory. Suddenly, the wedding party was transformed into an occasion of revelation, a moment when some were brought close to God.

I believe this story is about the cross, for in the Gospel of John, Jesus's hour of glory is when he is "lifted up" on the cross. John says this wedding was on the third day. The water is turned into wine, his blood for all people.

We're here because we want to be close to God. But how can we in our deceit, our sin, our blindness? How can we come close to God? The cross stands as God's act of coming close to humanity even in the face of humanity's self-designed attempts at salvation. In other words, this story speaks about Jesus as Messiah, Jesus in his messianic form, Jesus as God among us. And yet, I fear that the contemporary church is guilty of frequently using Jesus for non-messianic purposes.

The other day, I saw a sign advertising a garage. It showed a man with a gigantic wrench ready to fix your car. At the bottom of the sign it said, "A Christian business." The word *Christian* has become an adjective, modifying the noun, *business*. Christ is judged basically on the virtue of his utility, his helpfulness in getting things that we want, things that we wanted before we met Jesus. This is nonmessianic use of Jesus.

So we come to church hoping to find self-esteem, or peace of mind, or for help making it through next week. All of that may happen here. But it's not the main event. The main event is to come here hoping to meet or—more to the point of today's Gospel—hoping to be met by God.

Note in the story that Jesus is clearly in command of the situation. He gives the orders. He makes the sign. The Gospel of John presents Jesus as the Messiah who brings us close to the glory of God. Jesus bursts in as Messiah, devastating all of our self-salvations. In his temptation in the wilderness, he was tempted by Satan to turn stones into bread. Now, we want him to turn water into wine. Turning water into wine is impressive. Yet it is trivial, in itself. When you think about it, this is a rather trivial way to begin a Gospel—at an ordinary wedding reception with ordinary problems like the wine running short.

But by the end of the story, all of this has been swept away. Glory breaks out. Our trivial usages of Jesus are overcome and the Messiah shines through.

Is the church's Jesus merely the church's errand boy? Is Jesus the creation of the church, or is the church the new creation of Jesus?

Jesus is among us, not to provide wine, but to provide life, glorious life.

Relating the text

"Mainstream churches tend to assume that they naturally provide religious meaning. And in the false security of this establishment presumption, they no longer give careful and primary attention to this most critical (and problematic) function of church life. . . . People expect churches to be religious institutions, not social-service organizations or social clubs. . . . Mainstream churches have appropriated that 'don't ask, don't tell' approach to God that guides public discourse."

—David A. Roozen and Kirk C. Hadaway, *Rerouting the Protestant Mainstream* (Nashville: Abingdon Press, 1995), 76

The great French writer, George Sand, said of a friend: "He was a man who always longed for the pearl of great price during an age when people contended themselves with fake jewelry."

Evangelical writer David Wells has been critical of contemporary evangelical attempts to use God for our purposes in a therapeutic culture. Wells reminds us that Christian character cannot be built if we "exchange enduring qualities for a spate of exciting new experiences," if we are "guided by a compass of circumstance rather than belief." As Wells warns, a Christian faith that is "conceived in the womb of the self is quite different from the historic Christian faith. It is a smaller thing, shrunken in its ability to understand the world and to stand up in it."

—David Wells, *No Place for Truth* (Grand Rapids: William B. Eerdmans Publishing Company, 1993), 180

In the much-acclaimed Canadian film *Jesus of Montreal*, a group of young actors, none of whom are religious, at least at the beginning of the movie, take up the production of a play about Jesus—not the Jesus of the first century, but that of Montreal and the twentieth century. Gradually, in doing the play, in performing the roles, they become the characters they are portraying. It is as if the risen Christ comes to them, disrupts their lives, changes them, brings them glory!

After the resurrection scene, an actress says to the audience: "They were ready to die for their convictions. They too were crucified, beheaded, stoned. They were steadfast; Jesus awaited them in his kingdom. . . . They personified hope, the most irrational and unyielding of emotions. Mysterious hope . . . that makes life bearable, lost in a bewildering universe." Doesn't the same happen to us Christians? In acting as if we were disciples, true followers of Jesus, Jesus comes among us, changes us, makes us more than we could have been without him, and we, even we, see glory.

Yale theologian H. Richard Niebuhr offered a pithy summary of liberalism's message when he characterized in the following terms: "A God without wrath brought men without sin into a kingdom without judgment through the ministrations of a Christ without a Cross."

—H. Richard Niebuhr, *The Kingdom of God in America* (Chicago: Willett, Clark and Co., 1959), 193

"One who recovers from sickness, forgets about God."

—Ethiopian proverb

Third Sunday after the Epiphany
RC/Pres: Third Sunday in Ordinary Time

Nehemiah 8:1-3, 5-6, 8-10
Psalm 19
1 Corinthians 12:12-31a
Luke 4:14-21

People of the Word

Selected reading
Luke 4:14-21

Theme
Jesus came preaching. He launched God's promised revolution and inaugurated the God's kingdom on the basis of words. Even today, this Sunday in your church, the revolution continues; the realm of God takes form through preaching. Preaching is a primary means whereby God loves God's people through words.

Introduction to the readings
Nehemiah 8:1-3, 5-6, 8-10
During the rebuilding of the walls in Jerusalem, after the exile, a scroll is discovered. All of Israel gathers before the water gate and listens to the reading of the long-forgotten law.

1 Corinthians 12:12-31a
Paul writes to the congregation at Corinth, speaking to them about the diversity of gifts within the church.

Luke 4:14-21
Jesus returns to his hometown synagogue at Nazareth where he is handed a scroll. He reads and interprets the faith of Israel. The congregation will soon respond with anger.

Prayer

Lord Jesus, we are convened today because you have called us together. Each of us has, in some way, heard your word and sensed your vocation. Speak to us, Lord; speak to us so that we might speak for you in the world. Give us the right words to testify to your reign, and then give us the courage to preach that the world might know your name, might hear your summons, and come to your salvation. Amen.

Encountering the text

During renovations of the Jerusalem city wall, after the people returned from exile, a scroll is found. It is the lost scripture of Israel, lost and forgotten during the disastrous years of exile. The people are assembled and all day long they listen to the rediscovered word of God. As they listen, they are helped to discover the great gap between their lives and God's will for their lives.

Jesus returns to his hometown synagogue. What do his neighbors do? They hand him a scroll and ask him to read it to them. This is what Israel does in the synagogue.

We will have a good bit to say about the context and meaning of today's Gospel lesson from Luke in the context of our proclamation today as we walk people through the text, so we won't repeat it here. This Sunday's proclamation will be a meditation upon the significance and the challenges of preaching, a sermon about preaching that is primarily addressed to the listeners of sermons.

The beginning of Mark's Gospel—right after Jesus spends forty days in the wilderness and John is arrested—says, "Jesus came into Galilee announcing God's good news, saying, 'Now is the time! Here comes God's kingdom! Change your hearts and lives, and trust this good news!'" (1:14). What did Jesus do for a living? He went preaching. Jesus the Christ is God garrulous, loquacious, and graciously talkative.

Proclaiming the text

This Sunday's appointed Gospel is Luke's rather detailed report of Jesus preaching his first (and I presume last) sermon at his hometown synagogue in Nazareth. They hand him the scroll of the prophet Isaiah. He reads the stirring words, "The Spirit of the Lord is upon me . . . to preach good news to the poor." Then Jesus interprets the scripture, saying that this prophecy is taking place right now. He recalls two episodes from the work of Elisha and Elijah, great prophets of the past. The congregational response? Murderous rage.

From our Gospel I'd like to note a few things about sermons and those who listen to sermons.

First, the preacher speaks under the power of the Holy Spirit. What the preacher says is not just one person's outburst; it is divinely derived testimony. The preacher speaks under Spirit-induced compulsion. It's not a sermon unless the words of the preacher are empowered by the Holy Spirit and made understandable to the listening congregation through the work of the Holy Spirit. In some mysterious way, God tells the preacher what to say.

The Holy Spirit is the brooding wind, the descending bird from heaven, the empowering fire of God's closeness. The Holy Spirit is that mysterious force from God that brings new worlds into being, that enables truthful, creative, godly speech (preaching), and that enables hearing that could not be without God's near presence.

Second, the sermon is based upon scripture. Note that the Nazareth congregation didn't ask Jesus to share his feelings with them or to speak from
personal experience. They handed him a scroll of the prophet Isaiah and demanded that he work from that. Jesus quotes directly from Isaiah:

"The Lord God's spirit is upon me, because the Lord has anointed me. He
has sent me to bring good news to the poor, to bind up the brokenhearted,
to proclaim release for captives, and liberation for prisoners, to proclaim the
year of the Lord's favor" (Isa 61:1-2).

Third, Jesus clearly believes that these ancient writings provide an accurate
clue to what is going on in the present: "Today this scripture is fulfilled in
your hearing." This ancient, written word is presumed to be none other than
God's word here, now.

The gospel is the good news that is Jesus Christ. In a sense, every time someone faithfully preaches in a church, the church believes it's like that fateful
day in Nazareth all over again—Jesus is preaching to his people. As Saint
Paul put it, "We don't preach about ourselves. Instead, we preach about Jesus
Christ as Lord" (2 Cor 4:5). True, the preacher is not speaking directly for
God in the way that Jesus spoke. Any preacher, other than Jesus, is a flawed,
imperfect human vessel. Fortunately, that which makes preaching effective is
not the goodness of the preacher but rather the truthfulness of the news that
is preached, along with the energizing breath of the Holy Spirit.

In saying, "Today this scripture has been fulfilled," Jesus's sermon hits home.
It's one thing to say that God will move, act, and save one day, someday. It's
quite another thing to say God is doing so today, here, as you listen. Surely
there was an excited stir among the congregation. At last God is coming to
save, to set things right. And who is more deserving of that divine deliverance
than we are—with the heel of Rome on our necks, languishing in poverty
and oppression? Sure, it took about four hundred years for God to get moving and come for us, but now the preacher has announced our deliverance.
Hallelujah! It was about then that the preacher's sermon went south and the
good news got bad.

Fourth, Jesus preaches to a specific group of people in a specific time and place who in the sermon come face-to-face with a specific and always surprising God. Jesus said, "No prophet is accepted in the prophet's hometown." (A nasty little proverb sure to incite the home folks.) "Let's see now," says the preacher, thumbing through his floppy, black leather-bound Bible, "as I recall (quoting from your own scriptures) there were lots of poor widows right here in Israel during the famine when prophet Elijah was representing Israel's God, but Elijah fed none of those good Jewish women—only an alien woman of another nation and race." Sullen silence in the once adoring congregation.

"Again, quoting from our own cherished scripture, surely there were many sick among us during the days of the great prophet Elisha. The only person healed was this violent, non-Jewish Syrian army officer." To be reminded by the young preacher that God had come but had not come as we expected, that God had worked the wrong side of the street before and might well do so again was quite a blow to the spiritual sensibilities of the good synagogue-going folk at Nazareth.

Fifth, all hell breaks loose in response to the sermon. They rise up with one accord and attempt to throw him off a cliff. His sermon at Nazareth was not Jesus sharing his feelings or exchanging religious ideas (what preaching sometimes is today). Rather it was his "first inaugural presidential address," an official announcement of the coming invasion. And in so doing, he really rattled the cages of the faithful.

Now, you have never reacted this way to one of my sermons. But just knowing this little story of Jesus's sermon keeps me nervous!

Sixth, Jesus's sermon is about God. In an age when many of us show up at church expecting to hear sermons about how we can better our lives or how to muster the courage to get out of bed tomorrow morning, it's good to be reminded that Jesus spoke in Nazareth primarily about God and only secondarily, and then derivatively, about us. The primary purpose of scripture,

Luke 4 or nearly every other part, is God, not us: Who is the God we've got? What's God up to today?

Jesus's pronouncements of judgment show him to be a true prophet who loved God's truth more than popular acclaim. He criticized or condemned in order to instigate a dramatic movement of heart, mind, and hands called "repentance." Thus, he not only preached the good news as truth that could be known but also as truth that could free, though he knew firsthand that the truth could make us mad as hell, his sermon in Nazareth being a prime example. He was truth and light. But something in us, John warns, loves the dark and hates the truth.

The good news (gospel) not only was the content of Jesus's sermons but also was Jesus.

1. He is the truth. This preacher's sermons took on deep significance because of the preacher. He not only told us the truth about God but also enacted the truth about God. Thus, Jesus set high the bar for evaluating the truth of any preaching purported to be "in Jesus's name."

2. It's not his peculiar truth if it is not truth followed, obeyed, truth embodied, enacted.

3. Jesus would talk to anybody. It's not his truth if it's not true for all.

At Pentecost, when a mob in the street demanded an explanation for the ruckus in the upper room after the descent of the Holy Spirit and the birth of the church, Peter referred to an obscure passage from the prophet Joel: "I will pour out my spirit upon everyone; your sons and your daughters will prophesy, your old men will dream dreams, and your young men will see visions" (Joel 2:28).

Through most of our history with God, Holy-Spirit-induced-talk (preaching) was limited to a few charismatic or simply offensive truth-tellers: the prophets. But there will come a day, when Messiah comes, that God's Holy Spirit will be poured out on all. Young upstarts, women and men, maids, janitors, people who never got to the microphone will speak up and speak out. Everyone will preach truth to power. Everybody, a preacher. That promised age of free speech is now. The real preachers of Jesus are not ordained clergy like me but spirit-filled laity like you.

That's why Jesus's people tend to be big talkers. They'll go anywhere for the privilege of preaching and they'll talk to anybody. And they won't shut up, no matter what the government says. Jesus not only preached but also sent out his disciples to all the villages of Galilee to preach. The Christian faith is an auditory phenomenon. Saint Paul said that all faith "comes through hearing." So when we gather to worship Jesus there is some silence, but there is more time where we talk, shout, sing, and read about Jesus.

And then the service comes to a close and the preacher says to all the preachers: Get out of church and into the world and preach!

Relating the text

What is God's kingdom like? A sower went forth to sow. Did he carefully plan, diligently preparing the soil for the seed? Hey, it's God's kingdom! He slings seed everywhere, wasting lots of good seed with reckless abandon.

Of course, much of the seed is wasted—falling along the road (like I say, it was really messy agriculture), eaten by birds, choked by weeds. Miraculously, some of the seed, a small minority, germinated, took root, and produced a rich harvest. Miraculous, considering all the seed had against it. Though this seems poor agricultural production to me, Jesus found it thrilling.

As a preacher, working for Jesus the preacher, having nothing to arm me and help fight my battles but words, and desperately hoping for a hearing, I think this may be my favorite parable.

In today's Gospel, not only does Jesus cite two instances from Israel's own scripture of God showing mercy to outsiders, but he also begins his sermon by quoting the prophet who foresaw a day when even foreigners would be welcomed at Israel's temple and be "joyful in my house of prayer . . . for my house shall be called a house of prayer for all peoples." One can imagine how inclusive verses like these, extending the promises of God to outsiders, would go down amid a congregation full of people who bitterly hated their Roman overlords.

Jesus really was a prophet. Whereas prophets Elijah and Elisha had sometimes to stand up to some king and speak truth to power, prophet Jesus had to stand up to a more totalitarian and potentially violent adversary, such as people like us. I can't figure out how anybody could get the impression that Jesus is some sort of projection of our own wishes and felt needs; he is a poor servant of our fantasies about ourselves. He loves the truth as much as he loves us and he tells the truth no matter how bad it stings. "We never heard such as this!" was a typical response to Jesus's sermons. He loved to overturn expectations and to shake things up. He came not only full of "grace" but also full of "truth," says John. With Jesus you can't take the grace without being willing to subject yourself to his truth.

At one point Luke joyfully records how the Jesus movement is catching on: "Large crowds were traveling with Jesus." Right then Jesus preaches, "Whoever comes to me and doesn't hate father and mother, spouse and children, and brothers and sisters—yes, even one's own life—cannot be my disciple" (14:25-26). It's almost as if Jesus is saying, "Large crowds? I can fix that." Though Luke doesn't record the response to that sermon, anybody could figure it out. I find it a wonder that Jesus had even twelve who hung around for his next sermon. Do you?

On another occasion Jesus was preaching and during the sermon casually said, "Unless you eat my flesh and drink my blood you are unworthy of me" (John 6:53, paraphrased).

"That's hard to hear," said his disciples.

"Will you also go away?" Jesus asked. (I expect that after some of his sermons many found other things to do on a Sunday morning.)

"Where can we go?" replied his hapless disciples. "You have the words of life." That's the only sensible reason for listening to Jesus. Not that his sermons give your life meaning or put a lift in your step or explicate life's dilemmas, but rather because the one who is speaking just happens to be the God's Son, the savior of the world, Lord of life.

Fourth Sunday after the Epiphany
RC/Pres: Fourth Sunday
in Ordinary Time

Jeremiah 1:4-10
Psalm 71:1-6
1 Corinthians 13:1-13
Luke 4:21-30

Pardon Me While I Offend You with My Sermon

Selected reading
Luke 4:21-30

Theme
Not everyone received Jesus. In fact, most seem to have rejected him in his earthly ministry. People seem to have been particularly resistant to his preaching. Something about the person and message of Jesus provoked fierce resistance that finally led him to the cross. Wherever Jesus is faithfully preached, truthfully presented, there will be offense.

Introduction to the readings

Jeremiah 1:4-10

Jeremiah recounts the story of his call, a call that he resisted. Yet God said to Jeremiah, "I'm putting my words in your mouth."

1 Corinthians 13:1-13

This is Paul's great hymn to the supremacy of Christian love, the highest of all the godly virtues.

Luke 4:21-30

Jesus preaches at Nazareth and proclaims, "Today, this scripture has been fulfilled." The congregation's initial admiration turns to murderous wrath.

Prayer

Lord Jesus, we are gathered here, your body, your church. We are gathered with the sole purpose of being with you, listening to you, learning from you, being judged by you, and being gracefully empowered by you.

Lord Jesus, we know that in your earthly ministry, not everyone heard you gladly. Many walked away sorrowful, and angry too.

Therefore, we pray that you would give us the grace to be with you, as you are, rather than as we would have you to be, to listen to whatever you have to say to us, to learn whatever you want to teach us, and to accept your verdict upon our lives, grateful for your present, sustaining, empowering love. Amen.

Encountering the text

Jesus begins his sermon in his hometown synagogue by quoting from Isaiah 61:1-2, telling them "Today, this scripture has been fulfilled just as you heard it" (Luke 4:21). At first, the congregation is positive about Jesus's words. They can hardly believe that the one who reads and speaks so well is a hometown boy, Joseph and Mary's son.

Isn't it wonderful to hear that the one who announces such glorious benefits for our town is one of our own? Their "Doctor, heal yourself" is in no way a criticism of Jesus. Rather, it is a proverb something akin to "Look after yourself and your kin first before you attempt to help others."

The folk in Nazareth quite naturally assume that he will do the same wonderful acts for them that he performed at Capernaum. Yet the sermon takes a turn in verse 24. In the RSV, Jesus says that he is not "acceptable" (*dektos*) in his own hometown, which is an interesting play on words since it's the same word found in verse 19 about the "acceptable" year of the Lord. Jesus announces the "acceptable" year of the Lord, yet he is not "acceptable" at his own hometown synagogue.

After the preacher Jesus first announces that the long-awaited messianic age is here, in this "acceptable" year, the people's adulation turns to rage when Jesus announces the peculiar nature of the messianic age that is coming. The precise quality of God's reign is unacceptable to them.

The people at Nazareth believed that the Messiah would put their Gentile overlords to rout and set Israel up as the grand people God had promised they would be. But Jesus cites two examples of prophetic moments when God acted to redeem and to save two "outsiders"—Elijah gives food to a Gentile widow and her son (1 Kgs 17:8-16) though the prophet fed no Israelites. In verse 27 the preacher Jesus tells of the time when Elisha healed Naaman, a Syrian army officer, of leprosy (2 Kgs 5:1-14).

One can imagine the offense that the faithful at Nazareth took at such a sermon.

Proclaiming the text

The great Dietrich Bonhoeffer, hanged by the Nazis, wrote that preaching "allows the risen Christ to walk among his people." That's what we preachers do in a sermon, when we've done things well. The preacher lets Jesus loose. And, as today's Gospel reminds us, when Jesus walks or talks among the people, well, that's often when the trouble begins! Jesus preaches at his hometown synagogue in Nazareth, and he's scarcely three minutes into his sermon when the congregation got so angry they wanted to kill the preacher!

I hope you don't feel that way about this sermon at this point. Still, if I succeed as a preacher in allowing Christ to walk among you and to talk to you, well, you may be looking for some cliff to solve your "preacher problem"!

Church growth guru Paul Borden says that the challenge for us preachers is to "insert Jesus into conversation and then relinquish control." We preachers have got to have the courage to bring up Jesus in the sermon and then to let him walk where he wants to walk and to talk to whom he wants to talk.

I confess that this is difficult for us preachers! Preachers like me are communicators. That is, we want to speak in such a way whereby we lessen the friction, the cognitive dissonance between Jesus and the congregation. So that when the congregation exclaims, as they exclaimed in Nazareth, "How dare you talk that way to us!" I as a preacher say, "Now wait! Let me explain to you. Jesus didn't really mean the tough things that you think you are hearing him say. Let me rephrase what Jesus was trying to say if he had the benefit of a fine seminary education like me!"

Sermonic tension is hard for us preachers! We are pastors who want to care for people, to love people. We think of ourselves as reconcilers, peacemakers.

But Jesus? At Nazareth, he made some folks mad when he interpreted scripture in such a way that portrayed the work of God as a wide reach beyond the bounds of their definition of "insiders" and "outsiders." Well, they didn't like it. And they wanted to throw Jesus over a cliff in an effort to make him stop preaching!

So this Sunday's question is: Are you willing to listen to Jesus, no matter what he says to you? Are you willing to let Jesus walk among us, no matter where he goes, no matter where he takes us?

Relating the text

"Wherever Jesus encountered people, he filled them with a great sense of peace," said the preacher. "He who calmed the angry waves in the storm calmed troubled spirits of the people too."

I wondered just how much of the New Testament this preacher had read! It doesn't sound like he was familiar with Luke 4. True, often Jesus had a calming effect on people. He did still the stormy sea. But Jesus also stirred things up, evoked the demons, and led his disciples onto many a stormy sea.

Jesus still does. In your church and mine, Jesus continues to stir things up, to start trouble, and sometimes to evoke angry responses. "Wherever the gospel is faithfully preached," says Luther, "demons are set loose." If that's true, then perhaps I as a preacher should worry that I've never had a response to a single one of my sermons to match the response that Jesus received to his sermon at Nazareth!

I'm sure this is the preacher in me, but I could not help but feel some pity for Barack Obama during his campaign for president in 2008. Obama's preacher had him in all sorts of hot water because his preacher said some wild, challenging, outrageous things in some sermons and Obama was being criticized for not walking out in indignation at what his preacher had said!

I heard him reply to one reporter, when asked about his reaction—or lack of reaction—to his preacher, "Look, most Christians could tell you if we walked out of church every time our preacher says something with which we disagree, we wouldn't stay until the end of many sermons!"

Obama could have also cited Luke 4 in his defense! Obama's pastor was accused of making remarks that sounded anti-American and unpatriotic. Isn't that probably what the folk at Nazareth thought about Jesus's comments in Luke 4? Jesus was being anti-Israel, unpatriotic in implying that God also loved and cared for Canaanite women and Syrian army officers.

"Preaching is logic on fire."

—Saying by a Welsh preacher

The psychologist Scott Peck used to say that people get married for two reasons: to have babies and to have friction.

Perhaps that's a major purpose of preaching—to give birth (to new Christians, new ideas, new experiences with Christ) and to have friction (to bump against the truth, to be slapped with the Living Lord, to get jerked around by a holy and righteous God).

Most mergers of one denomination with another, in the past century, have ended up weakening the new, merged denomination. Take two different families, even when they share much of the same heritage, and have them move in together. So much energy is given to compromise and being fair to each group, and endless negotiation, and balancing that there's not much left to actually be the church.

On Pentecost I preach on Acts 2. There we were, all dressed up with the Pentateuch, the law, celebrating the gift of divine rules and regulations, "Jews from every nation under heaven," all settled in at "one place," the gavel comes down and the meeting begins. "Delegate from Mesopotamia, microphone one." "I yield to my distinguished colleague from Phrygia, or is it Pamphylia?" And the agenda cranks on.

Then God shows up and all hell breaks loose. Wind. Doors knocked off hinges. The whole building shakes, rattles, and rolls. Somebody yelled, "Fire!" Everybody starts talking at the same time. Look who's talking: old men from the nursing home, put on the shelf at retirement, maids, janitors, people who had never been in front of a microphone, everybody talking, everybody hearing new speech. A crowd out in the street smirks, "They're doing the same thing they did when Jesus was with them. They're drunk!"

Anytime the Holy Spirit shows up, some things are brought together, and some things are torn asunder. That's the fun and the challenge of gathering on Sunday and praying for the descent of the Spirit!

The seminarians were engaged in a discussion of student sermons in the preaching class. One of the members of the class had preached last Sunday in his church and had been saddened that a number of his rural parishioners expressed anger because of his sermon. One man had even walked out before the singing of the final hymns.

Attempting to be helpful, members of the class jumped into a discussion of what the preacher had done wrong. Had he overstated his arguments in the sermon? Had he spent enough time developing personal relationships with his people? Had he spoken in too strong or harsh a tone of voice?

The crusty old homiletics professor listened to the discussion and then finally said, "Did it ever occur to any of you that perhaps what he did wasn't wrong; it was right? I'm bothered by the assumption that many of you seem to have that there is some way to talk about Jesus without getting hurt for doing so. Let me assure you, none of you are smarter than Jesus. Jesus got into trouble for his preaching; so will you!"

Fifth Sunday after the Epiphany
RC/Pres: Fifth Sunday
in Ordinary Time

Isaiah 6:1-8, (9-13)
Psalm 138
1 Corinthians 15:1-11
Luke 5:1-11

Depart from Me

Selected reading

Luke 5:1-11

Theme

Before the living, holy Christ of God, we cower in unworthiness. After all, we are unworthy. Yet this gracious, forgiving God does not leave us in our sin and unworthiness but comes to us, embraces us, and takes us as his own.

Introduction to the readings

Isaiah 6:1-8, (9-13)

At worship in the temple, the young Isaiah is given a stunning vision of God and receives his call to be a prophet.

1 Corinthians 15:1-11

Paul tells the Corinthians how he was called to be an apostle and how he received the gospel from the risen Christ.

Luke 5:1-11

Jesus comes to his disciples while they are fishing, an amazing catch of fish results, and Simon is filled with wonder.

Prayer

Lord, to come before your presence is to be overwhelmed. We are weak; you are strong. We are filled with conflicts and doubts; you are a sure foundation.

Here in church, on Sunday, when we pause to consider your great plans for us, your image upon our lives, we also know how we fall short, we stumble, and we disappoint. Forgive us.

Here in church, when your word is opened, we feel judged, condemned, charged, and guilty. Of course, we are.

Yet, here in church, we are also embraced by your love. You came to us, your light shone into our darkness, and we beheld your glory. Do not leave us, Lord. Come to us. Let your light shine. Love us, and do not let us go. Forever, we pray. Amen.

Encountering the text

Today's Gospel speaks of an experience few modern people seem to have: an encounter with the awe-filled, wondrous, threatening holiness of God. Most of us have carved God down to more manageable proportions. Therefore, Simon's reactions to Jesus may seem strange.

Yet there are moments, usually in worship, when we know this experience of awe and unworthiness. We will attempt to name and evoke those moments in today's sermon. Today's text invites us to ponder the gap between our contemporary domestication of the living God of Israel into our patron as well as to celebrate the honest, life-giving experience of confessing our distance from this God as well as this God's having come near to us in the Christ.

- 128 -

Proclaiming the text

"Simon Peter . . . fell at Jesus' knees and said, 'Leave me, Lord, for I'm a sinner!'"

The first lesson tells of the day that a young man, about the age of a college student, entered the temple to pray. It was as if the windows of heaven opened. "I saw the Lord!" Isaiah said. The heavenly choir shouted, as we sang today, "Holy, holy, holy is the LORD of heavenly forces! All the earth is filled with God's glory!" (Isa 6:3).

On these all-too-rare, delicious moments, the veil is stripped away, and we cry out with Peter, when Jesus was transfigured before him, "Lord, it is good that we should be here!"

But today's scripture is about none of that.

Today's scripture, Old Testament and New, is not about the joy of being in the presence of God but rather about the terror. "It's scary to fall into the hands of the living God," says the Bible (Heb 10:31). A scary thing. Be careful. Worship would be easy if this were the weekly meeting of religiously inclined dilettantes who wish to further the study of deity, or a memorial dinner to resuscitate the memory of a departed hero. But no, to gather here is to risk falling into the grasp of the living God.

Here's a love that can blow you to bits, turn you inside out. No wonder we tiptoe around this presence, turn our churches into carpeted bedrooms, fearful that we might awaken this one. Note how we often chatter, nervously, before the music begins, the way people chatter when they're scared of what might come next. We transform our worship into the backslapping conviviality of a Kiwanis Club meeting; everybody smiling, reassuring one another that this is only church, only Sunday, only God, nothing over which to be alarmed.

Isaiah knew better; and in our better moments, we know better. To stand in the presence of God is to be brought to your knees. "Holy, holy, holy!" is followed by, "Mourn for me; I'm ruined! I'm a man with unclean lips, and I live among a people with unclean lips. Yet I've seen the king, the LORD of heavenly forces!" (Isa 6:5).

Here, under these great arches, in singing a great hymn, our defenses crumble. Our pretensions become as nothing; and we recoil from the gaze of the one who is so good, so just, so holy that we fall to our knees and say as did Peter, when he was face to face with the godliness of Jesus, "Leave me, Lord, for I'm a sinner!" (Luke 5:8).

Unclean lips. Sin. Here's an appropriate theme on this Sunday before we enter the season of Lent, though it may seem odd to have sin crop up here in these musings on worship, and God, hymns, and our Sunday service. Did you miss something? How did we move from thoughts on God, glory, and majesty to these unclean lips and sin?

My wife has said, as she sits in church on Sunday morning and watches the choir process, all scrubbed and vested, looking so angelic, that she finds it difficult to believe that these angels have been doing what they were alleged to be doing on Saturday nights in the dormitories!

We begin most of our Sunday services with confession of our sin. And any of us with even a shred of self-knowledge knows that we sin—sins of deceit, egotism, greed, and lust. (Preachers write many a sermon by turning, in our Book of Lists, to the entry "Sin," which is found, appropriately, right after "Sex"—adultery, anger, aggression, avarice.) Sin is all those little slip-ups and indiscretions that you do, that you know you shouldn't do. You have your list; I have mine.

But let us be clear: Isaiah's "Mourn for me!" and Peter's "Leave me, Lord, for I'm a sinner!" have little to do with our conventional definitions of sin. What is sin? The sin being confessed here has not to do with the occasional peccadillo, what your parents told you not to do, but rather the gaping chasm between who you are and who God is. We have counselors, therapists, and daytime television doctors to help you handle sin as misdeed. But what if our sin—with a capital *S*—and our real uncleanness is not what we did in the backseat of a Chevy in high school, but the gap between ourselves and God?

Freud noted that we project our parental experiences as God. Natural for us to think of God as the big mommy-daddy in the sky, making a list, checking it twice, knowing who is naughty and nice. But what if you come in here on a Sunday morning and find to your terror that God isn't like that at all, that God is that great "other," that over-againstness, whom Peter saw that day when he looked into the eyes of Jesus?

There are at least two ways to be terrified of God. Either you can be afraid of God because God is so harsh and cruel that you dare not slip up for fear of punishment, or God may be so wonderfully loving that you despair of all the ways you have betrayed that love in your own way of life. God's love is the searing light that penetrates our facade.

What if God, the one Peter saw projected back at him in the eyes of the rabbi, is like a mirror, a mirror of truth and self-knowledge that you are made to gaze upon? There you see reflected every moment of your life, every secret thought, all the good little things you have done for bad little reasons, the way you live, every second for you and you alone. My God, to be made to look upon that mirror, even for an instant, who could endure it?

"Mourn for me; I'm ruined! I'm a man with unclean lips . . . Yet I've seen the king, the LORD of heavenly forces!" The beauty of God's holiness turns to its brutality. By a little Sunday jaunt into church, a little listen to a little sermon, a nice little anthem by a pretty little choir, you saw God, and somebody in the third row from the left stands and screams (as did the Gerasene crazy person), "Get out of here, Jesus of Nazareth, what have you to do with us?"

God's holiness is the mirror through which our pretentious goodness is seen for what it really is. All of us who came here to catch just a glimpse of God get more than we wanted and cry, "Go away from me!"

You were warned. "It is a fearful thing to fall into the hands of the living God." Why could he not leave Peter with his nets, fishing? Why could he not let us be, content with our little lies, masks fixed firmly in place, quite happy to play our games?

Of course, I'm a preacher, one accustomed to climbing out and dancing on this shaky scaffolding once a week from eleven until noon. But some Sundays, even I lose my balance, slip into the chasm, forced to look at the mirror.

The night I was ordained was a grand occasion. The church was packed, and a brass ensemble accompanied the choir. Thirty vested clergy processed in behind the bishop. After the sermon came the point when the bishop called me to stand before him as he read the ancient words of the Ordinal: "Never forget that the ones whom you serve, as pastor, are the ones for whom he died."

There I was, wondering, "Will the bishop send me to a good church? Will the laity be enlightened enough to accept my advanced social ideas? Will I get an all-electric parsonage?"

The words thundered forth, obliterating my pitiful pretension: never forget, the ones you were lucky enough to serve are ones for whom he died.

And I said, "Leave me . . . for I'm a sinner!"

But you know, he never does. Across the gap between him and us, he reaches in love. He is no mere cold mirror of judgment, but a living God of grace. He touches the lips of young Isaiah, making him a prophet. Isaiah is wrong. He isn't lost; he's found. Jesus calls Peter to be a disciple, promising to teach him to catch more than fish. Refusing to leave this sinful man, he forgives him. Even when Peter denies him three times at the cross, Jesus forgives Peter. Because once the living God gets his teeth in you, he doesn't let go.

In my first church in rural Georgia, I stood one Sunday, as I will again shortly, and invited the congregation to the Lord's table. But nobody came forward for communion. After the service, I asked why no one came forward.

"I guess they just didn't think they were worthy," said one. "Oh," I said, "They're not. Nor am I."

We admitted all that up front, at the very beginning when we confessed our sin. We are unworthy even to gather up the crumbs under this table. Leave us, for we are sinful! Get out of here, Jesus of Nazareth!

But no, there's an invitation rather than a rejection. There's the bread. There's the cup. They are reminding you. You won't get rid of this God.

Relating the text

In his lament for his son Eric, killed at age twenty-five in a mountaineering accident, Nicholas Wolterstorff remarks that it was only in the midst of his own suffering that he saw that God suffers. He reflects on the old belief that no one can behold God's face and live. I always thought, Wolterstorff says, that this meant that no one could see God's splendor and live. A friend said perhaps it means that no one could see God's sorrow and live. Or perhaps, he reflects, the sorrow is the splendor.

—Nicholas Wolterstorff, *Lament for a Son* (Grand Rapids: William B. Eerdmans Publishing Company, 1987), 81

"Tolstoy wrote a moving reflection on Jesus' Sermon on the Mount, in which he said, 'The antagonism between life and conscience may be moved in two ways: by a change of life or a change of conscience.' Tolstoy chose to preserve his conscience; he began to live like a peasant. But such a fearsome choice, this young man admitted, was out of his reach. People in his situation, he observed, could stand the chafing between one's soul and one's life style more easily than they could face the awesome choice."

—Thomas G. Long, *Whispering the Lyrics: Sermons for Lent and Easter* (Lima, OH: CSS Publishing Company, 1995)

I enjoy watching people enter our chapel. Nearly half a million each year enter that large portal. And if they are here for the first time, I like to watch their eyes turn upward, their mouths drop open, overwhelmed by the glory and the majesty of this place. That's exactly what the Gothic architect intended—that these soaring arches and brilliant windows should overwhelm us with the glory of God.

It's an emotion one doesn't have often in contemporary religion with our pre-fab, multi-purpose gymnasium churches, where everything is scaled down to fit the needs of a covered-dish supper; where grinning, backslapping, glad-handing ushers seem more suited to work at a used car lot than in a house of God.

But to be here, beneath the monumental glory of it—the vast building, the great choir—is to want to cry out as Jacob when heaven's ladder was brought down to him, "Surely the Lord is in this place!" I'm not doing my job and the choir has flunked if there is not some Sunday when someone can say, "Surely, the Lord is here."

"Shepherds search for their lost sheep, but for their own profit. Men seek their lost property, but out of self-interest. Travellers visit foreign countries, but for their own benefit. Kings offer ransoms for prisoners, but out of po-litical calculation. But why have you searched for me? Why have you sought me out? Why have you visited this hostile earth where I live? Why have you ransomed me with your blood? I am not worthy of such effort. Indeed in my sin I have wilfully tried to escape from you, so you would not find me. I have wanted to become a god myself, deciding for myself what is good and bad according to my own whims and lusts. I have provoked you and insulted you. Why do you bother with me?"

—Tikhon of Zadonsk (1724–83), quoted in *The Way of a Pilgrim and Other Classics of Russian Spirituality*, ed. G. P. Feotov (North Chelmsford, MA: Courier Corporation, 2012), 217

"To adore. . . . That means to lose oneself in the unfathomable, to plunge into the inexhaustible, to find peace in the incorruptible, to be absorbed in defined immensity, to offer oneself to the fire and the transparency, to annihilate oneself in proportion as one becomes more deliberately conscious of oneself, and to give of one's deepest to that whose depth has no end."

—"Pierre Teilhard de Chardin, SJ, 1881–1955," *The Oxford Book of Prayer*, ed. George Appleton (New York: Oxford University Press, 1985)

Reinhold Niebuhr often warned us: "In the beginning God created man and ever since man has sought to return the compliment."

—Quoted in C. FitzSimons Allison, *The Cruelty of Heresy* (New York: Morehouse Publishing, 1994), 101

"O my Lord, since it seems you are determined to save me, I ask that you may do so quickly. And since you have decided to dwell within me, I ask that you clean your house, wiping away all the grime of sin."

—Teresa of Ávila (1515–82)

Sixth Sunday after the Epiphany
RC/Pres: Sixth Sunday
in Ordinary Time

Jeremiah 17:5-10

Psalm 1

1 Corinthians 15:12-20

Luke 6:17-26

Get Real

Selected reading

Psalm 1

Theme

Jesus speaks a new world into being, challenges the world's definitions of "the facts of life," and depicts a new reality called God's kingdom. Because of Jesus, Christians have a quarrel with the world's definitions of reality. As disciples of Jesus, we are to align our lives with the new reality that Jesus calls into being.

Introduction to the readings

Jeremiah 17:5-10

The prophet contrasts those who trust in the Lord with those who trust "in mere humans."

1 Corinthians 15:12-20
Paul speaks to the Corinthians of the relationship between Christ's resurrection and our hope.

Luke 6:17-26
Jesus heals and then preaches, preaching a sermon about the nature of God.

Prayer

Lord Jesus, grant us the grace to see the world as it really is, the world as you intend it to be, the world that you are working to create for us. Help us not to be distracted or deceived by bogus appearance. Keep revealing to us your intent for the world and for our lives. Keep turning us toward your light. Then, help us live in the light of that vision. Help us align our lives with the true shape of reality, this day and always. Amen.

Encountering the text

At first glance, Jesus's sermon on the level place is an obvious parallel to the better-known Sermon on the Mount in Matthew 5. Yet there are some differences. The blessings are presented in a different order. The "you" switches from plural, to singular, to plural again. Luke's God is "kind to the ungrateful and wicked people" (6:35) while Matthew's God "makes the sun rise on both the evil and the good and sends rain on both the righteous and the unrighteous" (5:45). So for both of these sermons, God is extravagantly gracious and merciful, even maddeningly so. Here is a God who takes sides with those whom we often exclude or put down. Here is a God who blesses those whom we curse and curses those whom we bless.

The sermon, particularly the verses that we focus upon today, is a depiction of God, rendered in the indicative rather than the imperative mode, of the nature of a gracious, forgiving God, a God who takes sides with the oppressed and who puts down the vaunted and the rich. In these verses, Jesus does not give any ethical instruction. If there is ethical instruction in this sermon, it is only by implication, as a response to a vision of God.

We will interpret the Sermon on the Plain as a depiction of a new reality, namely, God's kingdom, that moves in among us in the teaching and work of Jesus. Jesus begins the sermon by healing, and by releasing those who are captive to demons. Then he continues by preaching and thereby healing us of our sick, contorted notions of God and by releasing us in order that we might embrace a new reality that we would not have seen without his proclamation of that reality. Let us, in our sermon on Jesus's sermon, point the congregation to that reality.

Proclaiming the text

What's going on? What is real? Every time Christians gather, as we have gathered here this morning, that is the question that is on the table for consideration: "What is real?" Don't be too content with what you think is there, for the world as it appears before your eyes may be more shadow than truth.

"The good life consists," says popular psychiatrist M. Scott Peck, "of a lifelong dedication to the pursuit of reality, at all costs."

The world is forever telling Christians, "Get real." To the world, much of what we do here seems sadly out of touch with "the real world."

This is the point of view that says things like, "Well, I think prayer is fine, but sometimes you just have to get real." Or, "You religious people need to get off your 'pie-in-the-sky' thinking and face facts."

But that begs the prior question of, "Well, who gets to define reality?" Who gets to name the true facts of life?

We can only live in the world that we see. So debates about what's what in the world, about what is a fact, and about what is real tend to be arguments around the basic questions: Well, what do you see? What's going on? Who is in charge? Why are we here? Where are we heading?

Jesus comes down on a level place and begins to preach (Luke 6:17). You think that you've heard this sermon in Matthew, on a mountain, Jesus's Sermon on the Mount; but this one is a bit different, in some significant ways. You will note that, at least in the beginning of this sermon, Jesus doesn't tell us anything that we are to do. Lots of people think that is the whole purpose of a sermon, "I come to church and listen to the preacher tell me what I need to do to lead a better life," or something like that. But this sermon is about people who are "blessed" and people who are cursed. Jesus doesn't tell people what they are to do to be blessed; rather, he announces that certain people are blessed and that others are cursed. So, the sermon really isn't about us, who is in and who is out, who is behaving correctly and who is misbehaving. The sermon is about God.

The title of this sermon might not be, "The Sermon on a Level Place," but rather, "A Sermon about the Nature of God." God is the merciful one who is "kind to the ungrateful and the wicked" (Luke 6:35). Perhaps you thought if God is good, then that means that God punishes the wicked and socks it to the ungrateful. Well, think again, says Jesus. It is easy to be kind to people who are grateful for the kindness that we show them. It is easy to do nice things for good people. But this God that we've got is different from us. God is kind and good to the bad and the ungrateful.

It won't be many Sundays from now until we read the familiar story from Luke of the prodigal son. There, Jesus introduces us to an incredibly gracious and kind father. When the older brother wants to know why in the world the father is throwing a huge homecoming party for the returning wayward younger brother, the father replies, "We had to celebrate and be glad because this brother of yours was dead and is alive. He was lost and is found" (Luke 15:32).

Which is overstating it just a little. The facts are, the younger brother was not "dead"; he was out on a binge. Nor was he "lost." He didn't forget the way home one day after school. Rather, he ran away from home, took his father's hard-earned money, and headed west for a good time.

Which makes all the more remarkable (for the older brother, not remarkable, but exasperating) that the father is throwing a huge party to welcome home an ungrateful and wicked son. But we were warned. As Jesus says, God is kind precisely to the wicked and the ungrateful.

And, if you thought the facts were that God is in the business of punishing the wicked and stringing up the ungrateful, then God's mercy and extravagant forgiveness is exasperating to us. For it is exasperating to find out that God does not fit our idea of God.

Let us note that Jesus's entire sermon, at least the first half of it that we are listening to today, is a series of statements and assertions. The sentences, to quote my sixth grade English teacher, "are in the indicative rather than the imperative mode." Jesus is simply stating the facts of life, the way things are, reality.

Blessed are the poor—the same people, whom we overlook, disregard, despise, and consider failures.

Blessed are the hungry—the same hungry people whom we expect must be lazy or inept or they wouldn't be asking for handouts.

Blessed are those who weep—the same whiners and complainers who are always acting like they've had it worse than anyone else.

Blessed are you when people hate you—because you are abrasive, holier-than-thou, self-righteous, the way so-called "religious" people often are.

God—this God—blesses those whom we tend to curse.

Then the preacher moves to an even less attractive part of the sermon as he curses the rich, the content, the happy, and the morally upright (in short, people like most of us), but there's no need for us to spend time on all of that, right?

I expect it was a shock that day, for all the good, churchgoing, Bible-believing folk to see a portrayal of God that didn't fit their received Sunday school images of God. I expect it was a shock as great as climbing up out of the darkness of a deep, dark cave into the blinding light and reality of the sun at midday.

Perhaps this is the point of preaching. Not first to tell us what to do, but first to help us see. The acting follows the seeing. Perhaps that's why Jesus begins this sermon with healing (Luke 6:18), as a sign that a whole new world is breaking in to the old world, a new reality is shining through the darkness where those on the bottom are now brought to the top, and those who are poor, weeping, and despised are put at the center of what God is up to in the world.

So today's sermon doesn't tell you to go out and do anything, though, by implication, you may be thinking about something that you need to do. That's why Christians live as we try to live, not simply because Christ has commanded us to live in a certain way, but rather we live in a certain way because of the way we now know the world to be. We want to get in step with the way things are, reality, now that God in Christ has entered the world.

I know someone who is a cardiac nurse. She assists in the surgery and the care of people who have seriously ill hearts. Many of her patients don't make it through the delicate, risky surgery. Some of her patients have a very difficult time in their lengthy recovery. It can be depressing, difficult work. "How do you keep going?" I asked her.

"Walks in the park" was her reply. She explained, "I take an hour off for lunch and go to walk in the park. I see people who are happy, healthy. I see children playing and older people sitting on benches having a great time talking with one another. I am thereby reminded this is how things are meant to be. This is the real world. It helps me to keep going in very difficult situations."

Are her walks in the park an escape from reality, a trip into never-never land? No, they are a realistic engagement with the reality, a sober look at the way things really are and are meant to be that keeps her going in a shadowy world where it is easy for her to forget what's what.

That's a major reason why we gather here for worship on a weekly basis, to be reminded of what's what, to get a vision, to receive a picture of reality now that God in Jesus Christ has reached out to us.

Get real.

Relating the text

In the middle of modern-day Jerusalem, the members of the Bahai faith have built a beautiful, terraced garden. It is elegantly furnished with beautiful flowering plants and flowing fountains. Bahais from all over the world have contributed to its creation. Its striking terraces and beautiful vistas are quite a contrast to the hustle and bustle of the sometimes-violent streets of Jerusalem.

What good does that garden do? Why have they built it? It is an escape from the real world, a means of cloistering themselves from the realities, the facts of life in strife-torn, sadly conflicted Jerusalem.

The Bahais, who have suffered terrible persecution in places such as Iran and Iraq, say that the garden is their depiction and their reminder to everyone of the world as it is created to be, as it is supposed to be, as it will be when God gets God's way with the world. The garden is open to everyone as a sign, a signal, and a picture of what is real.

I think Jesus, the preacher on the plain, would understand.

What is going on? What is real? In one of his dialogues, Plato tells his famous Allegory of the Cave. We are like prisoners who are chained to the floor of a cave, forced to sit all day facing in one direction, toward the back wall of the cave. We can't move our heads far to the right or to the left. All we can do is to sit and stare at the wall of the cave. Behind us people move back and forth between us and the mouth of the cave. We can see their shadows reflected on the wall of the cave. But that's all we can see—their shadows, their reflections cast upon the back wall of the cave from the sunlight at the mouth of the cave. The shadows sometimes carry objects in their hands. We try to make out what they are holding in their hands, but all we can see are the shadows.

If we should be released from our bonds and turn around and look toward the mouth of the cave, the bright light would blind us. Gradually, our eyes might become accustomed to the light and we would begin then to see things as they really are, but it would be a long, painful process of gaining our sight, of seeing things as they are. For now, all we've got is the shadows, mere silhouettes, and outlines of things as they are.

Thus, Plato taught that we ought not take our perception of the world too seriously, as if what we perceived of the world were what is "really there." We ought to question the images that come before our eyes, for some of them are deeply misleading. They are only the shadow but not reality.

The way to get closer to reality, to things as they really are, is philosophy, taught Plato. Through reason and argument, through logic and disputation, philosophy enables us to cut through the shadows to the reality, or so Plato taught.

Christianity resonates with Plato's allegory of the cave. We know that what the world regards as reality is often only a shadow, a poor imitation of the real thing. However, we differ in that we believe that reality is to be found, not through careful philosophical reflection, but rather though God's gracious revelation. God shows us what the real world looks like. Thus, Jesus preaches his Sermon on the Plain, hoping thereby to enable us to see a whole new world, the real world, the world beyond the shadows and the sham. We believe that we only know what's what, what's real, through the gracious gift of God.

He works all day, every weekday, as a computer programmer. He sits before his computer screen, tapping at the keys on the keyboard, every day.

"In many ways, I despise my job," he says. "Sometimes the sameness, the relentless routine really gets to me. It's the same old stuff, day after day."

All of this was by way of explaining his hobby. On Saturdays and Sundays, he makes beautifully crafted, strong and sturdy old-fashioned wooden toys and rocking horses for children, which he gives to our town's center for the needy. Poor families are presented with these wonderful, hand-crafted toys for their children, all because of his generosity and skill.

"Actually, I do it for myself," he explains. "I'm glad that my work brings joy to others, but I do it mostly for myself. My work is so dull during the week. I don't think I accomplish much. But then, when I get in my workshop and begin working with the wood, when I get my hands on the wood and work it up into something beautiful, I am reminded of who I am and what I'm meant to be. When I'm making those toys, I sometimes say to myself, 'This is life as it is meant to be.'"

Perhaps, in the light of today's scripture from Luke, he could say, "This is the world as it is meant to be. This is reality. The other stuff I do, Monday through Friday, is the world as it is not meant to be."

Seventh Sunday after the Epiphany
RC/Pres: Seventh Sunday in Ordinary Time

Genesis 45:3-11, 15

Psalm 37:1-11, 39-40

1 Corinthians 15:35-38, 42-50

Luke 6:27-38

Choice, Chance, or the Hand of God?

Selected reading
Genesis 45:3-11, 15

Theme
It is not enough for Christians to conceive of our lives as the sum total of our astute human choices or as mere luck and chance. Behind the scenes, guiding and summoning, God works to redeem our lives, to move us from the bad that we often deserve to the good that God intends for us.

Introduction to the readings
Genesis 45:3-11, 15

In a dramatic scene, Joseph reveals himself to his brothers and weeps both in joy and in regret at the events of the past.

1 Corinthians 15:35-38, 42-50
Paul tells the Corinthians that our hope in death is the same as in life, that the God who loves us in Jesus Christ will continue to love us, raising us to new life.

Luke 6:27-38
Jesus continues his Sermon on the Plain with a command to love our enemies and to be as compassionate as God has been compassionate to us.

Prayer

Lord Jesus, as we look back on our life's journey, we are often impressed by how subtly, unobtrusively, and secretly you have worked behind the scenes to bring our lives along with yours. Though we have not always been aware of your leading, looking back, we know that you have led.

For your guiding hand, even when we were unaware of your guiding, for your encouragement, even when we didn't know you were giving us the strength to go on, for your correction, even when we were not conscious of your righting of our wrong turns, we give you thanks. Keep working with us, Lord. Keep drawing us toward you, keep leading us in the paths of righteousness, so that we might be able, at the end, to look back upon the twists and turns in our lives and say, "The Lord was in it." Amen.

Encountering the text

It's tough to do justice to the drama of the Joseph narrative without in some sense preaching the whole story even as we focus on one event in that story. Our challenge with this Sunday's first lesson is to speak about the end of the Joseph saga by recapitulating the whole story.

Genesis 45 is a key episode in the Joseph story that comprises Genesis 37, 39–50. Our first lesson for this Sunday is a climax in that well-wrought narrative.

Now all of the tensions of the story are resolved, and now the significance of the events prior to this moment are being revealed.

We can't really understand this episode without setting it in the context of the larger story. The story of Joseph is a long, carefully developed, coherent story that has a definite plot from beginning to end. Many scholars have therefore characterized the Joseph saga as akin to a modern novella. The saga shows unusual interest in character and personality development, in human emotions, and in the growth and development of character. Little wonder that Andrew Lloyd Webber transformed this saga into the popular musical *Joseph and the Amazing Technicolor Dreamcoat*.

By the end of the story a spoiled brat grows up into a generous, compassionate adult. The proud brothers who schemed against Joseph are now old men guiding an extended family in chaos. The murderous plot against Joseph and its aftermath are about to be resolved.

As you probably recall, the brothers were so jealous of Joseph that they conspired to murder him and then thought better of it, sending him into slavery. However, even in slavery little brother Joseph landed on his feet and prospered. He has been elevated to the second-highest office in Egypt.

There was a great famine and the brothers of Joseph came to Egypt looking for food. The tables are turned. The plot takes an unexpected twist. The story makes us wonder if there has been some agent operating behind the scenes, some unmentioned force driving the story to this conclusion. That surely is what the narrator wants us to think.

Most of this Sunday's first lesson is a speech by Joseph, filled with emotion because of the family reunion. When Joseph reveals his true identity, the brothers are both dumbfounded and shaking in fear. Will this powerful man now repay his brothers for the evil they did to him?

Joseph will forgive his brothers. The story will move on, and the family will be preserved through this act of forgiveness. Joseph gives a theological explanation for his actions: "God sent me before you to save lives. . . . God sent me before you to make sure you'd survive" (vv. 5, 7). The true climax of the narrative becomes explicit in Genesis 50:20, "You planned something bad for me, but God produced something good from it, in order to save the lives of many people, just as he's doing today."

Behind these twists and turns in the story of a human family, divine purpose is being worked out. That purpose only becomes obvious at the very end. God works behind the scenes to bring about God's intention for God's family. And yet human forgiveness also plays a role in moving God's intentions forward.

I suspect that we read Genesis 45 for this Sunday as a connection with the Gospel selection from Luke. In the ending of the story of Joseph and his brothers we see exemplification of Luke's "love your enemies." Here we have, notably within the Hebrew scriptures, the Old Testament, dramatic embodiment of Jesus's advice to "treat people in the same way that you want them to treat you" (Luke 6:31).

At the same time, there is no explicit command here in the story of Joseph. We are reading a story about a troubled family with a sad history. And yet surely the narrator intends for us to read this as a story about God. Joseph is not presented as a paragon of moral virtue. He is presented as someone living by his wits, attempting to survive and thrive, but someone who acts and lives as part of a larger pageant of God's salvation of the world.

May we proclaim this Sunday in such a way that our people come to see themselves and their histories in the same God-working-behind-the-scenes way.

Proclaiming the text

"You planned something bad for me, but God produced something good from it" (Gen 50:20).

In the last few weeks, at the round of receptions, conversations, and introductory meetings I've enjoyed asking people, "What led you to this church?"

My mother went to a Methodist church, at least I think it was a Methodist church.

I was looking for the Baptist church down town and somebody gave me the wrong address so I showed up here, liked it, and stayed.

I really like good preaching and the preacher before you was really, really good.

I was dating this guy. He went to this church so I came with him. We stopped dating, but I stayed here.

Nearly all the people I've talked with, whatever reason they give, interpret their reason as either a matter of choice—narrowing it down to three or four churches that seemed like they would be a good fit and then choosing this church because it was the closest to the house—or as a matter of chance—I could have joined lots of other churches, but there was this snowstorm and I couldn't drive too far that morning and showed up here.

By the way, I was chagrined that so few mentioned my great preaching as the magnet that pulled them in here! Oh well.

Choice or chance. That's the story of most of our lives to hear us tell it. In church or out. Choice or chance.

But what would you say if I told you that I believe you were here because God meant for you to be here? What would you say if I said that God means for you to be here, not necessarily here at the church or here in this town, but here? God has plans, purposes, and direction being worked out in you. You make your astute, well thought out choices. Good. But what if your choosing is not the only choosing being done in the world, your decisions not the only decisions being made?

The story of Joseph and his brothers is long and complicated. Today's scripture comes toward the very end of the story. We're slipping into the theatre in the last act when Joseph's brothers, seeing that their father has died, tremble, lest Joseph (now that the old man is gone) finally pay them back for all the nasty things they did to him.

Joseph puts their minds at ease. "Don't be upset," he tells them. "You planned something bad for me, but God produced something good from it."

If you read the whole story of Joseph and his brothers, beginning some twelve chapters earlier, you would see why Joseph's brothers had cause to fear little brother Joseph, daddy's fair-haired boy. Jacob loved Joseph, the last of his children, with unashamed favoritism. And those dreams!

Imagine your kid brother saying, "I had a dream. We were binding sheaves of wheat in the field. And your sheaves all bowed down to my sheaf."

"Really?" said Joseph's brothers.

"Then I dreamed that the sun, the moon, and eleven stars bowed down to me."

"How interesting," said the eleven brothers.

"I wonder what Freud would say about my dream?" Joseph asked.

The brothers said to themselves, "We'll give him something to dream about!"

One day, when Joseph had been sent out to the fields with lunch for his brothers—his father was opposed to little Joseph doing any hard work—the brothers took Joseph and that pretty coat of his and threw him in a pit to die. Later, they thought better of it and pulled him out of the pit in order to sell him as a slave to some Ishmaelites who took this bratty, big-mouthed, dreaming little brother to Egypt.

There, Joseph's brains were recognized by Potiphar, an officer of the Pharaoh, and Joseph prospered. Unfortunately, Joseph's other attributes were recognized by Mrs. Potiphar and she tried to—I'm sure you're not interested in this steamy part of the story. At any rate, Potiphar threw him into prison for trumped-up charges of conduct unbecoming a slave.

Joseph languished in jail for many years, interpreting dreams and, no doubt, endearing himself to everyone whom he met. Finally, Joseph got out of jail by interpreting a dream of the Pharaoh who was so impressed with Joseph that he put him in charge of the entire Egyptian welfare program during the big famine—a famine that Joseph predicted through advanced dream interpretation.

And who should show up in Egypt looking for food? Joseph's brothers. They didn't recognize the powerful man who gave them the food (which enabled their family to survive) as their own little brother. Eventually, Joseph revealed himself to them, and when he did, they figured that they were done for. The pit, the slavery, the prison.

But wonder of wonders, Joseph said, "Don't be upset and don't be angry with yourselves that you sold me here. Actually, God sent me before you to save lives." Their attempt to put this dreamer to death had been used by God to keep Jacob's family alive. They meant it for evil; God meant it for good.

For a few thousand years, people have loved this long, complicated story of Joseph and his brothers. If we had the time and the talent to tell our story, my story, your story, they, too, would be long and complicated, full of twists and turns. And could we tell our story with such unflinching realism and honesty as the story of Joseph and his brothers? Whenever we look at our lives, we tend to indulge in a good bit of cover-up and deceit. We grew up in a happy home, with loving, understanding parents, adoring brothers and sisters, like a family in a television show from the 1950s.

Here is a story about a real family that's more like the ones you and I have, if we had the strength to tell it. In any family, even the best of them, there is envy, unfairness, competition, struggle, and the threat of violence. Home is not just the alleged "haven in a heartless world." It is also a place of deep feeling and dark secrets, love and hate mixed, the sideward glance, the downcast eyes, the anger that bubbles up, and the rage mixed with popcorn by the fire and presents around the tree. How does anybody make it out alive except by dreaming and holding fast to the dream?

What I'm pointing to is that, even in the best of families, the best of lives, there are always twists and turns, setbacks, and sorrow. And why is it that sometimes those whom we love the most hurt us most, and we they? The one who is your brother is also the one who casts you into the pit. It's a true story about that.

Yet it is also a story about certitude in the midst of real life: "You planned something bad . . . but God produced something good from it." A story that began with resentment and betrayal turns out to be a story about the preservation of God's people. There is some deep, dark presence behind the story, some hand greater than the brothers' guilt and evil deeds, and some author greater than the actors. The dream lives!

The dream isn't stumped, thwarted by the brothers. The bratty little dreamer isn't the hero. The hero of the story—the One who makes it worth retelling—is the Author of another plan, a plan hidden but sure. Joseph tells his brothers, "Don't be upset . . . God sent me before you to make sure you'd survive." God's plans will triumph, but we're not told how. Not even the story or the Bible can do that. We're told that God's plans do triumph.

"God," says Luther, "can shoot with the warped bow and ride the lame horse."

Oh, we're so accustomed to thinking of life as choice or chance. Life is what I do and decide or else a roulette wheel of sheer luck. Is that why we often feel so helpless and hopeless? If life is all up to us, then we know enough about ourselves and our brothers to know we are doomed. A terrible paralysis comes from thinking that it's all up to us. If the fate of the world and the outcome of the future is solely of my doing, or even yours, then a college course in the history of Western civilization should convince us that we are without hope. No wonder we feel frail and fearful before the bomb, AIDS, the ecological crisis, thinning ozone, and even exams. It's all choice or chance.

But Joseph, at the end of the story, is able to look back on all the twists and turns and proclaim, "Don't be upset"! You meant it for evil, but God meant it for good. I'm not talking about the silly notion that everything that happens and everything you do occurs because God planned it that way. I'm talking about the amazing resilience of God's purposes for us. God's intent for the world isn't stumped by our plans.

Calvinist though I am not, I do believe in a kind of predestination, but only in the backward view. While I don't believe that everything that happens in this world happens because God wants it that way (there are still too many murderous brothers to believe that), I do believe that sometimes, when we look back at the twists and turns in our lives, it is amazing how well it all fits, as if there was a hand, an overriding purpose, or a divine intent. As God means it to be so.

Saint Augustine said that our lives are like a yard full of random chicken tracks in the mud, going this way and that in confusion. Seen through the eyes of faith, straining to see the purposes of God, our lives take on pattern, coherence, form; we discover a certain design, a direction as if led by some unseen hand. Then we know with Paul that "God works all things together for good for the ones who love God, for those who are called according to his purpose" (Rom 8:28).

How about your life? How about the twists and the turns that you have made along your life's journey? Are you willing to be as imaginative and as faithful as Joseph seems to be by the end of his life story? Sometimes others were meaning it for bad, sometimes you yourself were messing up and doing wrong, but through it all God was meaning for good, working to bring you home, even while you thought you were wandering.

So make your decisions, your careful choices, and take your lumps when you make a wrong turn or things don't turn out like you planned. Just remember, God . . .

Relating the text

Southern Methodist University's Old Testament scholar John Holbert says, "The story of Joseph is not merely an illustration of how we are to forgive our enemies. . . . Joseph is a complex human being, like Abraham and Jacob before him, like Moses and David after him. Our human actions are never simple but are fraught with complex emotions and needs. . . . How are we like this man Joseph, bent on revenge, filled with our own power, yet convinced that we are called to act on behalf of God? That is the dilemma the story of Joseph, and it is the dilemma of anyone who would be honest with himself and God."

—Roger E. Van Harn, ed., *The Lectionary Commentary: Theological Exegesis for Sunday's Texts*, vol. 1 (Grand Rapids: William B. Eerdmans Publishing Company, 2001), 75

"The narrative comes to a climax. When Joseph has both the power and the motive to avenge his brothers' betrayal, he decides not to retaliate but to re-establish the relationship that his brothers had severed. Throughout the book of Genesis, the stories of conflict and reconciliation: the values of courage and compassion overcome those of accusation and retaliation."

—Gail R. O'Day and David L. Petersen, eds., *Theological Bible Commentary* (Louisville: Westminster/John Knox Press, 2009), 23

I think it important to note that Joseph doesn't look back upon all that happened in his life and say of all that happened, "This was good." It would have been wrong for him to say that about what his older brothers did to him. Rather, Joseph says that God was busy meaning it for good, taking the bad that was produced by his brothers and moving it toward something good.

I saw an advertisement for a credit card that featured a set of human hands with a small globe in the center of the hands. There was a big headline over this picture: "You have whole world in your hands . . . Mastercard."

That's how we modern, North Americans enjoy conceiving of ourselves: it's all up to us. We've got the whole world in our hands.

Yeah, right.

As I attempted to comfort her, six months after her divorce, she said to me, "Well, looking back at this point, my divorce was best thing happened to me. Not that it was good, but that it wasn't the end of my life."

What? How can someone say something like that about so bad an experience?

"It was bad at the time, terrible. But with time, not that the wound heals, but you start to take the long view, to put things in perspective."

Seen through the eyes of faith, we take the "long view," and sometimes that enables us to see that, though it was meant for evil, God meant it for good.

Eighth Sunday after the Epiphany
RC/Pres: Eighth Sunday in Ordinary Time

Sirach 27:4-7 or Isaiah 55:10-13
Psalm 92:1-4, 12-15
1 Corinthians 15:51-58
Luke 6:39-49

Blessed and Cursed by Jesus

Selected reading
Luke 6:39-49

Theme

Jesus is revealed to us in what he blesses and in what he curses. The Christian point of view is not unreserved, nondiscriminating affirmation; there is also a time for judgment. As Christians we are called to imitate Christ, in God's topsy-turvy realm, to embrace those whom he embraced, and to condemn that which he condemns.

Introduction to the readings

Isaiah 55:10-13

Through the prophet Isaiah God says that God's word will go forth in fruitfulness, accomplishing the purposes for which God sent the word.

1 Corinthians 15:51-58
Paul proclaims the grand mystery of God's redemption of our dying. We will be changed!

Luke 6:39-49
Jesus ends his Sermon on the Plain with a couple of parables that illustrate the blessings and the woes of his sermon.

Prayer

Lord Jesus, we come to you, seeking not only your blessing upon our lives but also your correction and even your rebuke. Therefore, we pray this day for your promised blessing on all who are poor, for all those who hunger, and for those who weep. Use us as part of your blessed work to satisfy their need and to move them from tears to laughter.

Lord Jesus, we pray that you would both correct the rich, making us uncomfortable with our riches, and help us acknowledge our hungers, even though we have more than enough. We also pray that you would help us see how much of our laughter and joy is evidence of our ignorance of those in tears and want.

Even as you descended to the plain to bless and to rebuke your disciples, come down to us and bless and rebuke us today, giving us the grace to hear both your blessing and your rebuke without resenting you for them. Amen.

Encountering the text

The Gospel this week is the conclusion of Luke's sermon, on "level ground" (6:17). This week's pericope is a series of parables that illustrate Jesus's opening blessings and woes. They don't make much sense without some consideration of those blessings and woes. Therefore, I recommend that you focus on the verses at the opening of the Sermon on the Plain as a way of highlighting the topsy-turvy nature of God's reign. You may want to use some of the parables in your proclamation this Sunday as a more concrete, narrative illustration of Jesus's opening verses, but I think you will find that confrontation with the opening beatitudes and woes will be challenge enough for the sermon!

Luke's sermon is a parallel to Matthew's Sermon on the Mount from Matthew 5–7. One of the things that makes Luke's version of the sermon distinctive is that Luke has Jesus immediately follow beatitudes with woes. Though God is "kind to ungrateful and wicked people" (6:35), and gracious to people without regard to their merits, Jesus is judgmental toward some in the second part of the sermon.

Noting those who are blessed, we can assume that Jesus is pronouncing grace toward the victims but not toward victimizers. There are no instructions about how to strike, steal from, or abuse others. To the vulnerable and to those who receive the world's abuse, Jesus teaches how not to be a victim—that is, to turn the world's ways on their head and to take charge of the situation by loving, caring, and giving. We are not given the authority to judge or condemn the behavior of others, but it is clear that God blesses certain sorts of people who have been abused by the world. There is no gracious acceptance of the abusers. God shows favor to some, but there is also disfavor for others.

The sermon opens with four beatitudes and four woes that remind us of the blessings and curses that were set before Israel in Deuteronomy 11:26, 28. The poor are blessed, along with those who are despised and rejected. We certainly expect Luke to highlight Jesus's compassion for the poor. This is typical of Luke's Gospel. But we are a bit surprised to find the four blessings followed by four woes. The rich, the full, and the laughing, those who experienced such blessing in this world, are condemned.

This sermon has a definite eschatological cast. Jesus is giving no instructions for us in the present but rather is painting a picture of the last things. It is fair for the preacher to draw out some implications from this picture of what God is ultimately up to in history, but perhaps we would do well to let the congregation draw its own application and instead follow the path of Jesus's Sermon on the Plain in its depiction of who God really is and what God is up to in the world. God's reign has already begun. As Jesus said in his sermon in Nazareth, "Today, this scripture has been fulfilled" (4:21).

Many people may have been conditioned to think that they come to church to hear instruction about how they are to live their lives, what they are to do in order to show that they are Christian. But perhaps this is one of those Sundays, and one of those sermons, when we gather primarily around God's word to hear about God before we draw any implications for our own behavior.

Is this sermon to be received as good news or bad news? I suppose the main factor is where we happen to be standing when we hear this sermon! In the gospel there is good news for some, bad news for others. Where are we when we hear the news?

Proclaiming the text

After the community Martin Luther King Service in January, a person was being interviewed by a reporter in front of the church, and the person, explaining her presence at the service, said, "Dr. King taught us to love everybody, impartially, without regard to who they are, the color of their skin, or anything else, just to love and accept them, to embrace and affirm them. He was just like Jesus in that."

Well, I'm not sure that statement was really fair to Dr. King. He certainly had some choice words of condemnation for southern segregationists! Whether or not that's true of Dr. King, it's certainly not true of Jesus.

Do not get Jesus confused with the department of motor vehicles. When some little bureaucratic toady is dealing with you, he is supposed to treat you as if you were anybody else, impartially, disinterestedly, without prejudice. That's generally what we call justice: everybody is treated exactly the same, without regard to who they are or how they act. When we say we want a more just society, I think that's usually what we're talking about. For us, justice is that place where everybody is nobody in particular. Where nobody has a face or a particular history, such as the department of motor vehicles.

Well, that may be what we want, but what does God want? Faceless, bureaucratic equality may be how we run our kingdoms, but how does God's kingdom work?

Jesus, in today's Gospel, comes down and stands on a level place. Matthew has Jesus do this sermon up on a mountain, but in Luke, Jesus gets down on our level and preaches. Students know that you can tell a lot about a professor, such as what that professor cares about, by reading between the lines and listening carefully to the professor's lecture, analyzing what the professor says. Well, that's what I want you to do this morning with Jesus. What do you think that Jesus thinks from what Jesus teaches?

First half of the lecture: "He looked up at his disciples and said: 'Blessed are you who are poor, for yours is the kingdom of God. Blessed are you who are hungry now, for you will be filled. Blessed are you who weep now, for you will laugh. Blessed are you when people hate you, and when they exclude you, revile you, defame you on account of the Son of Man. Rejoice in that day and leap for joy, for surely your reward is great in heaven; for that's what their ancestors did to the prophets'" (6:20-23 NRSV).

Second part of the lecture: "But woe to you who are rich, for you have received your consolation. Woe to you who are full now, for you will be hungry. Woe to you who are laughing now, for you will mourn and weep. Woe to you when all speak well of you, for that is what their ancestors did to the false prophets" (6:24-26 NRSV).

Alright, Jesus's lecture consists of two parts. Part one is a series of blessings: "Blessed are you who are poor, for yours is the kingdom of God."

"Oh how blessed," we might say, or "how happy," or how, in the Greek, *makarios* are those whom the world curses, people like the poor, the sick, the unemployed, the grieving, and the dispossessed. "Blessed are you who are hungry now, for you will be filled. Blessed are you who weep now, for you will laugh. Blessed are you when people hate you." Now in the kingdoms in which we live, such people are cursed or at least pushed down to the bottom. It's a curse to have to put your children to bed hungry at night, to have to come home and tell your family, "No, there was nobody who needed me today. I didn't find any work today." That's a damning experience for sure.

Somebody was telling me the other day—a person who has been unemployed for a number of months—when I was commenting on how unfortunate her time "between jobs" was, she said, "You know, being out of a job is bad, real bad, but what's worse is the way that people avoid you when you're unemployed. It's like they think you must have done something wrong. You must have been a lazy employee, or you must have had conflict with the boss. People don't want to catch what you've got, and it's no fun to be around people in pain."

She said, "The loss of a job is bad, but the loneliness is worse."

That's how we deal with those whom Jesus blesses. Jesus tells people, in God's kingdom, those who we put on the bottom are blessed—the poor, the hungry, the weeping, the hated. Clearly, Jesus takes sides. He is partial to the poor. He is prejudiced toward those whom we are prejudiced against. Blessed are you who hunger, who weep, and who are poor.

And if that were all there was to Jesus's lecture that day, I suppose that this sermon would be remembered as one of the sweetest things that Jesus ever said, because we all respond positively to anybody who has a good word to say to the less fortunate.

If you'll notice in Matthew's version of this sermon, that's how this sermon ends, with this series of beatitudes, this series of blessings.

Today, though, we've walked away from kinder, gentler Matthew's account of this sermon to what Luke remembers. For Luke the sermon goes on from a series of blessings to an opposite mirror image. Jesus moves on to curses. Curses?

Jesus is known not only by what he affirms but also by what he rejects. After blessing those whom we curse, such as the hungry, the poor, and the sorrowful, Jesus—there's no other way to put it—curses those whom we bless, that is, the rich, the content, and the happy.

God's future sure looks different from our intended future. Today, tears for some and laughter for others. Tomorrow the tables are turned.

Where's the grace, all of that warm-hearted, all-embracing acceptance that we have come to expect from a fair-minded God? I also find it curious that when Jesus really unloads and begins cursing people, Jesus doesn't say, as I might say, "Curse you fornicators, adulterers, thieves, and cheats." He says, "Curse you successful, happy, and full. To hell with you well-fixed."

Jesus doesn't say that God is going to punish these otherwise successful people. Jesus doesn't say, "You ought to go out and try to act more poor," or, "You ought to try to grieve each day." The whole sermon is in the indicative rather than the imperative mood. This sermon is not urging us to do anything. It's just an announcement of who God is and what God's up to. God's kingdom is coming and here is the way God's kingdom looks. This is the bias on which the universe has been cut, says Jesus. This is more real than that false-front that you call reality. Jesus is announcing that this is where God is and here is where God is not.

When our choir went to Poland a few years ago to sing, we were stunned by the remarkable piety of the people in Poland, standing for three hours for worship services in these big ice-cold churches. And yet, as we crossed over the line into the Czech Republic—a country that's more democratic, more economically prosperous—some noted that you could almost feel the piety dissipate. Quite a difference in the Czech Republic from the poverty, misery, and despair we felt in Poland. Observing the sort of care-free, casual quality in the Czech Republic, and less piety and devotion, somebody said, "You know it's kind of embarrassing. It's almost like the Christian faith is prejudiced toward the poor and the suffering."

A pastor in Africa was talking about the remarkable growth of churches in Africa; they were booming. I lamented the state of the mainline church in

North America. And he said to me, "Well, here there is just so much. You have so much freedom, and so much free time, and so many things, and it's just so much, and the Christian faith just doesn't seem to do that well in that environment."

Jesus, in his Sermon on the Plain, gets down on our level and talks about the peculiar shape of the realm of God, the final rendition of God's future.

Well, what do you think about the sermon in Luke? Matthew forgot about the curses and just remembered that Jesus blessed a lot of people that day. Luke has Jesus turn from blessing to cursing. Whether this is good news or bad, grace or judgement, I suppose, depends on where you are when you get the news.

He was top of his class in law school, and a law firm flew him down for an interview. The interview went well. He liked the firm, and the firm liked him, until the second day of the interviews when somebody casually mentioned one of their big clients, and he, the law student, said, "Isn't that the company that's in charge of the casinos and gambling in this state?"

They said, "Yeah, and they pay well, very well. It's all legal."

So he said, "It's legal, but do you think that's moral? I don't know that I could represent well somebody who makes money off the misery and ignorance of others."

He never heard another word from the firm. But Jesus did give a word: "Blessed are you when people hate you, and when they exclude you, revile you, and defame you on account of the Son of Man."

She decided not to go to college but went to work for a center that helped the city's homeless in a great northeastern city. Every night there were just too many people and too few beds, and the hours were long. One morning in August she woke up and collapsed when she got out of bed. She began crying and couldn't stop. It was possibly because of overexposure to the raw edges of human need. A professional was consulted and said she was suffering from depression. Somebody else who knew her well said, "It's burnout."

Jesus called her "blessed." You heard the lecture, didn't you? "Blessed are you who weep now, for you will laugh."

He was the janitor in a company. He didn't have a big office or a high-paying position. But as he cleaned the floors and emptied the wastebaskets, he observed things. He watched people of one particular race come in and apply for jobs. He watched as none of them were hired. Their race was different from the race of those in charge, those who called the shots.

He thought about it and prayed about it, and then he made an appointment and met with the president of the company. He told the president what he had seen and the comments he had overheard.

"I know you want us to be better than that," he said. "I am sure that you want us to be an example to everybody else."

The boss listened. Though he asked no questions, the boss seemed to be agreeing.

The next day the janitor was fired.

"Just not happy in this company," the boss said. "Not really our type. It will be easy to replace him. He's way in over his head. A loser."

But Jesus called him "blessed." "Blessed are you when people hate you, and when they exclude you, revile you, and defame you on account of the Son of Man. . . . For that is what their ancestors did to the prophets."

Jesus appears to be taking sides. He appears to be prejudiced. Jesus seems to lean toward the world in a peculiar, particular way. And this Sunday, while we listen to Jesus's sermon, following Jesus means that we must confront the prejudices of Jesus.

And I don't think that we can love the poor and the powerless without also admitting that there is much to condemn among the rich and the powerful.

There can't really be grace if there's not also judgment. If we are going to be a church that speaks up for justice, then we have to speak out against injustice. At least that's one implication of Jesus's blessings and curses.

Carlisle Marney, a great Baptist prophet and my mentor when I was young, told a group of us clergy, "The trouble with you guys is not what you little preachers manage to affirm, but what you fail to reject. You go on about your ministry, and you're always saying 'bless, bless, bless.' . . . But you can't say that without there also being a time when you join Jesus in saying, 'damn, damn, damn.'"

Relating the text

Marcus Buckingham wrote a fine book on management, *First Break All the Rules*. A recurring theme in Buckingham's book is that many of the "rules" that managers work by need to be broken in order for management to lead in ways that are most beneficial to the organization. One of the rules that ought to be broken, says Buckingham, is the bureaucratic truism, "Treat everyone the same."

A leader has the responsibility to notice and to empower those employees who are most important to the life of the organization. Not everyone who works in a company is of equal value to the future and vitality of the company. A leader must, in a sense, "play favorites," identifying and undergirding those who have the gifts and the skills to move the organization forward.

Today's proclamation asserts that Jesus takes sides, plays favorites. In noticing those whom we often fail to notice, in calling them "blessed," Jesus changes our point of view. Jesus lifts up those whom we, in our North American culture, often put down.

What might the church learn from Jesus's refusal to "treat everyone the same"?

A person was telling me the other day, she's had six months of cancer treatments, she hadn't responded well to the therapy, and things are not going well. My heart went out to her, and she said, "You know, it's odd. I feel closer to God now than at any time in my life." There's a reason for that. It's as if she's finally gotten on God's level. She's descended down to the plain, down to where Jesus preaches his sermon.

As chaplain, I talked with Duke students about their parents and the guidance their parents have given them about what they ought to do with their lives. Primarily students say that their parents say to them: "Dear, whatever you do, I just want you to be happy." It's a great blessing if your children grow up and they're happy. And yet, in today's Gospel Jesus curses the happy.

Barbara Walters used to have television specials in December that presented the ten most influential Americans of the year. It was Ms. Walters's way of honoring those who, in her words, "contributed the most to America" and were the most admired. And I can tell you, there wasn't a hungry, weeping, grieving, empty one among them. They were all people of great power, prestige, and possessions, people who had happily impacted America.

Well, as we see in the Gospel, Jesus had some choice words for people like that: "Those of you who are rich, damn you! You've already received your consolation. You have already had the best that this world has to offer. What could God give you?"

"You were so good at working the kingdoms of this world to your personal advantage, well now, in God's kingdom, curse you. If you've had your fill, if you are stuffed with all that can be consumed here, well, to hell with you!"

By the way, I teach preaching at a seminary, and I don't think I would bless a student who preached a sermon like the Sermon on the Plain. Be the student on a mountain, or on a plain, or in a church.

Transfiguration Sunday
RC/Pres: Ninth Sunday
in Ordinary Time

Exodus 34:29-35
Psalm 99
2 Corinthians 3:12–4:2
Luke 9:28-36, (37-43a)

Blessed Befuddlement

Selected Reading
Luke 9:28-36

Theme
Jesus Christ, God's love incarnate, is the great mystery that always remains a mystery to us. The closer we come to understanding God, the more mystified we are that God is for us. To be a Christian is to be in love with the grand mystery that is God—Father, Son, and Holy Spirit. The mystery of God is not a problem to be solved or a question to be answered but rather a relationship to be enjoyed.

Introduction to the readings
Exodus 34:29-35

Moses descends, with shining face, from Mount Sinai with the two tablets of the covenant.

2 Corinthians 3:12–4:2
Paul speaks of the joy with which we behold God "with unveiled faces" through the work of the Holy Spirit.

Luke 9:28-36, (37-43a)
Jesus leads three of his disciples up a mountain, and there he is transfigured before his wondering disciples.

Prayer

Ever-living, ever-loving God, grant us grace to worship you as you are rather than as we would have you be. Give us the courage to see you as you would appear to us rather than as we would like you to look. Guide us into the depths of your mystery. Help us to scale the heights of your glory. In all things, help us to love you as our God, our guide, and our savior. Amen.

Encountering the text

Whatever we have to say about today's text, the transfiguration of Jesus on the mountain, can we all agree that it is a very strange, mysterious story? In our first lesson we see Moses going up the mountain. There, on the mountain, God reveals God's way to Moses. At last the distant God comes close and speaks. At last the veil is lifted, and there is direct address.

And of course this passage from Exodus is a setup for this Sunday's Gospel. Jesus leads his disciples up a high mountain, as if to bring them closer to God on high. And there, wonder of wonders, the disciples converse with Jesus, Moses, and Elijah. There is a voice from heaven, "This is my Son, my chosen one. Listen to him!" God speaks and reveals. The disciples are moved from wonderment and enjoyment to awe and fear.

Is this story of the transfiguration a kind of parable for how it is sometimes in the church's worship? We meet. We converse with God. We listen. And sometimes, by the grace of God, there is a voice, a revelation. The living God speaks, reveals, intrudes, and interrupts.

Yet even in the speaking, even amid revelation, there is always the mystery. We can never hope to explain such moments. We preachers ought to be careful not even to try to explicate such events. And yet, somehow the fact that they are inexplicable and very mysterious makes them seem all the more real.

And even if we hear the voice clearly, there is a sense in which the closer we come to God, the more distant God seems to us. We are not God, not even close. So the more we know of God, the more we respect our distance from God.

Today's proclamation will be a celebration of that grand, ineffable mystery that is God in Jesus Christ.

Proclaiming the text

Most of my sermons have as their purpose the clearing up of the fog of confusion. They promise to get to the essence of a thing, to make the complicated simple, to explain what something really means. Marcus Borg begins his book *The Heart of Christianity* (Nashville: Harper Collins, 2009) with, "There are no serious intellectual obstacles to being Christian. There is a way of seeing Christianity that makes persuasive and compelling sense of life."

I'm a preacher. My job is to help you see God more clearly, to understand more nearly the truth of God. Well, this is transfiguration. You heard the story of Jesus, miraculously transfigured before his befuddled disciples on the mountaintop. Do you really think I've got a clear explanation for that? Forget it!

We preachers have yet to fathom the significance of the fact that Jesus's primary, distinctive method of communicating the gospel was the anticommunicative form of parable.

Matthew says, "Jesus said all these things to the crowds in parables, and he spoke to them only in parables" (Matt 13:34). He only talked in parables? Is this an exaggeration? No, it's an observation of Jesus as communicator. Jesus refuses to say anything to you except in parabolic form.

A sower went out to sow and began slinging handfuls of seed everywhere. Of course, seed sown with that sort of recklessness is sure to perish—on rock, among thorns, and trampled along the path. (What sort of farmer sows seed on a highway?) Some of the seed, a small fraction, actually germinated. Jesus concludes, "If you've got ears, use them."

The kingdom of God is like a rich man who employs a poor man who, when threatened with termination, swindles his boss out of large sums of money, calling in his boss's creditors and having them write off their debts so they will be indebted to the employee when he gets fired. The boss hears about the crime, calls the little crook in, and says, "You genius, you! Good work!"

A farmer's got a tree that hasn't produced fruit in three years. "Cut it down?" says the longsuffering farmer.

"Master, let me dig around it and pile high the manure (*koprion*), and let's see what happens."

The disciples, feeling the *koprion* getting rather deep around them, ask, "How come you teach in these riddles?"

Jesus responds, "You have been given the mysteries of God's kingdom, but these mysteries come to everyone else in parables so that when they see, they can't see, and when they hear, they can't understand" (Luke 8:10). What?! Why would Jesus talk in a way that cultivates confusion?

Sometimes when we're trying to understand something, we attempt to explain through analogy. And Jesus seems to do this in his parables. He says, "God's kingdom is like . . ." That's analogy. Work from what we know to understand what we don't know. This is like that. Want to know what B means?

You already know what A means. Well, B means something analogous to what A means. Now you know B.

But Jesus appears to use analogy as a means of assuring us that whatever the reign of God means, it's not what we thought. Oh, we preachers try to explain, to lessen the distance between you and God. We hope to help you understand God. Trouble is, in the modern world, sometimes we attempt to understand or explain in order to control. We say that we want to "get a grip" on some subject. Or when we've finally figured something out, we say, "I got it." Got it!

But what if that which you're trying to understand (God) can never be gripped, grabbed, or seized by you? What if we're not so much here in worship this morning to "get" God but rather here daring to expose ourselves to the possibility that during this service of worship God might "get" us?

A teacher of Zen told his cocksure students one day that they could never know Zen until they were willing not to know. They must be honest about their ignorance before they can have any wisdom. "A full jug holds no wine," he told them.

The Bible says, "The beginning of wisdom is the fear of the LORD" (Prov 9:10). What is this biblical "fear"? Could it be the fear that, when it comes to knowing about God, it is wisdom to know that we are not in control? We don't know.

What happens when you say (as the disciples on the Mount of Transfiguration surely must have said), "What was that?" You admit to ignorance, confusion. Sometimes that confusion creates room. The admission of the mystery is the beginning of growth. I remind you that the tempting promise of the serpent back in Genesis was that if they ate from the forbidden tree of knowledge, their eyes would be opened and they could "be like God" (Gen 3:5).

So far in Luke's Gospel, Jesus has been patiently teaching his disciples, explaining to them the nature of the reign of God. Sometimes he has used parables, pithy little stories. But rarely do these parables seem to help them understand anything more clearly. In fact, sometimes the parables seem to confuse them all the more.

And now Jesus takes his disciples up a mountain, as if to take them up to a higher level. Once there, Jesus does not teach or explain anything. In fact, he befuddles them. He is transfigured before them. His garments glisten. There is a light from heaven and a voice too. Moses and Elijah come back from the dead and appear before them. It's all very, very befuddling.

Now, I know what you're thinking. "Well preacher, now is when you come up with it. Now is when you earn your salary and explain this weird Bible story to us. Tell us, preacher, what does this story really mean? How can we use it in our daily lives? How are we to make sense of this story?"

But what if I can't explain it to you? What if—and I think this is the point I'm trying to make—what if I don't attempt to explain it to you?

What if this strange story of Jesus transfigured on the mountaintop is itself a kind of parable of Jesus? What if this episode is not meant to explain Jesus but rather to point to Jesus? What if this is more like a picture that we're to look at and encounter rather than some problem to solve?

Nobody I know looks at some great work of art—stands there before the canvas—and then exclaims, "I got it! I got it!"

Rather, if it's a truly great work of art, sometimes you walk away muttering, "Wow. It really got me."

The transfiguration is a kind of parable of us here at worship. We gather here in our church, just wanting to be with Jesus. Maybe we think of Jesus primarily as a wonderful teacher, or an inspiring moral example, or a good guide along life's way, or all the other rather mundane ways of thinking about Jesus. We come to church to get our explanations, or our rules, or our principles for life.

And that's okay, as far as it goes. But sometimes Jesus takes it to another level. Sometimes he leads us beyond our answers and rules and certainties. It's as if he takes our hand and leads us up into another realm. He shines before us, mysterious and wonderful, beyond our ability to explain or understand. And maybe that's when worship, when church, when being a disciple of Jesus is as good as it gets. And we exclaim, as those first disciples exclaimed on the mountaintop, "Master, it's good that we're here."

Peter said on the mountain, "We should construct three shrines: one for you, one for Moses, and one for Elijah." The Gospel writer says that "he didn't know what he was saying." He was talking nonsense.

Well, maybe that's worship, as good as it gets, when we no longer know what we are saying, when we are out of our minds. We have sailed beyond mere thinking and rational thought. We are in ecstasy. We are in another realm with God, with a mystery greater than we know how to describe.

I know that the old King James Version of the Bible didn't give a very good translation of John 1:5. It says that Jesus came into the world as light shining in the darkness but the "darkness comprehendeth it not." It's far better linguistically to update this old English with "and the darkness did not overcome it," as in the Revised Standard Version and other newer versions.

But I still think that older phrase speaks to what it was like to have Jesus come into our darkened world. Jesus came to us and was pure, shining light. But the darkness "comprehendeth it not." The darkness, our darkness, couldn't figure Jesus out. We couldn't comprehend God coming to us as a crucified savior.

That we couldn't fully comprehend, explain, or figure him out is, in a way, confirmation of his divinity. Jesus befuddled us and confused us, not only on the Mount of Transfiguration but when he ate with and welcomed sinners, when he died for us sinners, and when he showed us a way that was not our way. We just couldn't comprehend him.

We still can't, thanks be to God!

Relating the text

We are modern people who want explanations, answers, clear analysis. Alas, for us preachers the Bible has no interest in this modern reductionist project. Perhaps that's because the point of intellectual clarity, in modernity, is control.

"The Heart of . . ."

"The Essence of . . ."

"Basic . . ."

"Read this book, and you will be like God. You will know God. You will be able to manage God."

The Bible is strangely content to let the complicated stay complicated, even to make it more complicated. Scripture is opaque, demands interpretation, wants preaching.

For instance, Luke begins his Gospel saying that he is going to write an orderly account of "the events that have been fulfilled among us" concerning Jesus. With that, Luke launches into a strange digression about a childless old couple named Elizabeth and Zechariah, one of whom is encountered by an angel who tells the old man that his long-childless wife is pregnant, and when Zechariah asks, "How can this be?" the angered angel strikes the old man mute.

Not the most promising beginning for an "orderly account" of Jesus!

Thomas Jefferson was a thoroughly modern man. Jefferson was a deist; he believed that God had created a universe that was a wondrous machine and then retired, leaving us in charge. Jefferson the deist decided to create his own Bible. He cut out the "primitive" Hebrew scriptures. Turning to the New Testament, he snipped out everything that did not square with a modern, rational man's devotion to reason and natural law. This meant the miracles had to go. Healing stories were out. You probably aren't surprised that Jefferson's Bible was a slender volume, composed mostly of the moral teachings of the man of Nazareth. Christianity was reduced to morality, a faith without revelation or theology. It was a practical faith, a faith without a God who was in any way present or active. We were in charge now. The world was thereby demystified, and God was silenced. We could run the world as we pleased.

Reformer John Calvin spoke of the "hiddenness of God" whereby we encounter God in a hidden, obscure fashion, awaiting that full, radiant revelation that is Christ. Martin Luther also spoke of the "hidden God." But for Luther, God is hidden "in the despised man, Christ." God is most hidden, for Luther, precisely when we encounter God most vividly and directly in Christ. We do not, cannot ever fully comprehend the God who is encountered in the crucified Christ. Thus, the nearer God in Christ comes to us, the stranger God seems.

A friend of mine had an aunt who was certainly no theologian, but every time that the theologian Paul Tillich spoke in the area of Cambridge, Massachusetts, his aunt went to hear Tillich lecture. She sat there, transfixed by the German theologian's remarks.

"You mean that she was able to understand what Tillich was talking about?" I asked.

"Are you kidding?" replied my friend. "My aunt never understood a word of what he was talking about. But she said that she loved listening to him because she knew that whatever it was he was talking about, it was very, very important."

First Sunday in Lent

Deuteronomy 26:1-11
Psalm 91:1-2, 9-16
Romans 10:8b-13
Luke 4:1-13

Tempted

Selected reading
Luke 4:1-13

Theme

Perhaps, in the now postmodern world, we are ready for a reconsideration of the concept of Satan. While the existence of a satan, a devil, may be a notion many have rejected, on this First Sunday of Lent, as we remember Jesus's temptation by Satan, the idea of Satan may be an idea worth reconsidering as we ponder the mystery of evil.

Introduction to the readings

Deuteronomy 26:1-11
Having arrived at the threshold of the promised land, an offering of thanksgiving is prescribed for the Hebrews.

Romans 10:8b-13
Paul joyfully proclaims the triumph of God's salvation in Christ to the Romans.

Luke 4:1-13
Out in the wilderness, Jesus is tempted by Satan.

Prayer

Lord Jesus, you have invaded the whole world with your presence. You came to us because we could not come to you. Yet when you came to us, you were not the savior that we were expecting. We therefore rejected you, turned away from your love, and once again attempted to go our own way.

Lord Jesus, you were tried and tested, but you did not deter from your vocation. You were always true to who you were called to be.

Keep being yourself, Lord Jesus. Keep loving us sinners, keep reaching out toward us, keep invading our world with your presence. Our best hope, our only way, our salvation is that you would keep being who you are.

And we have great faith that you will. Amen.

Encountering the text

Today's Gospel deals with Satan's temptation of Jesus in the wilderness. This is one of the comparatively few places in the New Testament where Satan is depicted.

We will use this text as a means of talking about the notion of Satan, an accuser, a devil as a personification of evil. Is our modern inability to conceive of Satan another aspect of our denial of the reality of evil?

Today we reflect upon the existence of evil in our world. We will do so through a reexamination of the concept of Satan.

Proclaiming the text

The preacher began her sermon, on this First Sunday in Lent, by saying, "Luke says that, at the beginning of his ministry, Jesus was tempted by Satan in the wilderness. Now we modern people may find it hard to conceive of a devil, a 'satan,' who tempts us. But we need not believe in the personification of evil in order to believe that evil is real."

And as I sat there listening to this sermon, I thought to myself, "You know, I find it quite easy to believe in a personal satan, in the existence of a devil. Maybe it's because I'm now over fifty, but I'm not shocked at all that, at the beginning of his career, Jesus met Satan."

Several years ago, a best-selling book by Princeton professor Elaine Pagels, *The Origin of Satan* (New York: Random House, 1995), explored our continuing fascination with the devil. Pagels tells the story of how Christians borrowed the notion of Satan from the Jews and then, in a peculiar perversion, applied it to Jews, demonizing their Jewish adversaries as collaborators with Satan against Christians. Then they demonized their pagan enemies, Christian heretics, anybody with whom they had disagreement.

Pagels says that Satan is merely the ancient Jewish and Christian name for the "other," for anyone who is different from us and whose existence poses a challenge to our identity. Church history is a long record of the ways in which we have demonized those whom we did not understand or whom we understood as a threat to us. So white people depicted the devil as black, even though there is no mention of color in the Bible. The Bible says that Satan often "disguises himself as an angel of light." Evil hides among the good. Scott Peck, in his book about evil, *People of the Lie* (New York: Touchstone, 1998), says that one good place to look for evil is at church, not because church is inherently evil, but because it's just that church is where evil attempts to hide itself among the good.

Here is where I think Pagels has written a poor book. For Pagels, Satan is little more than our demonization of the human propensity to regard other people as a threat, a result of the "profoundly human view that 'otherness' is evil." We take those whom we don't understand and label them as satanic. The concept of Satan, for Pagels, is only an example of the way in which we tend to project our evil ideas upon others and call that Satan.

What she does is to reverse the traditional Christian view that Satan is somehow mixed up in the origins of evil to mean that our evil is the origin of Satan. The modern world has a long history of reducing religious faith to nothing more than psychological or social problems, and Pagels does just that. If Satan is only a projection of our evil tendencies, then why isn't God only a projection of our good tendencies? It's all only a projection anyway.

How on earth does a projection of our imaginations have such power over us? When Jesus was confronted by Satan in the wilderness in today's Gospel, certainly Matthew may be saying that Jesus was face-to-face with some of his own internal conflicts. Jesus surely loved life, wanted to avoid pain, wanted to be loved and accepted. Who doesn't? And it is true that those human desires—to avoid pain, to be loved, to be accepted and successful—are the origins of some of the most satanic temptations.

But by saying that Jesus was confronted by Satan, that the evil that confronted Jesus had a face, a personality, Luke meant us to know that the resistance against Jesus was organized, subtle (note that Satan quotes scripture just as well as Jesus!), a genuine threat to Jesus. In resisting Satan, Jesus wasn't just overcoming his own natural inclinations; Jesus was confronting and defeating the principalities and powers, the evil not just within the human heart, but the evil within the whole universe, evil even greater than that of our own creation. Pagels says that belief in Satan has tempted Christian people to demonize those who are innocent, who are merely different from us, and thereby such belief has contributed to human sinfulness.

Yet there is another side to the coin, says Harvard's Jon Levenson, a great Jewish scholar. If Satan tempts us to do things that, in our better moments, we might not have done, might Satan also energize us to do good things that, left to our own devices, we might not have done ("The Devil in the Details," *Commentary* [September 1995]: 54–57)?

Levenson illustrates by invoking the blessed memory of Dietrich Bonhoeffer (1906–45). Bonhoeffer was dismissed from his teaching post by the Nazis. He lectured awhile in America but decided to return home to Germany at the outbreak of World War II to work against the Nazis. Earlier, in castigating a Christian organization that was working with Hitler, Bonhoeffer did not shrink from using the inflammatory term *anti-Christ* to describe Hitler and those Christians who collaborated with the Nazis.

Eventually, Bonhoeffer paid for his existence with his life. But Levenson wonders if Bonhoeffer would have been as clear and courageous in his resistance if he had merely explained Hitler and his followers as those who were merely the unknowing victims of inner psychological distress. No, Bonhoeffer believed in the existence of the demonic, in the possibility of evil having a face, a name.

Levenson, perhaps because he is a member of a people who have suffered unspeakable evil at the hands of others, is willing at least to consider the possibility that evil is real, that evil may have a personality, a face, a name—Satan. He says, "Given the mysterious capacity of human beings for unspeakable evil, a belief in Satan and his works may lead not only to acts of demonization, but also to acts of redemption. In explaining away the true challenge posed by the satanic to the divine—and posed, as well, to us—Elaine Pagels unwittingly contributes to the sentimental view of religion."

Many years ago, I wrote a book on sin, evil, and the Christian life, *Sighing for Eden* (Nashville: Abingdon Press, 1985). In that book I took the rather conventional view that, when discussing sin and evil, the idea of the existence of a personal devil, or Satan, was not very helpful. The evil is more in us, than outside of us, I said. Besides, those who say, when they have done wrong, "The devil made me do it," are probably just trying to excuse their own sinful behavior.

I received a letter from a woman who had been a pastor for a few years. "What you say about there being no real Satan may be true. However, as a woman pastor, I have come to believe that, if evil doesn't have a name, Satan, or the devil, it ought to. I came into the ministry because God called me here. I have sacrificed and worked to gain the skills to be a pastor. The churches I have served are full of good people, at least better-than-average people who are in the church wanting to be good and to do good. For the most part, my ministry among them has been well received. But not completely. I have seen good people do some terrible things. I have witnessed a depth of cruelty, some, but not all of it directed toward me, that has shocked me. I am now willing to believe that our lives are not entirely our own, that we are in the grip of something, someone who leads us down dark paths. In short, I am more willing than you to conceive of Satan."

Her letter hit home to me. It is fine for me—someone who has rarely encountered real injustice or cruelty, someone who is well fed and in good health—to dismiss the idea of Satan as outmoded, naive, and unnecessary. Yet for someone who has been the recipient of real evil, it is possible for evil to have a face and a name—that is, Satan. It is no kindness to tell someone who has encountered real evil that evil is only some warped projection of our human psyche, a result of improper education or poor child-rearing practices. The pain and anguish suffered by the victims of injustice, sin, and evil are real, so real we even have a name for it.

Paul wrote these anguished words after he had become a Christian:

"I don't know what I'm doing, because I don't do what I want to do. Instead, I do the thing that I hate. But if I'm doing the thing that I don't want to do, I'm agreeing that the Law is right. But now I'm not the one doing it anymore. Instead, it's sin that lives in me. I know that good doesn't live in me—that is, in my body. The desire to do good is inside of me, but I can't do it. I don't do the good that I want to do, but I do the evil that I don't want to do. But if I do the very thing that I don't want to do, then I'm not the one doing it anymore. Instead, it is sin that lives in me that is doing it. . . . I'm a miserable human being. Who will deliver me from this dead corpse?" (Rom 7:15-20, 24).

I expect that you know, from your own experience, the sort of inner turmoil that Paul felt. Jesus knows, for he felt it himself at the beginning of his ministry, in the wilderness.

Thus, when we pray the Lord's Prayer, we ask to be rescued in the time of trial, to be delivered from evil. Some versions of the Lord's Prayer say, "Deliver us from the evil one." Thus, the prayer makes explicit that there is a conspiracy against God's good kingdom in which a personification of evil (Satan) makes sense. First Peter says to young Christians: "Be clearheaded. Keep alert. Your accuser, the devil, is on the prowl like a roaring lion, seeking someone to devour. Resist him, standing firm in the faith" (1 Pet 5:8-9a).

In praying to God to deliver us we acknowledge that God is greater than any foe of God. The power of evil must be admitted and taken seriously yet not too seriously. Perhaps that is why, though the Lord's Prayer honestly focuses upon trial, temptation, and evil, it never mentions Satan by name. And that's probably the way we ought to think about Satan. Evil is not a mere projection of our conflict egos. Evil is real. Yet the cross and resurrection of Christ tell us that evil does not have the last word. Evil is a threatening power, though a defeated one. Though the battle rages Monday through Saturday, every time we come to church we say that we know who has won the war.

When we pray for deliverance from evil, we acknowledge that we have not the resources, on our own, to resist evil. The Lord's Prayer is so honest. The power represented by the name Satan has real power over our lives. The good news is that, just as Jesus was able to resist the wiles of Satan, to reject his tempting offers, we can also resist. In our weakness, we reach out and there is deliverance.

Isn't that how Alcoholics Anonymous puts it? "We had to reach out to a power greater than ourselves." Note that one of the ways Alcoholics Anonymous enables us to reach out "to a power greater than ourselves" and the chief means through which that power intervenes on our behalf, is by putting us as individuals in a group. The community enables us to be free from Satan. Jesus stood alone in the wilderness against Satan. But we don't have to stand alone. Standing alone, as isolated individuals, we are no match for the devil.

Maybe that's why you are here this morning. You are not alone. The church stands with you amid Satan's temptations, in whatever wilderness you find yourself. Jesus, who knows what it's like to be face-to-face with evil, stands with you.

Here, the good news this First Sunday in Lent: although temptation is real, Satan does not have the last word. Thanks be to God, through Jesus Christ, we are more than victors. Amen.

Relating the text

Theologians display a variety of approaches to the idea of the devil. Walter Wink says that the expression "The devil made me do it" constitutes evidence that we have in fact "delivered ourselves straight into his hands. When we fail to make conscious, committed choices for God, we default on our 'dominion' over the world, and Satan becomes like a holding company that has taken over billions of mortgages in arrears through foreclosure. The satanic is actualized as evil precisely by our failure to choose."

—Walter Wink, *Unmasking the Powers: The Invisible Forces That Determine Human Existence* (Minneapolis: Fortress Press, 1986), 34

John Newport similarly contends that Satan's powers are limited: "He can tempt, deceive, accuse and attack us, but he cannot force us to do something against our wills. We cannot truthfully say, 'The devil made me do it.'"

—John Newport, *Life's Ultimate Questions: A Contemporary Philosophy of Religion* (Dallas: Word, 1989), 194

Daniel Day Williams would argue that projecting the image of the devil in order to avoid responsibility is part of the problem. Reason dispels superstition about demonic personalized entities, he says. The assertion of demonic possession in the face of reason leads to witch hunts and injustice.

Belief in demons and supernatural powers can itself be demonic.

—Daniel Day Williams, *The Demonic and the Divine* (Minneapolis: Fortress Press, 1990), 23

Second Sunday in Lent

Genesis 15:1-12, 17-18
Psalm 27
Philippians 3:17–4:1
Luke 13:31-35 or Luke 9:28-36, (37-43a)

Repent

Selected reading
Luke 13:31-35

Theme
Christians are given the power by God to be honest about our sin, to confess all the ways that our lives have betrayed the love of God. And then we are given the gift of forgiveness, the ability to start over. The good news is, we can repent.

Introduction to the readings

Genesis 15:1-12, 17-18
This is the story of God's gracious covenant with Abraham.

Philippians 3:17–4:1
Paul reminds the Philippians that "our citizenship is in heaven," therefore we ought to live accordingly.

Luke 13:31-35
Jesus, warned of a plot against him, weeps for the city of Jerusalem, calling the people to repent.

Prayer

Lord, during these forty days of Lent, enable us to see all the ways that we have forsaken you, have turned away from your will for our lives, and have betrayed your love for us. Give us the courage to count our sins, to be honest about our faults, and then to return to your way. Loving Lord, whose property is always to forgive, grant us the grace to see not only the error of our crooked ways but also the wonder of your gracious embrace. So might we be renewed, returned, restored, by your love. Amen.

Encountering the text

Here, at the beginning of Lent, our Gospel, Luke 13:31-35, looks ahead to Jesus's passion. Jesus is "determined to go to Jerusalem" (9:51). We are on a journey with Jesus that will lead to the cross. Luke borrows most of this pericope from Matthew with the exception of verses 31-33. Though that "fox" King Herod is after him, Jesus must continue to do his work, must continue, through signs of mercy and love, toward the consummation of his ministry. The Pharisees, who are depicted as the steadfast enemies of Jesus, here attempt to befriend Jesus, to warn him of the impending crisis. You are in big trouble when even your enemies are concerned for your safety! Jesus responds with "go tell!"—a kind of retort to the Pharisees' concerns. Jesus remains steadfast to his mission.

The lection ends with a lament for Jerusalem. Jerusalem has turned away prophetic truth before and may well do so again. But there is still time to repent, to turn, to return. Jesus moves quickly from any concern for his own safety to concern for Jerusalem. He invokes the tender image of the mother hen protecting her brood (9:34).

Jesus recounts the history of Jerusalem with the prophets. A major prophetic message was the call to "repent." As Jesus portrays these final days, this is Jerusalem's last chance. It is high time for turning, for repentance. Will Jerusalem at last turn and return to the Lord?

No doubt there were many in Jerusalem who took some sort of consolation in the temple, the great, solid rock that represented Israel's relationship to Yahweh. Yet Jesus sees an end to such security. Here is a warning to any who take security in the solidity of religious membership, institutions, and traditions. All must repent. His warning therefore is more than prophetic fatalism. It is a prophetic call to change, to turn. There is still time to change; furthermore, Jerusalem can change. There is the good news amid these prophetic, Lenten warnings. Good news. We can repent.

Proclaiming the text

Jesus moves steadily toward the capital city, toward Jerusalem, toward his fate on the cross. And as he does, without a thought for his own fate, he takes a moment to warn us about our fate. He takes a moment to call us to repent.

Lent is the season of repentance—forty days of honest reflection on our identity as sinners, yet sinners who, by the grace of God, are being redeemed in Jesus Christ. We are being redeemed through the work that Jesus goes to do in Jerusalem, yet we will not be redeemed unless we repent. Jesus calls us to repent.

Once the church seemed preoccupied with this message. There was a day when, if you asked someone, "What do they do at church?" they would respond, "Church is where you go to be told that you are a sinner and that you need to get down on your knees and repent."

I don't hear that message too often in churches today. Today, we are usually told that we are basically good people who are doing the best that we can, and the best that we can is good enough for God. God loves us, just as we are, blemishes and all. Talk of sin is so depressing, a put down.

But this was not the message of Jesus. He was on his way to Jerusalem, where we will find that our sin is so serious that we will conspire to put God's Son to death on a horrible cross. And he was put there, not for the things that we usually call ugly and evil, but for the things that we call good. Therefore, his cross stands as a stark warning to us of the perils of our sin.

Yet, by the grace of God, the cross stands for us as a sign that God forgives, that Christ takes our sin on himself, bears it, and forgives.

That is our only hope in our sin. Jesus moves to Jerusalem, not to punish, but to call to repentance. He promises a people who have a long history of turning against the prophets, of ignoring the truth, forgiveness and new life.

I think that one of the most detrimental, evil notions among us is the simple conviction, "People don't change."

This, so far as I can tell, is one of the main reasons why people stay trapped in the hell of addiction. Once a drunk, always a drunk. You can't fight genetics. We arrive here in this world fixed at birth, finished. All of life consists of simply replaying the tapes that were implanted in your brain when you were born. Life consists of a whole host of determinisms. Once your gender, or your socioeconomic level has spoken, what can anybody do? Don't you see, even at the end, even as he moves toward his certain death, Jesus calls on people to change. He calls on Jerusalem to repent. One might have thought after all of the teaching, after the centuries of prophetic warnings, it would be too late. But it's not too late. There is still time to repent.

And there is time for you as well. Jesus may have more faith in you than you have in yourself. I know. Old habits die hard; you can't teach an old dog new tricks. I know.

But I also know that, in Jesus, there is a power unleashed in life. There is a power greater than that of our own devising. When God created us, Genesis says that God's image was stamped upon us. Admittedly, we have defaced that image terribly with our sin. Yet God intends to have God's way with us. By the grace of God, we can change.

I therefore want to call you to honest consideration of your life. How have you wandered far from God's way? What are those habits, those inclinations, those propensities that need to be changed if you would live the abundant life?

The good news is, Jesus means to have you, to have all of you, you as you are meant to be. The good news is, you can change.

Relating the text

In his remarkable study of growing "new paradigm churches," a veteran sociologist of religion notes the way that these congregations plan for conversion, attempting to create occasions for repentance and turning to God:

"Conversions are not going to occur unless a church affirms their efficacy and regularly provides occasions that trigger their occurrence. While this may seem self-evident, mainline churches are not going to grow through conversion if they do not affirm 'born-again' experiences; if they do grow, it will be for other reasons, such as the appeal of their social outreach programs, the beauty of their formal worship, or the quality of their children's programs. In contrast to many mainline churches, new paradigm churches are highly conversion-oriented; they believe that they have an answer to people's felt needs, and this conviction is perhaps intensified by the fact that so many of the pastors have drug addiction and other vices in their backgrounds. These pastors understand firsthand the needs of people with such trouble-filled lifestyles, and they have the vocabulary to communicate, at a very personal level, the solution to these individuals' problems."

—Donald E. Miller, *Reinventing American Protestantism: Christianity in the New Millennium* (Berkeley: University of California Press, 1997)

Ernest Hemingway's *A Farewell to Arms*, a virtual ode to hopelessness, contains the following remarkable sentence: "The world breaks everyone, and afterward many are strong at the broken places." Repentance can be painful. It does involve a kind of breaking. Yet Christians claim that it is in such breaking, in such stooping and humility, that our true selves are discovered. Here is a stooping that leaves us standing taller, a breaking that makes us strong.

—Ernest Hemingway, *A Farewell to Arms*

The gates of hell are open night and day;
Smooth the descent, and easy is the way:
But to return, and view the cheerful skies,
In this the task and mighty labor lies.

—Virgil, *Aeneid* 6.124–41 (translated by John Dryden)

Third Sunday in Lent

Isaiah 55:1-9

Psalm 63:1-8

1 Corinthians 10:1-13

Luke 13:1-9

Judgmental Jesus?

Selected reading

Luke 13:1-9

Theme

Jesus loves us enough to accept us as we are. But Jesus loves us so much that he will not leave us as we are. Jesus loves us enough to tell us the truth about our situation. Jesus holds up before us our true, God-given vocation and holds us accountable to that vocation. Sometimes Jesus judges us and calls us to repent and change because Jesus loves us.

Introduction to the readings

Isaiah 55:1-9

The prophet Isaiah speaks to suffering Israel on exile. Surprising, Isaiah calls even suffering Israel to repentance, to change, to return to the covenant with God.

1 Corinthians 10:1-13

God is faithful. Even when we are unfaithful, God is faithful. This is the good news that Paul proclaims to the Corinthians.

Luke 13:1-9

Jesus responds to a report of a terrible tragedy, in which Pontius Pilate has massacred a group of innocent people at the temple, with a parable about a barren fig tree. Jesus calls upon people to repent.

Prayer

Lord Jesus Christ, you come to us with gracious love. You take us as we are. But in love, you do not leave us as we are. You love us enough to judge us, to correct us, to hold us to account. Give us the grace to see your judgment of us as part of your grace toward us, to see our lives in the light of your truth, to grow, to change, and to be reborn into the people you would have us to be. Courageously let us listen to what you have to say to us, to receive what you have to give us, even if what you have to tell us is the truth, even if what you desire to give us is judgment. Amen.

Encountering the text

This Sunday's Gospel presents a real challenge for us. Here is how I would describe that challenge: the contemporary North American church has succeeded in sentimentalizing Jesus to the point where we have taken the romantic "gentle Jesus meek and mild" of the nineteenth century and reworked it into Jesus our good friend, our buddy, our therapist, who always affirms and never criticizes, always blesses and never curses.

Today's Gospel presents us with an unsettling, judgmental Jesus.

At the end of Luke 12, Jesus says clearly that he has come to cast fire on the earth. He warns people to read the signs of the times that predict coming judgment.

While Jesus is speaking about signs of judgment (12:54-59), news comes to Jesus about Galileans killed by Pilate as they were offering their sacrifices. What did these people do to deserve such tragedy?

In the Gospel lesson, the figure of Pontius Pilate appears. This is the only place in the Gospels where Pontius Pilate, the executioner of Jesus, his judge, appears prior to Jesus's death. We will therefore focus somewhat on Pontius Pilate, contrasting our judgments with Jesus's judgments. Judgment and repentance are appropriate Lenten themes, which we will follow this Sunday, wherever they lead.

Proclaiming the text

A recent survey among young adults in America, asking them why most of them were reluctant to participate in church, revealed the following: the main reason given was that "Christians are too judgmental."

Now today's Gospel refers to the notorious biblical judge Pontius Pilate. Pilate, you will remember, was the Roman official who judged Jesus for death. We know from biblical historians that Pontius Pilate was an efficient and brutal enforcer of Roman law and order against the occupied Jews. Luke does not tell us why Pontius Pilate murdered these Galileans. We hear nothing about this massacre in ancient sources, probably because killings of this sort were commonplace. That's the way Pilate managed these Jews. When you've got a foreign army occupying somebody else's country, even though you may not want to be brutal, it is terribly hard to be an enforcer of occupation values without resorting to grave violence.

Of course, this is a prelude for another violent act of Pontius Pilate—that is, the coming crucifixion of Jesus. Pilate had to give the order for the crucifixion of Jesus, for crucifixion is a specifically Roman punishment used especially for Jews who threatened Rome's power. The Gospels show Pilate as hesitant to give the order, but he did it. John's Gospel portrays Pilate as a philosophical cynic. When Jesus mentions "truth," Pilate asks, "What is truth?" Caiaphas, the high priest, is portrayed as less cynical than Pilate. Caiaphas's priestly colleagues fear that, due to Jesus, the Romans are going to move into action and make havoc upon the Jewish people during Passover.

For Pilate, it is mostly a matter of power. As he says to Jesus, "Don't you know that I have authority to release you and also to crucify you?" (John 19:10).

Jesus responds, "You would have no authority over me if it had not been given to you from above" (19:11).

Pilate is the embodiment of worldly power. He wields his power as if he were responsible to no one.

By the way, Pilate was eventually removed from his position, shortly after he crucified Jesus, because his cruelty and excessive use of power was too much, even for the Romans.

So today Jesus is told of Pilate's horrible action against the poor Galileans, who were just trying to worship God at the temple. Surely Jesus knew all about Pilate and his terrible history already. Then, as now, when there is some great tragedy, some great disaster, people talk.

"Did you hear about what happened in New York?" And one reason we talk is to try to make sense out of such tragedy, then, as now. "Jesus, did you hear about what Pilate did to those Galileans up at the temple?"

And while we talk about these tragedies, usually we have a question in the back of our mind: "I wonder what those people did to deserve this."

Elsewhere in the Gospel of John the disciples of Jesus encounter a blind man and ask Jesus, "Who sinned so that he was born blind, this man or his parents?" (John 9:2).

Jesus is not drawn into a discussion with his disciples about who sinned or caused this tragedy. Rather, he throws the whole question back at them: "I tell you, but unless you change your hearts and lives, you will die just as they did" (Luke 13:3). A whole generation stands before the judgment of God. Judgment looms over this story. The Pharisees are depicted as collaborating with the Romans in order to get Jesus out of the way, lest they provoke the Romans in any way to come down on their heads with their power. Ironically, just a few years later, despite all efforts to keep the Romans at bay, the Romans brutally come down on the heads of all Jerusalem, destroying the city, laying waste the temple, and devastating the people.

Jesus moves toward Jerusalem, where the rulers of the world, embodied in Pontius Pilate, the powerful people, will judge him. But ironically, Jesus will eventually exercise power over them. He will judge the world. The followers of Jesus will help, in their own peaceful way, to dismantle the empire that has placed Pontius Pilate in charge.

Jesus's words are as harsh as those of John the Baptist, who began this Gospel. John began Luke's Gospel by screaming in sermons, "You children of snakes! Who warned you to escape from the angry judgment that is coming soon?" (3:7).

That's a tough sermon. And here, Jesus is not a sweet, sentimental savior, but rather is a fierce prophet of truth, a scathing preacher who preaches judgment.

On this Third Sunday in Lent we might like to speak about the suffering of the world, preferably our suffering, to have pleasant theological discussions about spiritual matters. But Jesus won't let us. He wants to talk about judgment. We come in here wanting to judge him, wanting to make a verdict upon his way. Does it make sense? Is it practical? Is Jesus an adequate answer to the deep questions that life puts before us? And so on. And then Jesus turns the tables and questions us, pronounces a verdict upon us: you must repent, and you must let go of your devices and cling only to God.

Pilate thought he was judging Jesus. But before the end of the story, on the cross, Jesus is unmasked and judges Pilate.

And this day Jesus judges us.

Jesus has set his face to Jerusalem. That is the story immediately before this one. He is going to Jerusalem to suffer and die. And on his way, he puts before us a question: "Will you walk with me? Will you go the way I am going?"

He said, "All who want to come after me must say no to themselves, take up their cross daily, and follow me. All who want to save their lives will lose them. But all who lose their lives because of me will save them" (9:23-24).

And so we are reminded that Jesus not only did some tough things and suffered some tough things but also said some tough things. And today he says them to us. Not only does he say, "I am the light of the world," but also he turns to us and says, "You are the light of the world." And he promises to hold us to account for letting our lights shine before the world in such a way that all might see our good works and give glory, not to us, but to the God who enables us to do those good works.

A peculiarly Lenten question is: will you follow a savior who not only dies for you and loves you but also judges you, who promises not to leave you until you are transformed into the person God creates you to be?

Relating the text

I had always wanted to see Monreale (Italian for "Royal Mount") outside Palermo in Sicily. A few years ago we got to go there and enjoy the spectacular mosaics. I say "enjoy" because it was an enjoyable experience of one of the world's great centers of art.

Yet I'm not sure that I could say that I "enjoyed" being exposed to the Byzantine image of Christ the Pantocrator. Hovering over the church, floating in a gold background in the apse, is a figure of Christ, arms outstretched. Christ is not only the creator of all but also the judge of all.

There are beautiful mosaics depicting hundreds of stories form the Hebrew scripture and New Testament. There are charming scenes of Abraham, Jacob, and the children of Israel, as well as all of Jesus's parables and the stories of Jesus and his disciples.

And over all, with all the lines of pictures flowing toward him, is the Christ, Christ the judge. All the images flow back toward him, and everything must finally answer to him and must be judged by him.

It is an image that is utterly missing from the iconography of today's church, at least all of the churches in which I worship. We stress Jesus as the image of God's love, a sign of God's descent to humanity, a sign of God's determination to be with humanity. But what of God's determination finally to judge humanity? What of God's determination not to leave us to our own devices but to judge us by a higher standard of righteousness than our own? In short, what of Christ the judge?

We were watching a television program on burgeoning "new paradigm churches," many of which are found in Southern California. A young man who is the pastor of one of these fast-growing churches was being interviewed. His church gathers each week and is led in music by a rock band. It is a church with a median age of under thirty.

The reporter asked the young pastor to what he attributed the phenomenal growth of his congregation. The pastor replied, "I think you've got a generation of young adults that never had anybody look them into the eyes and say directly to them, in love, 'You really, really suck.'"

Though I might have put the matter more delicately, I could see his point. We've told people for so long that they are basically good, that they are making progress, and that they are nice people who always mean the best. But they know better. Are we now at a point where we might speak the truth? Might we once again speak of judgment and repentance and of our need as sinners for a gracious, forgiving God?

It's a good, Jesus-derived message to us for this Sunday in Lent.

You might consider ending this Sunday's sermon with a general prayer of confession in which the congregation is asked to confess some of the ways that we as a church have been unfaithful to the way of Christ.

You might also, as pastor, point to some of the ways that your congregation is repenting of past infidelity in its present work.

I know a congregation that once kept African Americans from entering its doors. Today its pastor is African American, and it is one of the most culturally diverse congregations in town. It seems to me to be an example of both repentance and of Jesus's implicit promise that, given his grace, we can change.

I can testify that one of the greatest challenges of being a parent is summoning the energy to discipline your children. It's much easier to overlook inappropriate behavior, to look the other way when your children misbehave, than it is to take the time (and the energy) to sit down with your child and try to explain, in ways that the child can understand, why the child's behavior was inappropriate.

My heart really goes out to single parents who are forced to work two jobs or long hours in order to provide for their children. I am in awe of those who still hold their children accountable, who dare to discipline the children because they love them.

Christians believe that God loves us so much that God refuses to leave us alone. God keeps working with us, keeps attending to us, correcting us, showing us a better way.

I think of those times, in my years of schooling, when some teacher gave me a grade that was lower than the grade I thought I deserved. How dare that teacher judge my work to be merely average when I thought it was excellent!

But some of the worst grades that I received were followed by the teacher saying to me, "Well, I gave you a B but not happily. You can do better. I was disappointed that you did not put more into this paper, and I think you are disappointed too."

How I wished that teacher had simply failed me. That way I could blame the teacher or turn my anger toward the teacher. But with that speech, I had no one to blame but myself. The toughest words of judgment are words of disappointment, words that are true.

Fourth Sunday in Lent

Joshua 5:9-12

Psalm 32

2 Corinthians 5:16-21

Luke 15:1-3, 11b-32

What Is God Like?

Selected reading

Luke 15:1-3, 11b-32

Theme

In his parables and teaching, in his life and his death, Jesus reveals to us the true nature of God. God is the loving Father who receives us in our sin and shows mercy upon us, even in our sin.

Introduction to the readings

Joshua 5:9-12

At last, after forty years of wandering, Israel enters the promised land. The manna ceases on the day they eat the produce of the land.

2 Corinthians 5:16-21

Paul says now that Christ has come we regard no one from a human point of view. This is Paul's classic statement of the "new creation" that is ours in Christ.

Luke 15:1-3, 11b-32

Jesus, criticized for receiving sinners and eating with them, tells one of his most memorable stories, the story of the prodigal son, which is the story of the boy who was lost in dissolute living yet was welcomed home by his father.

Prayer

Almighty God, we confess that we have held many wrong ideas about you. We believed you to be almighty power, and yet you came to us in mighty love. We thought that you would not receive us in your righteousness, yet you received us in our sinful rags. We deserved your just and harsh punishment for unrighteousness, and you invited us to a joyous party.

We confess that you are not the God we expected. We thought that you desired our fear and respect, only to be surprised that you cherished our love and affection.

Bring us, in these forty days of Lent, to see the fullness of your glory, to acknowledge the depth of your love for us, and to respond to you as you are rather than as we feared you to be. Amen.

Encountering the text

I confess that I'm always a bit relieved when we come to the Fourth Sunday in Lent, and our Gospel, in Year C, is Luke's greatest hit—the story of the prodigal son. I say "relieved" because Lent can be a most somber affair with the focus on our sin and Jesus's cross. It's somewhat of a relief to get to Lent Four and this grand—and controversial—party for the homecoming of the prodigal son.

And who gives that scandalous party? It is the waiting father who receives the prodigal back home. And Jesus says that God is like this. Our proclamation will basically walk the congregation through this beloved, familiar story of God, hoping to lift up the truth about the identity and intentions of God.

Proclaiming the text

In my experience many of you are here this morning because you are bugged by a question: "What is God like?" Fortunately, your question is one that Jesus answered directly.

A man has two sons. The younger son says, "Father, give me my share of the inheritance." In other words, "drop dead." (Is there any other way to put the old man's will into effect?) And the father gives it to him. Many of you had to leave home in order to grow up, so you ought to be able to identify with this story.

Out in the "far country," Jesus says the boy engages in "loose living" (RSV). Let me allow your imagination to work with that phrase, "loose living." Though Jesus doesn't, feel free to supply whatever forms of "loose living" appeal to you—loose girls, loose boys . . . chocolate cake. I'm assuming that some of you know from personal experience about this "loose living"!

With all the money wasted on loose living, the young man is reduced to the level of a pig. See him in rags slopping the pigs. Eventually it was hungover, empty-pockets, wake-up time: Monday morning. The boy then comes to himself. He says, "Wait a minute. I don't have to starve out here. I have a father, a home." And he turns back toward home. And I expect some of you know what that's like.

He has written a little speech for the occasion. "Now look, Dad. Before you start yelling, let me explain why she answered the phone when you called my room," or "Dad, er, uh, I mean, Father, I have sinned. I am unworthy to be called your son. Treat me as one of your hired servants."

But the father isn't interested in speeches. "Chill, Howard," says the father. "Save the flowery speeches for your law school application. Come on in. I'll show you a real party."

The story is a shocker. Remember, the question was, "What is God like?"

And in response to our perfectly good theological question, Jesus tells a wild story about the homecoming of a ne'er-do-well—welcomed with a party. It isn't what we expect. We want the father to be gracious but not overly so. Homecomings for prodigals are fine when the lost are dressed in sackcloth and ashes, but we don't want to see them in patent leather pumps and a tux. Our question is that of the older brother: "Is it fitting to throw a party for a prodigal?"

Jesus answers our deep, serious question, "What is God like?" by telling a story about a party thrown by a father for a prodigal. Jesus, in telling this story, expends more verses describing the party than on any other aspect in the story. But it's this part that is the scandal.

Put this parable in context. One day Jesus's critics cried, "This man eats and drinks (i.e., parties) with sinners! What kind of savior are you?"

You expect Jesus to back off saying, "But I'm going to redeem these prostitutes and tax collectors! Make them straighten up, be more responsible, more middle class like you and me."

No. He tells them that God loves to party with sinners, loves to tell parables of parties when a woman found a lost coin, of a bash after finding a lost sheep, and of the most questionable blowout of all—the party for the prodigal son. So, "they began to celebrate." End of scene one. In the return of the wayward son from the "far country," Jesus dramatizes a return from exile. Israel's long deportation is ending. Come home and join the great kingdom party!

Thus comes the older brother's perfectly understandable reaction. With nostrils flared and a look of indignation, "Music! Dancing! Levity! And on a Wednesday! What are you doing in that tux?" he asks the servant.

"Your kid brother's home. The old man has given everybody the night off and there's a party."

"A party! Doesn't that old fool know that we've got turnips to dig? How does he expect me to keep down overhead when he goes and blows two grand on a party to welcome home this son of his who blew his hard-earned money on whores?"

One moment. I don't believe Jesus said anything about whores, did he? Jesus just said the younger son blew his money in the far country on "loose living." Perhaps all this means is that he slept in late and ate high-cholesterol snacks.

But see? The converse of the older brother's, "See what a good boy I am," is always, "See what this son of yours has done: harlots, whores!"

He was angry and wouldn't go in. The father comes out into the darkness and begs him to come party. "Lo these many years have I served you," he sneers to the old man, "turning your turnip business around, putting the books in the black."

"Come on in, Ernest," says the father. "So what? You're the biggest turnip grower in the county. Big deal. At least your kid brother has been to the city and tasted the wine. Come on in. Let's party."

We know this story as the story of the prodigal son. But I remind you that Jesus doesn't give this parable a title. It could as well be called the story of the ridiculously gracious father. The most interesting character in the story is not the prodigal son or the older brother. It's the father. He's the real prodigal, in that his love is extravagant, more excessive than either the younger brother's loose living or the older brother's moral rectitude. It's a story about a parent who is excessive in his persistence to have a family, an old man who meets us when we crawl home from the far country after good times go bad, or who comes out to the lonely dark of our righteousness and begs us to come in and party. It's a hopeful, joyous story of homecoming. It's a somber warning to those who would rather sulk in the dark than come in and join the homecoming dance.

"You are always with me. Everything I've got is yours," pleads the father out in the dark with the older brother. The father is willing to miss the first dance in the hope that his firstborn might relent his vaunted self-righteousness and join the party.

You have probably heard me say before: the Bible never questions, "Is there a God?" The Bible's question is, "Who is the God who is there?" John says that nobody has ever seen God—until we met the one who told this parable. God is the long-suffering parent who waits for the younger son to come home when good times go bad and who pleads with the older boy to come in, hug his brother, resume the family, and "make merry." The story's claim that God is the parent who refuses to stop silently waiting or earnestly pleading for you collides with modern self-understanding that our lives are our possessions to do with as we please. We are owned, the story implies, sought, even loved. The story also collides with the modern view of God as a detached, rule-driven, distant potentate who can't stand for the kids to have a good time.

Jesus's story doesn't have an ending. We are not told if the younger brother ever grew up and bought a Buick or if the older brother ever loosened up and joined the party. We sometimes doubt that they "lived happily ever after." Jesus doesn't end the story because this is the story that you finish yourself. And you are finishing it, even if you didn't realize it. I'm betting that the one the father is awaiting, the one he is begging to come in and party, is you. This story says: you do not journey alone. There is one who names you, claims you, has plans for you, waits or prods, invites or blesses you. This one, sooner or later, will have you.

We, the lost, have been found. Come to God's party.

Relating the text

A father receives a wastrel son back home and throws a grand party to welcome him. Is this a joke? Parables—these pithy, strange little stories from everyday life—are the most distinctive, and peculiar, aspect of the teaching of Jesus. Parables are close cousins of another distinctive literary form—that is, the joke. Mark says that Jesus never said anything in public that wasn't a parable. There are religious teachers who, when asked a theological question, respond with thoughtful, general principles that are high-sounding, serious, and uplifting. Paul leaps to mind.

Why did Jesus explain God with unexplained stories, most of which lack neat endings or immediately apparent points? It's as if Jesus says that God is not met through generalities and abstractions; God is met amid the stuff of daily life, in the tug and pull of the ordinary, at a party for a son who really deserves nothing but a stern rebuke.

Yet God is usually encountered, if the parables have it right, in ways that are rarely self-evident, obvious, or with uncontested meaning. In parables the joke is on us.

Don't be troubled if you can't figure out these parables; the disciples who first heard them didn't get it either. Jesus comes across at times as this Zen-like teacher whose greatest desire is not to pass out the right answers but rather to tease and to provoke even more questions. I'm sure that it comes as little surprise that a frequent response to his parables was befuddlement. Perhaps Jesus was attempting to talk about matters (God, God's kingdom) that can't be simply explicated without damaging the truth of what he was trying to talk about. Perhaps what Jesus was trying to do in his parables was make more than a mere intellectual point.

Here is an interpretive principle: scripture always and everywhere speaks about God and only secondarily and derivatively speaks about us. I doubt that Jesus's parable of the prodigal son is a story about better family life or how to be a better father. It is a story about God. What is God like? What is the nature of God's kingdom? Scripture's point tends to be theological before it is anthropological. The stories of scripture tend to be stories about God.

"Maybe the reason it seems hard for me to forgive others is that I do not fully believe that I am a forgiven person. If I could fully accept the truth that I am forgiven and do not have to live in guilt or shame, I would really be free. My freedom would allow me to forgive others seventy times seven times. By not forgiving, I chain myself to a desire to get even, thereby losing my freedom."

—Henri J. Nouwen, *The Road to Daybreak: A Spiritual Journey*
(New York: Doubleday, 1988), 68

"Have I rejoiced with and for my neighbor in virtue or pleasure? Grieved with him in pain, for him in sin? . . . Have I revealed any evil of anyone, unless it was necessary to some particular good I had in view? Have I then done it with all the tenderness of phrase and manner consistent with that end? . . . Has goodwill been, and appeared to be, the spring of all my actions toward others?"

—John Wesley, "A Scheme of Self-Examination Used by the
First Methodists in Oxford" (c. 1730)

"It was the summer of 1930 . . . when Pop had made over to me the portion of my inheritance and threw open the door for me to run away and be a prodigal, or be a prodigal without running away from any earthly home, for that matter. I could very well eat the husks of swine without the inconvenience of going into a far country to look for them."

—Thomas Merton, *The Seven Storey Mountain*
(New York: Harcourt, 1948), 89

Fifth Sunday in Lent

Isaiah 43:16-21
Psalm 126
Philippians 3:4b-14
John 12:1-8

The God Who Saves

Selected reading
Isaiah 43:16-21 (related to Philippians 3:4b-14)

Theme
The God of Israel and the church is the God who rescues, heals, delivers, and saves. There is something about this God that is determined not to be God alone. In even the most dismal circumstances, people of faith look with hope to the God who saves for their future.

Introduction to the readings

Isaiah 43:16-21
The poet and prophet Isaiah proclaims to suffering Israel a brighter, glorious future. Israel will return home and will be saved so that they "will recount my praise."

Philippians 3:4b-14
Paul stresses the Christian life as a matter of living into God's promised future, of leaving something behind so that a life far better might be fully embraced.

John 12:1-8
Jesus is anointed as if for burial by a woman who loves him. Thus, we are given a preview of the events that await him in the coming week.

Prayer

Lord Jesus, in these days of Lent, we have been made to look at all the ways we sin. Our distance from the ways of God has been made clear to us. We have our good intentions, our better inclinations. But time and again we turn away. We live as we want to live, not as you call us to live. We sin.

Therefore, Lord Jesus, we give thanks that the Gospels reveal you to be a God who saves. You got into lots of trouble because of the sort of company you kept at the table, because of the ways that you welcomed sinners.

We have heard your welcome, Lord Jesus. We have sensed your call. We give thanks that you, even yet, love sinners like us enough even to die for us so that, in your love, we might live for you. Amen.

Encountering the text

I find it curious that this Sunday's first lesson from Isaiah 43 was proclaimed to suffering exiles in bondage. Though little in their present situation gave them reason to hope, Isaiah boldly declared a dramatically changed future for them. They will be released from the grip of Babylon (Babylon fell to Cyrus in 539 BC), and they will joyously return home. "The LORD says," a straight way will be made through the desert for God is going to do an entirely "new thing." The language echoes other references earlier in scripture to the exodus. It will be as if there is a new exodus, a new world, a new future will be offered to those who have suffered terribly.

Thus, we have a promise of deliverance, salvation. The first lesson from Isaiah 43 relates well to Philippians 3, which is Paul's promise of a new future and new creation now that Christ has come. The deliverance will be costly, as today's Gospel, John 12:1-8, presages. Jesus will suffer because of his desire to save people like us. Yet the dark events of the coming weeks, as Christ goes to the cross, is nothing less than our deliverance, our salvation, our future given as the gift of a God who has steadfast love.

How is it possible to preach hope in the middle of a hopeless situation? How is it possible to preach salvation in circumstances in which there seems to be little evidence for deliverance and healing? To do so is surely one of the greatest acts of faithful imagination.

Proclaiming the text

A friend of some years approached me with a question that had become his obsession. He told me that he grew up in a small-town church. As a youth, he said, "I accepted Jesus as my personal savior and I knew that I was saved." He was active in church until his late teenage years when other interests drew him away. As a young man, when he married he returned to the church, partly because of his wife's piety.

Now in midlife, he had become obsessed with the question, "Am I really saved?" He had begun to doubt that he had ever had a true conversion experience. He had engaged in a study of the Bible, but that had filled him with more questions. He had tried to discuss his plight with a number of pastors and friends, but they all seemed to have different points of view, which confused him all the more. He used to pray but had stopped because it felt like he was just "talking to myself."

"What if I died tomorrow?" he asked. "I'm not sure that I would be saved and go to heaven."

I told my friend that God had sent him to me to reassure me that we needed another book on salvation!

My heart went out to this brother who was in real torment and consternation. I could make a number of observations about his struggle with salvation, but for now I'll just note the absence of one key player: God.

My friend characterized his struggle as his lonely battle to understand, his solitary attempt to decide, his need to feel, and his efforts to be certain. I asked my friend to consider the possibility that his turmoil might be God-induced, that God might be using this turbulence to move him to some new plane in their relationship. Perhaps his struggle was validation that God was indeed real and that God was working to draw him closer. Perhaps.

The modern world teaches us to narrate our lives without reference to God. It's all our decisions, our actions, our feelings and desires. Celebration of human potential is the dominant, governmentally sanctioned story but is not the story to which Christians are accountable. It is the conventional North American story that, at every turn, is counter to the gospel. Thus, there are few more challenging words to be said by the church than *salvation*. Salvation implies that there is something from which we need to be saved, that we are not doing as well as we presume, that we do not have the whole world in our hands, and that the hope for us is not of our devising.

I'm certain that most people think of the word *salvation* as related exclusively to the afterlife. Salvation is when we die and "get to go to heaven." To be sure scripture is concerned with our eternal fate. What has been obscured is scripture's stress on salvation as God's invitation to share in God's life here, now, so that we might do so forever. Salvation isn't just a destination; it is our vocation. Salvation isn't just a question of who is saved and who is damned, who will get to heaven and how, but also how we are swept up into participation in the mystery of God as Jesus Christ. Get a biblical concordance and check the references to *heaven* and you will find that almost none of them are related to *death*. *Heaven* is a name for when or where one is fully with God: salvation.

Look up *salvation* in the concordance and you will find a wide array of images. All of the Gospels are stories about the peculiar nature of salvation in

Jesus Christ. Salvation is a claim about God. God's self-assigned task is making "salvation happen in the heart of the earth" (Ps 74:12). God is addressed as "God of our salvation" (Ps 65:5). For some, salvation is rescue, deliverance, and victory. For others, it is healing, wholeness, completion, and rest. Isaiah speaks of salvation as a great economic reversal in which God gives a free banquet for the poor (Isa 55). The God of Israel saves, rescues, heals, and delivers.

One of the main testimonies about Jesus is that "Jesus saves." Jesus's earthly ministry was characterized by a constant, relentless reach. Jesus saved people that nobody thought could be saved. He loved people that everybody thought were beyond love.

Is it any wonder then that one of the earliest and most persistent charges against Jesus was "This man welcomes sinners and eats with them" (Luke 15:2)? Jesus is crucified for welcoming sinners to his table, and not only for welcoming but also for actively seeking them. At the end, with whom did he choose to dine at his Last Supper? Sinners. And in his resurrection, at a new beginning, with whom did he choose to dine at his first meals (Luke 24:13-35)? Sinners. His door was too wide to suit many of the faithful.

In the beloved parable of the prodigal son (in Luke 15, which was read last Sunday), when the boy was still far away, the father ran to welcome his prodigal son. The son had a penitent speech prepared for his homecoming. But the father did not allow the son to speak. Running to him, he embraced him, welcomed him, not simply back home, but to an extravagant party, treating him not as the wayward son he was, but as the prince the father intended him to be.

What if the father had simply waited for the boy? What if the father had not run to meet him? What if the father's forgiving, embracing response was to be made a principle for all our dealings with sin and injustice? Then where would we be? Would there not be moral chaos and parties every night? Is the father's behavior ethically irresponsible?

Let us confine our thought to that which Jesus said, rather than upon idle speculation. Let us cling to the story Jesus tells. Jesus says: God is like the father who ran to embrace his wayward son and invite him to a party.

Plato noted, and Freud reiterated, that the human animal, from the first, seems to have this insatiable longing, this great yearning. The infant demands attention from the world, insists on being noticed. The human is a fragile animal who cannot survive alone, who must make connection first with the mother, then with one human being after another. Plato said that this was the beginning of all human thought and culture, the explanation for all human achievement, and the source of much human misery, too. We must connect.

Yet here's the great mystery: the God of Israel and the church also connects. It is not so much that God "must" connect, but there is something about this God that wants to communicate with us, to self-reveal to us. God's generativity doesn't end with Genesis 1. Today, right here, in our church, in your life and mine, God is busy connecting, seeking, reaching, saving.

This is our hope, in life, in death, in life beyond death: Jesus saves. And in the next couple of weeks, as we follow Jesus, we will all see the extraordinary lengths to which he will go to save us. Thanks be to God! Amen.

Relating the text

With Pharaoh's chariots pursuing them, the children of Israel falter on the bank of the sea. Moses encourages them with, "Don't be afraid. Stand your ground, and watch the LORD rescue you today" (Exod 14:13). Upon arriving on the opposite shore, safe from the Egyptians, Moses leads Israel in a hymn, singing, "The LORD is my strength and my power; he has become my salvation" (Exod 15:2).

Jesus begins his famous sermon with, "Happy are you who are poor, because God's kingdom is yours" (Luke 6:20). To those who can do nothing to purchase the kingdom, he gives it to them for nothing. Matthew is not spiritualizing the beatitudes when he adds poor "in spirit." Poor is poor. To those who haven't got much spirit, to those who are inept at spiritual matters, who can do little to further their case before God, who by their poverty have no control over their future, Jesus promises everything, his whole glorious kingdom (Matt 5:3).

The Nicene Creed states explicitly that all Christ did and said, including his death and rising, was done *pro nobis*—for us and our salvation. "He came down from heaven for us men and our salvation," is one translation of how the Nicene Creed characterizes Christ, the incarnation. To be near us, Christ had to come down to us. There is distance between us and God. We are not with God in heaven, much less are we gods who dwell in the vicinity of deity. Even though we were created by God, in the image of God, God must risk opposition, overcome something, go somewhere in order to come near to us sinners, in order to replenish, restore, resurrect God's intended image in us. In salvation, God comes, becomes Emmanuel, and fully embraces what the human can be. "God with us" is yet another way of thinking about salvation.

John Duns Scotus said that Jesus died for sinners, but God would have become incarnate for us even if we had not sinned, our sin not being the whole point of the incarnation but rather God's determination to be with us.

At the risk of being sentimental, I think we ought to consider Jesus not simply as some payment back to God for the debt we owed to God, though we are indeed indebted to God for everything.

Rather, the incarnation of Jesus Christ is God's great love letter to us. Having tried to get to us in so many ways, through so many attempts down through the ages, God comes to us, ventures out toward us in Christ.

True, our response to God's loving overture in Christ was ugly and sad—we crucified the very one whom God sent to say and to show, "I love you." Still, even our bloody rejection of Christ makes God's reach toward us all the more remarkable.

There really does seem to be in God this rather relentless determination to have us, to get to us, to be with us, even if God has to suffer horribly to do so. Jesus saves.

There is so much of Jesus's life here among us that is left out of the Gospels. We know next to nothing about his childhood and youth, save for a very brief mention of it early in Luke's Gospel. Most of what is told about Jesus could easily fit in this morning's newspaper with lots of room left for the quotes from the stock exchange.

Considering our high level of interest in the minute details of a person's life and our use of the early years of a person's life to explain the significance of a person's whole life, this lack of biographical information about Jesus is extraordinary.

I expect that the reason why we know so little biographical information about Jesus is that the whole point of the Gospels is not biography but soteriology—a presentation of salvation. It is as if the Gospels are determined to tell us only what is most important about Jesus. And the most important thing about Jesus is that Jesus saves.

The Gospels are not stories of the life of Jesus. They are proclamations of amazing good news: Jesus saves. Jesus saves sinners. Jesus saves people whom nobody thought could be saved. Jesus does something about the age-old problem that exists between us and God. Jesus saves.

Passion/Palm Sunday

Liturgy of the Passion
Isaiah 50:4-9a
Psalm 31:9-16
Philippians 2:5-11
Luke 22:14-23:56 or Luke 23:1-49

Liturgy of the Palms
Psalm 118:1-2, 19-29
Luke 19:28-40

Shouting Rocks

Selected reading

Luke 19:28-40 (Liturgy of the Palms)

Theme

Palm Sunday is a reminder that Jesus is not just a spiritual leader. He is also making a political claim. Jesus Christ is Lord means that other claimants to the throne are not lords. Christians are those who proclaim Jesus as Lord, who shout to the world that a new king has come and a new reign has begun.

Introduction to the readings

Isaiah 50:4-9a

The prophet Isaiah stands and speaks God's truth to the people. Even though they resist the truth and wish that they could avoid the truth, the prophet speaks. The true prophet speaks what God wants the people to hear, not always what the people desire to hear.

Philippians 2:5-11
In this great hymn, Paul praises the Christ who, though he was God, humbled himself, taking the way of the cross in service to God, in the salvation of humanity.

Luke 22:14–23:56 or Luke 23:1-49 or Luke 19:28-40
Our Gospel lesson is the dramatic story of Jesus's passion—the arrest, trial, and crucifixion of Jesus. When Jesus's critics urge him to silence his exuberant followers, Jesus says that if they were silent even the stones would shout forth his praise.

Prayer

Lord Jesus, on this day you were welcomed in triumphant procession into Jerusalem. Give us the grace, Good Lord, to welcome you into our lives, into our homes, and into our communities. Enable us to put our trust in you that we find, in you, the Lord of our lives. Amen.

Encountering the text

At last Jesus makes his promised move on Jerusalem. Most of his ministry has been out in the hinterland, out in Galilee. Now he enters the capital city. Jesus is welcomed, not by the city dignitaries, but rather by children waving palm branches. Those who welcome Jesus work themselves into a frenzy. Their exuberance is evident as they shout, "Blessings on the king who comes in the name of the Lord!"

Did they say *king*? They have turned a procession with a Galilean rabbi bouncing in on the back of a donkey into a royal victory parade.

It is more than the religious leaders can take. They are outraged at the blasphemy, the impudence. "Tell your fanatical followers to shut up!" they say, or words to that effect. Jesus responds, "I tell you, if they were silent, the stones would shout."

This Palm/Passion Sunday we will settle on one verse in the story of Jesus's triumphant entry into Jerusalem, the verse that proclaims that, if his followers were silenced by the authorities, "the stones would shout." This may seem to you like not enough of a verse to preach on. However, I find it a sufficiently evocative phrase with which to catch up some of the significance of Jesus's Palm Sunday parade.

Palm/Passion Sunday is one of the most "political" Sundays of the year. On this day there is a question before the church: "Who is in charge? Who rules?"

The little children shout that the new "king" is Jesus.

A couple of years ago on Palm Sunday, after the palm branches had been distributed to all the children and the choir was in place in the narthex preparing to process with the children on the first hymn, someone said, "Quiet! Children, quiet! The service is beginning!"

Don't you find it curious that Jesus said, in effect, "Children, shout! Rocks, start screaming!"

The reign of God is coming to us; what can we rocks do but shout?

Proclaiming the text

I have a friend who teaches biology at a rather forlorn community college. Many of his students have been abused by the educational system. However, my friend enters into his work as a professor with great enthusiasm. Rather than complain about the quality of his students, as some lesser teacher might, he takes them and their educational limitations as a challenge.

"I could teach biology to a rock," he bragged to me.

So I am willing to believe that a truly brilliant teacher could teach a rock biology. But could you teach a rock to shout?

As Jesus enters Jerusalem on Palm Sunday, bouncing in on the back of a donkey, his followers and admirers clip palm branches from the trees, waving them as he comes before them. This waving of palm branches is a sign of welcome and hospitality. Many in the crowd began to shout, "Blessings on the king who comes in the name of the Lord."

Jesus's critics are obviously unnerved by this political demonstration. They have worked out an arrangement between the faith of Israel and the power of Imperial Rome. They do not want the common political fanatics to disrupt the alliance they have constructed. So Jesus's critics say, "Scold your disciples. Tell them to stop!" They want Jesus to tame the outburst, to tone down the uproar. During Jesus's earthly life, it is estimated by scholars that there were at least sixty armed rebellions against the Roman occupation forces. People waving palm branches and shouting was a threatening sign, particularly when they were shouting that there was a new king in town.

Upon receiving the demand that he calm his followers, Jesus says something interesting: "I tell you, if they were silent, the stone would shout."

There is something about Jesus that can make even a rock want to shout.

Jesus had gotten this sort of thinking from the Hebrew scriptures, in which trees clap their hands for joy, the hills skip into a dance, the waves cry out, and the mountains shout. The Bible teaches that matter can sing.

Every time I camp out in the woods, I am impressed by how loud nature is. I have never understood people who go out into the wilderness seeking "some peace and quiet." Nature is alive with sound. Long before daylight, the creatures begin calling to one another. Throughout the night, there are various cries, rustling, and scuffling in the wilderness. On the rare moments when I have gone scuba diving this is the thing that impresses me: even the deep water is alive with all sorts of sounds. No way that you could shut up all of the stuff.

One of our great hymns sings, "The heavens are telling the glory of God." This God has made even the material universe to sing, to speak up, to testify.

Those who want to keep a lid on things, those who have a stake in the status quo and the present order, always try to keep things quiet. They don't like noise and commotion. When Jesus entered into Jerusalem, he was entering the town as a king, a new ruler, an adversary who threatened the throne. Children, the least and the lowest, the powerless in society, began to praise and shout, which really threatened the powers that be. "Be quiet!" said the authorities. And Jesus said, "If they were silent, the stones would shout."

Many times I have seen parents bring little children into the church service, saying to them, "Hush, now. Quiet down. Now is the time for church voices." I am sure that they think of "church voices" as low, soft-sounding voices, but here Jesus defends his followers with their raucous outburst. Here Jesus says that if his followers were silent, even the stones would shout. That would imply that "church voices," being the voices of Jesus's followers, need to be loud, abrasive, raucous voices.

Does Jesus not say, "Whoever is ashamed of me and my words, shall make me ashamed of him"? Does Jesus not say that they would drag us before princes and in the courts and we would not know what to say, but the Holy Spirit would tell us what to say and give us words to shout?

It appears to be the nature of this God to have a witness, to enable testimony. Little children on Palm Sunday looked at Jesus and saw who he really was. He was coming into town to take charge. He was riding in on the back of a donkey to rule. And they shouted that their deliverance was at hand. And when these little witnesses were threatened and intimidated, Jesus defiantly replied that even if the powers that be were successful in shutting them up, the very stones would cry out.

Have you ever heard a stone sing?

A few years ago, on vacation in Paris, we arrived on a Sunday morning, and that evening we were walking down one of the streets on the Left Bank. It didn't feel like Sunday to us. The streets were thronged with tourists and weekend merrymakers. There, on one of the side streets, we encountered an ancient church. We were astounded to read that the church was nearly one thousand years old. It was a beautiful example of late Gothic French architecture. As we stood before those venerable, moss-covered, ancient stones, admiring their antique beauty, we heard singing coming from within the church. Here, in supposedly secular France, there was a Sunday evening church service. They were having Mass. We went up to the church, pushed the door open, and were surprised to be greeted by a wave of songs coming from a packed interior. The congregation was made up of many different colors of people and a higher percentage of young people than I had seen in most of the churches I had visited in the United States in the couple of months before.

"It's hard to believe we're in France," said my friend.

We had heard that there was nobody in the French churches but a few old people. That evening I found out that was a lie. The church was full, full of praise, a living, breathing testimony to the continuing vitality of the church.

So when I hear Jesus say that he can teach even stones to shout, I think of that evening and that church.

It is the nature of this God always to have a witness, always to raise the dead, always to have somebody to testify and tell the story. There are people in this congregation who think they are not good at public speaking. There are people right here who are shy, reserved, and self-effacing. And yet, the Holy Spirit has given you some good words to say; and by the power of God, despite resistance, you have stood up and testified. You have been a witness. I'm not calling you a "stone," but I am saying that your testimony is in itself proof of the power of God to have God's word spoken to a disbelieving word. Jesus said that he could make even the stones to shout if the shouting people around him were silent. What would a stone say when it shouts? What would be its witness?

Relating the text

We were participating in a three-hour worship service in a large African American church in one of the poorest parts of the city. I asked the pastor, half in jest, "Why do black people make so much noise when they worship?" We had been subjected to throbbing—and at times thundering—music throughout the service. My friend had preached a long sermon in which he whooped, shouted, strutted, and even screamed.

My friend shook his head in sadness and replied, "It really makes you white people nervous when we get happy, doesn't it? Why is our worship so loud? We've got people here who have spent their whole lives keeping quiet. They are expected silently to wait on tables, to make up rich people's bedrooms, and to clean their houses for low pay without complaint. They are never asked what they think about anything. They're never invited to come to the microphone and render a verdict on what's going on in the world. They are voiceless. Silent.

"So we get them down here in the church, and we give them a microphone. We tell them that here, this is free space, God-created space, and if they want to strut and they want to shout, they can because Jesus has made them royalty."

From what I've observed, shouting seems to be a fairly typical response to Jesus. When Jesus sets foot in town, the voiceless speak up. And as Jesus says, all creation can shout his glory.

Today we remember Jesus's entry into Jerusalem and we remember how he was received into the city. We remember that when Jesus entered Jerusalem, the religious rulers (that is, people like us preachers) felt threatened by his entry and rebuked his followers for their enthusiasm.

Much of the time in the church is consumed with history, with memory, with remembering our past so that we might move forward. And yet, sometimes we remember in order to forget; we remember in order to learn from our past errors and mistakes. Theologian Harvey Cox once put forward an intriguing proposal in regard to our acts of remembrance: "We should read history more as a cautionary tale than as a treasure house of available inspiration. We Christians today need to understand our history as a compulsive neurotic need to understand his—in order to see where we veered off, lost genuine options, glimpsed something we were afraid to pursue, or denied who we really are."

—Quoted by David Augsburger, *Dissident Discipleship: A Spirituality of Self-Surrender, Love of God, and Love of Neighbor* (Minneapolis: Brazos Press, 2005), 130

In the morning I go to work at my office and I pass McCoy United Methodist Church. Well, it's not a church anymore. It's just an empty building. McCoy lost nearly all of its members more than a decade ago, and the building was given to the city of Birmingham, Alabama. McCoy sits there, on the street corner, a real Gothic testimony. But a testimony to what? McCoy was one of the most active and vital churches in our Conference. But the neighborhood changed racially, and the congregation of McCoy refused to change with it. At one point, guards were placed at the door to keep African Americans from entering McCoy. It was even said that one of the Birmingham bombings during the 1960s was planned by a couple of men in a downstairs Sunday school room in McCoy.

But now McCoy church is closed. And what do those stones say? Today they say to me that God is not nice to churches who refuse to be faithful to the commands of Christ. That's what the stones say.

Passion/Palm Sunday

Liturgy of the Passion
Isaiah 50:4-9a
Psalm 31:9-16
Philippians 2:5-11
Luke 22:14-23:56 or Luke 23:1-49

Liturgy of the Palms
Psalm 118:1-2, 19-29
Luke 19:28-40

Fools for Christ

Selected reading
Luke 22:14-23:56 (with special emphasis on Luke 23:28)

Theme
The way of Jesus is not the world's way. The way of Jesus is a narrow way that the world considers to be foolish. Yet this Sunday, as we follow Jesus toward the cross, we affirm that his way—his foolish way—is the true way to life.

Introduction to the readings
Isaiah 50:4-9a
What is to be taught? The truth of God, even though the people did not want to hear the sometimes hard truth of God.

Philippians 2:5-11

Paul praises the Christ who, though he was God, humbled himself, taking the way of the cross on our behalf.

Luke 22:14-23:56 or Luke 23:1-49

Our Gospel lesson is the dramatic story of Jesus's passion—the arrest, trial, and crucifixion of Jesus.

Luke 19:28-40

The liturgy of the Palms is the story of Jesus's triumphal entry into Jerusalem.

Prayer

Dear Jesus, on this day we welcome you into our worship, even as pilgrims welcomed you into Jerusalem; we follow behind you on your dangerous way, even as your disciples followed you to the cross. Give us the grace, Lord Jesus, to despise the praise of this world and to dare to walk with you. Make us willing to be foolish enough to follow you, confident that your cruciform foolishness is wiser than that of the world. Amen.

Encountering the text

Today, Passion/Palm Sunday, we suggest a thematic sermon on the foolishness and difficulty of following Jesus. As Jesus comes into Jerusalem, his followers welcome him into the city and walk behind him. We do the same this Sunday. As we welcome Jesus, or walk behind him, are we prepared for his countercultural, narrow way?

Today's Gospel is the longest of the year. It is a magnificent, dramatic story. This is the culmination of Jesus's ministry, of all that he has taught and all that he has said. In one sense, the story is enough just by itself, read well in your church. Let today's sermon be a time to reflect on this dramatic, saving story from the angle of its foolishness, noting the deep irony that lies behind all that we do or say this fateful day, the irony of a crucified savior, of a God who reigns from a cross.

Proclaiming the text

What does Jesus look like to you today, this fateful day when he comes into Jerusalem with the disciples? Jesus arrives in the capital city bouncing in on the back of a donkey, not on a powerful warhorse in a royal entourage.

His followers break palm branches, wave them as signs of welcome, hail him as king, but you wonder if they did so in comical irony. King? Some king, bouncing in on the back of a donkey. He looks foolish.

"He is just the perfect pastor," the undergraduate said to me in effusive tones as she told me about her pastor. "His car is always a total mess, with books and papers strewn all over it. He is never anywhere on time. Last month, he forgot to show up for a wedding! Some nights, when he can't sleep, he will call me and see how I am doing in college. He says I am the only person he knows who stays up that late. You never know what he is going to say next. He's just the perfect pastor."

I marveled at the effect of this messy, unpunctual disorganized pastor upon the life of this very fastidious, upwardly mobile, ambitious student. Perhaps, in knowing this disordered pastor, she was catching a glimpse of other possibilities for the future, an alternative world. Something else.

There was a pulpit search committee that had spent months searching for a new pastor of a large, prestigious Presbyterian church. Dozens of candidates had been considered and eliminated. No one was to be found who was smart enough, good enough, good-looking enough, and competent enough to be their new pastoral leader.

One night, when the committee had gathered for its usual meeting, one of the members said, "We have been sent an interesting letter of inquiry and a resume, and I would like you to consider this person." Then he began to read from the letter. The letter said:

"I would like to be considered as your new pastor. I've only been in the ministry for a few years, and I must admit that my years of ministry have been rather tumultuous. I did not grow up in the church but was drawn into the church as an adult through a rather dramatic religious experience, so dramatic that I was incapacitated for a number of days after I met Christ. Then I quit what I was doing and began to roam about preaching the Gospel. Some people liked my sermons, but a lot didn't. I have been arrested on at least four occasions and had served time in three different jails. On one occasion, after one of my sermons, the congregation was so incensed that they dragged me out of the pulpit, beat me, and escorted me out to the edge of the town before dumping me. In the churches that I have served, I think that I have been a loving pastor, but also a strict one. I've had to chase more than one member out of the church for immoral actions. I certainly don't mind calling an ace an ace and a spade a spade when it comes to disciplining church members. I write this letter to you while I am in jail. I hope to be released from jail sometime soon, but I have found that when it comes to jail time, one never knows. However, I hope that you will consider me as your new pastor. As soon as I get out of prison, I would certainly like to have gainful employment."

Well, the committee was incensed. "How dare someone write a church of our caliber, with a presumption that we would be desperate enough to hire somebody like that?" one of the members wanted to know.

"Is this some kind of joke?" another asked.

"A jailbird, as our new pastor! I would love to see the Session get hold of that!"

"Who is this guy who wrote this?" one demanded.

The person holding the letter said simply, "It's signed, St. Paul." The great missionary to the Gentiles, the one who founded so many churches, created Christian theology, and spread the Gospel throughout the Mediterranean world, was also the one who boasted that he was a fool for Christ's sake (1 Cor 4:10). He was the one who boasted that the wisdom of the world is pure foolishness, from a Christian point of view, whereas the foolishness of the cross is true wisdom.

"I believe that a member of my church works for you and your company," I said to the business executive.

"John Smith? Yeah, he works with us. John is one of my vice presidents. I don't know if you have found this is true, but I have certainly found that John is pretty much a fool. For every ten ideas that he brings to me related to the company, I'd say only about one idea ever pans out and means anything. He really can be a fool," the executive said.

"Well forgive me for asking," I said, "But if John is such a fool, why would you make him a vice president in your company?"

"Why? Because John is the only person we've got who ever comes forward with any new ideas."

Perhaps it takes someone who is somewhat of a fool to be able to see alternative possibilities. Paul says that, "The cross is foolishness," and he means that it is the supreme alternate possibility to the world's wisdom (1 Cor 1:18).

I was urging a Duke undergraduate to go with us on our spring mission trip to Honduras. She had initially shown some interest, telling me that she might consider going with us this year. Her older sister had gone with us a few years ago and I was eager for her to go as well. When I finally got back in touch with her, I was surprised to hear her say, "I'm not going on any mission trip. I've decided. That's that. I'm not going."

"May I ask why?"

"Because Jane went with you to Honduras, and it totally destroyed her life. When she came back from working with the poor, she wasn't the same person. She completely changed the course of her life. It disrupted my family, upset my parents, and things have never been the same. I just don't want to bring that much disruption into my family."

It was one of the best reasons I have ever heard for not going on a church mission trip. The way of the cross is the way of foolishness. As Bonhoeffer said, "It is no small thing that God allowed himself to be pushed out of the world on a cross."

And yet, with all of this talk about foolishness, fools, and cross bearing, there ought to be a warning. When you look at our church, this building, its beauty, its order, and its stability, you are apt to be confused by such talk. When we gather on Sunday morning, everything looks so stable, so pure and solid, and this form can be an illusion; it can obscure how foolish this particular way is in the world.

Despite the cross, despite Paul's clear, outrageous labelling of the way of the cross as a way of foolishness, there does seem to be built right into the church this relentless tendency for the church to degenerate from Christ's body into the Rotary Club. There is that tendency to take the gospel foolishness and repackage it as just another brand of worldly wisdom, common sense, something on which all thinking people ought to be able to agree. At least the Rotary Club meets at a convenient hour of the week and serves lunch!

Paul's words remind us that we are called, as Christians, for more than buttoned-down life respectability.

Many years ago, as the United States was arming and preparing for another invasion of Iraq, a group of us clergy were discussing the possibility of an invasion. What should we, as spokespeople and followers of the Prince of Peace, do in this situation? There was widespread frustration in the group. Some urged rather active resistance and dramatic protest. Others urged quieter, more respectable support of the administration. Some said that as clergy, we ought to stay out of such political matters. What do we know? The debates went on and on. What could we do that would make a difference? What can we do that shows that we are on the right side of this issue?

Then, as the discussion was ending, one of the ministers said, "We could pray."

In a moment, the sheer foolishness of the gospel became more apparent. In a world that wants to be effective, that wants to do something for good, that wants to right the wrong and to fight injustice, it is easy to forget that Christians may have a peculiar notion of what makes sense, and what ought to be done.

This day Jesus goes to do something, something final, decisive, world shaking, and life changing on our behalf. For us and our salvation he is going to do something foolish. Bounding on the back of a donkey, hanging in scorned agony on a cross, he looks like a fool rather than the savior of the world.

Will you welcome him and follow him this day?

Relating the text

I was before a group of South Carolina pastors doing a Bible study of the book of Acts. We got to Acts 5, which is that nasty little story of a squabble in a church meeting, during which two board members, Mr. Annanias and Mrs. Saphira (whose parents founded this church), dropped dead after the preacher told them to drop dead.

There was murmuring in the group of pastors. What kind of story is this? Is this a Christian story? What kind of pastoral care is this? Where's the grace? Where's the compassion? Two people dead at a church meeting!

Off the top of my head I asked, "Has anybody here ever had to kill anybody in order to have church?" Silence. Then he spoke. "I preached on the race issue. There were rumblings, demands that I stop. I preached. Three families left the church. One joined another church. Two left the church forever and never joined any church. My wife asked, 'I know it's an important issue. But is it worth driving three families out of the church?' Is it worth provoking death, while preaching new birth?"

This is a hard saying. Who can listen to it?

This gospel. This Jesus. These words. This life. Hard.

To be a disciple is to find oneself stretched between the horns of a dilemma. On the one hand, "This is hard! Who can listen to it?" and in the middle,

"Will you also go away?" followed by "Lord, to whom should we go? You have the words (sometimes hard words) of eternal life."

"We've always enjoyed thinking of ourselves as 'the thinking person's church'" she said. "We're in a university town, and we've always attracted lots of university faculty. Our pastor has her graduate degree and has even published a couple of books. Well, anyway, Jane Johnson is a real matriarch in our congregation, has been there since the church was founded in the late 1950s. Jane is in her late eighties, and we had noticed that she had begun to fail just a bit, not as sharp as she used to be.

"Well, we had this problem with homeless people breaking into our building at night, particularly on cold nights. We had bought new locks for the doors, but one of them had kicked in the door, causing all sorts of damage. Our neighborhood has gone down over the past few decades. It's a real problem.

"Well, Jane got on this tangent, started calling up members, went on a real campaign to simply unlock the doors of the church at night and let the homeless people come on in and spend the night! 'We're taking so much effort to take care of the church that we're going to fool around and kill the church as a church!' Jane was telling people.

"Some of us are beginning to think that Jane may be losing her grip on reality," she said.

Eugene Peterson writes, "Christ is the way as well as the truth and life. When we don't do it his way, we mess up the truth and we miss out on the life. We can't live a life more like Jesus by embracing a way of life less like Jesus."

—Eugene Peterson, *Christ Plays in Ten Thousand Places*
(Grand Rapids: William B. Eerdmans Publishing Company, 2005), 313

Good Friday

Isaiah 52:13–53:12
Psalm 22
Hebrews 10:16-25 or Hebrews 4:14-16; 5:7-9
John 18:1–19:42

The Thirst of God

Selected reading
John 18:1–19:42

Theme
This day, Good Friday, the day of crucifixion, is the most dramatic demonstration of the lengths that God will go to for us. In saying, from the cross, "I thirst," Jesus not only demonstrated his humanity in his agony but also showed how far God was willing to go to save us, to reach out to us, to have us as we are. We come to church this day thirsting for God; God also comes thirsting for us!

Introduction to the readings

Isaiah 52:13–53:12

Isaiah the prophet speaks of a suffering servant who will be despised and rejected and yet will carry our sicknesses and bear our sufferings.

Hebrews 10:16-25

The letter to the Hebrews speaks of a day when the covenant of God will be written on human hearts and the Lord "won't remember their sins and their lawless behavior anymore."

John 18:1–19:42

This is John's account of the arrest, trial, and crucifixion of Jesus.

Prayer

Lord Jesus, in your love, you came to us, reached out to us, and searched for us. Yet we turned away from your outstretched hand, we still wandered, and we even nailed you to a cross. This day is for us a vivid testimonial to the lengths to which you will go for us. Help us not turn away from the horror of this day, your terrible crucifixion, that we might experience the glory of this day, the wonder of our salvation. Speak to us, even from the cross that we, standing at the foot of the cross, might know the depth and breadth of your love. Amen.

Encountering the text

The Gospel for this day always presents us with a rich—almost too rich—array of narratives and images. We will focus on one of the few things that Jesus says during all of the events of his crucifixion: "I thirst." In one sense, this is a seemingly insignificant detail in a dramatic drama. Yet we preachers come to the biblical text with the conviction that it is fertile, thick, revealing literature. Seemingly small details can, through the eyes of faith, be rich and rewarding revelation.

Today's "Proclaiming the text," therefore, has a twofold focus: the demonstrable humanity of Christ and the crucified Christ as evidence of God's determination to have a people. The cross shows the lengths to which God will go for us, the depth and breadth of God's love for a lost and wayward humanity.

Proclaiming the text

"I thirst" (John 19:28 KJV).

How can it be that God's Son, the second person of the Trinity, would be thirsty? In most of our dealings with Jesus, we are very spiritual. Now, as Jesus suffocates and bleeds to death, things get physical. "I thirst."

How like Jesus, the Word made flesh, the incarnation of God, to mix the fleshly with the spiritual, the earthly with the heavenly. On the cross, we encounter one of the most horribly physical events in the most sacramental of Gospels. Someone may be able to think that Christianity is something "spiritual," ethereal, floating off into never-never land, that is until we gaze upon this wretched body, nails through sinew and flesh, heaving in final agony, in sweat and blood upon a cross, because of us.

And let's be honest. There is something about us creatures that wants to make Jesus-God un-carnate. Let's worship Jesus—a great spiritual leader, a marvelous teacher of high wisdom, a purveyor of some of the noblest notions ever uttered. Thus, we attempt to keep Jesus high and lifted up, floating somewhere above the grubby particularities of life. He can mean as little to us as Plato. He can be exclusively spiritual and therefore irrelevant.

But not with the words *I thirst*. When will we ever learn that, if we are going to meet God, we will meet God in the flesh? We live in air-conditioned homes. At any given moment, millions of us are on medication that dulls our experience of bodily pain and presence. I get a pain, I pop a pill, and I can go right on deluding myself about my essential carnality.

I think this is one reason why the Gospels are so terse in their descriptions of the crucifixion—none of the explicit, sentimental blood and gore of Mel Gibson's *The Passion of the Christ*. They just report "they did this," then "they did that," without gory detail. Lots of room left for our imagination; little opportunity given for us to make too much out of our cruelty. Nothing now but the simple words *I thirst*.

This brief word from the cross is curious in light of Jesus's repeated statements that he was the ultimate thirst quencher: "Whoever drinks from the water that I will give will never be thirsty again" was a claim that he made many times (John 4:14; 6:35). "All who are thirsty should come to me!" (John 7:37). The "thirst quencher" is now thirsty? This "I thirst" must mean more than simply that Jesus was, after all, not only divine but also human. In his saying "I thirst," we may be at the very heart of his divinity, that which makes Jesus God, one with the Father, and so very much unlike us.

In the Bible, to "thirst" is usually for more than water. To thirst in scripture is to yearn, to long for, to be desperate with desire. Jesus, in the beginning of his Sermon on the Mount, blessed a certain sort of holy desperation. "Happy are people who are hungry and thirsty for righteousness" (Matt 5:6). Blessed are those who want God's will to be done on earth as it is in heaven as if they were desperate for a drink of water after a week in the desert. The psalmist prays, "My whole being thirsts for God, for the living God" (Ps 42:2).

I am remembering from my youth a long and grueling hike up a dusty trail in the mountains on a hot day. We had all taken water with us, but all of our water was gone a little over an hour into the hike. We had to keep walking for another hour or so. When we finally came to a mountain creek, everyone burst into a gallop, and reaching the creek, we threw ourselves into the creek, pushing and pulling one another out of the way, falling in face down, lapping up the water like the thirsty animals that we were.

In a Honduran village I watched brave women, trudging halfway up the steep mountain, day after day, with huge tin watering cans on their backs, desperate for life-giving water for their families.

When, in New Orleans after Hurricane Katrina, civil unrest broke out, the general in charge said, "You keep potable water from people and they will destroy the city to get a drink."

Jesus blessed people who were that way about the righteousness of God. He blessed people who were eaten up with the desire to be with God, to see God's will done on earth as it is in heaven.

C. S. Lewis said that the trouble with many of us is not that we are bad, just that we are "too easily pleased." We are too satisfied with things as they are, too adjusted and accommodated to the status quo, not thirsty. For us, it is a sign of immaturity for a person to be too eager, too single-minded in pursuit of something. The mature learn to step back, to live with balance and cool discretion. Most of us long for balance in our lives, equilibrium, and serene contentment. But that was not the way of Jesus. Jesus blessed those who thirsted after God like a thirsty animal.

Ever seen a person truly thirsty for righteousness? I was at a conference on justice and spirituality at Messiah College in Pennsylvania. We sat around for a couple of days, a group of scholars and students, discussing biblical concepts of justice, having historical lectures on the prophets of Israel and their meaning. Toward the end of the second day, in a panel discussion on *dikaiosune* in the letters of Paul, a sophomore rose up from his seat and started shouting, "Do you people know what Israel is doing in the occupied territories? I've just come back from Ramallah. Here we sit talking about justice and not one hand is lifted in concern, not one word about the suffering and injustice there!"

We informed the student that such outbursts were not appreciated in academic gatherings. We urged him to behave in a more rational manner, to see all sides of the issue without settling down on any of them, to step back, cool off, tone down, and act more intellectual.

He stormed out, just about to die for some justice, thirsty for a drink that only God could give.

"Our hearts are restless (thirsty) until they find rest in thee," said Augustine.

Here, at the cross, we are now not splashing about in the shallow end of the pool. Here even the most complacent minds realize that Jesus has led us into deep waters. Here religion is significantly more than something "spiritual," more than an uplifting thought or noble idea that we can all sit around and discuss and then go home and forget. Here religion has somehow taken hold of our whole being, consumed us, knocked us off balance, and demanded our last anguished breath. Jesus says, "I thirst."

In Jesus's deep anguish and in his thirsting, they offered him a sponge with vinegar on a stick. But Jesus was thirsty for more than water. Jesus had a deep, blessed thirst that God's will be done on earth as in heaven, that God's righteousness might be fulfilled to the brim, a holy thirst that could only be assuaged by lifting up the blood-red cup of salvation and drinking it to the dregs.

But maybe Jesus isn't talking about our thirst or our hunger. He says "I" thirst. Not you, not me. He said, "I thirst." God Almighty, the Son of the Father, is thirsty. The mocking soldiers offered him a sponge soaked in vinegar just to scorn him in his thirst.

But maybe he wasn't thirsty even for water. Maybe he was thirsty for us. Is that not a fair summary of much of scripture—God's got this thing for us? God is determined—through creation, the words of the prophets, the teaching of the law, the birth of the Christ—to get close to us. God has this unquenchable thirst to have us. Even us.

Sorry, if you thought when we say *God* we have in mind some impersonal power, some fair-minded and balanced bureaucrat who is skilled at the careful administration of natural law from a safe distance in eternity. Our God is intensely, unreservedly personal. The God of Israel and the church refuses ever to be an abstraction or a generality. In the Bible, God gets angry, makes threats, promises, and punishes. Only people do such things and, when we do them, it is a sign of our personal worth, not of our grubby anthropocentric imperfection.

That's one of the things we mean when we say that "Jesus is Lord" or "Jesus is God's only Son." We mean that this God is shockingly personal, available, and present. And to say that is in no way a detraction from the Father's immense deity. There are gods who could not risk getting this close to us. We are killers who tend to kill our would-be saviors. Because we so want to be gods unto ourselves, we are rough on any who would presume to rule over us. So most "gods" are careful to keep their distance from us through abstraction and generalization.

This God, the one whom Israel and the church know as Trinity, is so great as to be utterly personal, available, and present to us. This God is against balance and reserve. This God thirsts for us, wholeheartedly gives himself over to us, unabashedly gets close to us. You can't get much closer to us, to the real us, than a cross.

When Christians say that God is transcendent or distant, this is what we are trying to say. The hiddenness of God is precisely in God's nearby self-revelation as God on the cross. It's God's difference from our expectations for gods that makes God hidden to us. We are blinded to God on the cross by our assumption that if there were a true God, that God would be somewhere a long way from us, not here before us, naked, exposed, and on a cross. I'm saying that Jesus's "I thirst" is another way of revealing God's utter self-giving availability to us.

So, in Psalm 23, when the psalmist says, in most of our traditional translations, "Surely goodness and mercy shall follow me all the days of my life: and I will dwell in the house of the LORD forever," I discovered that the Hebrew word translated most of the time as "follow" can also be rendered as "pursue." In fact, in a number of other places in the Hebrew scripture, that's just how it is translated: "Our enemies pursued us."

That certainly colors God's goodness and mercy in a different way, doesn't it? It's one thing to have goodness and mercy tag along behind you all your days, but it's quite another to be stalked, tracked down, cornered by goodness and mercy pursuing you just when you thought that you were at last on your own. Here we are, all self-sufficient and liberated, only to climb up the mountain to find goodness and mercy ready to jump us from a bloody cross.

"Are you able to drink the cup that I am to drink?" he asked his disciples. Our answer is an obvious, "No!" His cup is not only the cup of crucifixion and death, but also the bloody cup that one must drink if one is going to get mixed up in us. Any God who would wander into the human condition, any God who has this thirst to pursue us, had better not be too put off by pain, for that's the way we tend to treat our saviors. Any God who tries to love us had better be ready to die for it.

Earlier in this very same Gospel, it was said, "The Word became flesh and made his home among us. We have seen his glory." Now the Word, the Christ of God, sees where so reckless a move ends: on a cross. "I thirst, I yearn to feast with you," he says, "and behold, if you dare, where it gets me."

When I was giving lectures at a seminary in Sweden some years ago, a seminarian asked, "Do you really think Jesus Christ is the only way for us to get to God?"

And I thoughtfully replied, "I'll just say this, if you were born in South Carolina and living in a terribly violent culture, yes. There really is no way for somebody like me to get to God, other than a savior who doesn't mind a little blood and gore, a bit of suffering and grisly shock and awe, in order to get to me. A nice, balanced savior couldn't do much for a guy like me. I need a fanatic like Jesus. For we have demonstrated that we are an awfully, fanatically cruel and bloody people when our security is threatened. We have this history of murdering our saviors. So I just can't imagine any other way to God except Jesus."

God's in this fix, on this day, because God's so thirsty for us.

Relating the text

I've got a friend who refuses to watch nature programs on television, even *National Geographic* specials on the survival of hippopotami. He calls them "Nature Exploitation Shows." He thinks that it is morally debilitating for us to watch a tiger hunting down and killing a zebra or a crocodile devouring a water buffalo. He is unmoved when I say, "Well that is nature. Tooth, claw, and nail nature." He thinks that, as modern people, we have seen so many millions of images of this sort of "natural" violence and bloodletting that we have become immune. Now there is nothing within us that is moved by jaws crushing bone and ripping bloody flesh. It is just another evening of television.

His could be a good rationale for avoiding the evening news. After you have seen your thousandth child sitting in the rubble of her village in the West Bank, after, for the two hundredth time, you have seen the screaming mother running through the streets of a town in Iraq holding her baby after our bomb hit her house, you begin not even to have a twitch of sympathy. You are numb.

In case we would try to do anything like that with the suffering of Jesus, he cries out with these words, "I thirst."

In Honduras, an esteemed surgeon, who was also a devout Catholic, one day in the clinic picked up a naked little boy, a child of no more than four or five, and asked me to touch the boy's bloated belly. With tears in his eyes, the surgeon said, "This little boy has no more than a month to live with malnutrition this advanced. His little, empty stomach is about the most obscene thing I've ever seen."

Only the sacramental worship of a God in the flesh could teach a modern Western person like him the obscenity of human starvation.

Pontius Pilate

Selected reading

John 18:1–19:42

Theme

Jesus stands before Pilate on Good Friday. Two kingdoms clash in this fateful encounter—the kingdom of this world and God's kingdom. Pilate personifies the world's way, the way of violence and force, of power and politics. Jesus embodies another way, which is God's way. Pilate appears in the Apostles' Creed as a reminder of the clash between the crucified Messiah and power of empire.

Introduction to the readings

Isaiah 52:13–53:12
Isaiah speaks of the suffering servant who was "like a [sheep] silent before her shearers," thus bringing to mind Jesus who, before Pilate, was silent.

Hebrews 10:16-25
The writer to the Hebrews speaks of a law written, not on tablets of stone, but rather upon the hearts of the people.

John 18:1–19:42

John tells the dramatic story of Jesus's trial by Pilate, which led to Jesus's torture and crucifixion.

Prayer

Lord God, on this day we gather to recall Jesus's crucifixion. There is something in us that would like to believe that what happened to Jesus on this day was unrelated to us, something done by others, something that could never be done by us.

Convict us, Lord. Show us the error of our ways, the manner in which we have betrayed Jesus, have crucified him with our failures and sins, our half-hearted discipleship.

We hear the voices in the crowd calling "crucify him!" and the voices we hear are our own.

Be with us, Lord. Forgive us for our sin against your Son, our savior, Jesus. The fate of our souls is in your hands this fateful day and always. Amen.

Encountering the text

This Friday's reading is the rich, dramatic story of Jesus's trial and crucifixion as told by John. On a number of times in this Gospel, Christ has said that when he is "lifted up," then it will be his "hour." Now, in this story, Jesus is being lifted up on an ignoble instrument of Roman torture. Yet through the eyes of faith, we see this great defeat and these horrible hours of torture and pain as his greatest victory.

Crucifixion was a peculiarly Roman form of punishment, well-suited for humiliation of revolutionaries and rebels against the Roman occupation forces. We shall recall that in our exposition of this story, illuminating our interpretation with a clause from the Apostles' Creed: suffered under Pontius Pilate.

In this drama, Pilate, representative of the repressive state, and Jesus, harbinger of God's kingdom, go head to head, one on one. Who will remain standing at the end of this battle? Who will be the victor this night?

John presents Jesus and Pilate as two warriors engaged in combat. Pilate is a representative of the most powerful of worldly empires. Jesus represents a "kingdom not of this world." Whose politics will triumph this night? That is the Good Friday political question. The fate of the world rests upon the answer.

Proclaiming the text

How did somebody like this make it into the Apostles' Creed? Except for Jesus and the Virgin Mary, the only other person mentioned by name in the Apostles' Creed is the Roman bureaucrat who was most responsible for the death of Jesus, Pontius Pilate. Why did he get in the Apostles' Creed? The theologian Karl Barth says that Pontius Pilate enters into the creed somewhat "like a dog into a nice room!" (*Dogmatics in Outline* [New York: Harper & Row, 1991], 108).

As someone who has ventured from time to time into the cesspool of ecclesiastical politics, I can tell you, politics intrudes into the church; and when it does, it is not pretty. On Good Friday politics intrudes. Who was Pontius Pilate? He was a person of not much consideration, a government bureaucrat who had been sent by Rome to keep these troublesome Jews in their place in the occupied territory of Judea. During his rule, Pontius Pilate kept a lid on Judea, mostly through a beloved form of Roman punishment for troublesome non-Roman criminals and revolutionaries—crucifixion.

The local religious authorities had declared Jesus guilty and sentenced him to death, but they lacked the power to carry out that sentence. They appealed to Pontius Pilate for the execution, and he consented, thinking that by doing so he could quiet the revolutionary passions of the crowd. Pilate was just following orders. He initiated none of the evil that was done against Jesus, but he was its most notable accomplice. Even though he acknowledged that Jesus was innocent, he handed him over to one of the most vicious and cruel forms of capital punishment ever devised.

Pilate does not worry about following the established law, but rather he yields to the pressure of the screams of the mob. Consulting his public opinion polls, he commits a great evil.

Jesus suffered at many hands. He suffered rejection by his own family and friends when he preached his first sermon in Nazareth (Luke 4). He suffered misunderstanding and eventually betrayal by his own disciples. He suffered the taunts of "Crucify him!" by the crowd. But all we remember was that he "suffered under Pontius Pilate."

By mentioning the suffering of Jesus and the name of its perpetrator we are reminded that the great mystery of our redemption, God's saving us from our sin and death, God's war against our evil, did not take place in heaven but in history, right here in our world. The world, the real world, where there is political intrigue and compromise, cowardice and cruelty.

The implication is that if we would meet God, then we would need not go away to some spiritual retreat, aloof and detached from the grubby facts of life in this world. Rather, if we would see God, we would need only to open our eyes to God's work in human history; more precisely, in the very worst of human history, where people meet in smoke-filled rooms and do things under the table and make grubby political deals and compromises. It was right there that God came out to us.

We are free not to close our eyes to this grubby, seedy side of human life because God has not closed God's eyes to this side of us.

In Jesus Christ, almighty God entered into our political shenanigans. The affirmation that "the Word was made flesh" really meant what it said. As Barth says, to mention Pontius Pilate, along with the suffering of Jesus, is an affirmation that "we are not left alone in this frightful world. Into this alien land God has come to us."

Pontius Pilate, with the Roman legions backing him up, is the representative of all worldly, militarily based power, the power of the state, the power mechanisms of the modern nation. Pontius Pilate represents all of that. In his unprincipled, vacillating, political cowardice, Pontius Pilate is not one of our most noble images of the government. In him, the futility and the folly our state pretensions are based on are exposed. In that brief but fateful episode, as Jesus stands before Pontius Pilate, God's kingdom and our kingdoms meet, clash, and struggle with one another. By the end of the story, one kingdom triumphs, while another trudges into the dustbin of history. The name of Jesus Christ would be remembered and revered; however, the name of Pontius Pilate would be obliterated, were it not for his mention in our creed.

Surely we are meant to see this as commentary on the fate of the state. Pontius Pilate represented the all-powerful Emperor Tiberius. We live in a world in which politics seems to be everything. It is the main concern of our news reporting, our almighty protector from the cradle to the grave. We need to mark well the fate of Pontius Pilate, for his fate is, according to scripture, the fate of all of our governmental protections.

Earlier, when questioned about our allegiance to the government, Jesus had said, "Render to Caesar what is Caesar's, but render to God what is God's." Such a statement might lead some to conclude that the state has power over an area of human life, while God has power over another. Christians are to keep the two areas separate. But if that is a valid intention of Jesus's words to "render unto Caesar," and I am not sure that is the correct interpretation, then that interpretation cannot be sustained now, here, as Jesus stands before Pontius Pilate. Here, that which we called law and order, state power, the domain of the government, all of that is being called into question, criticized, and challenged. Here we see state power in its most negative form. Jesus becomes the light, the spotlight that highlights how cruel the state can be. We who have just lived through the bloody twentieth century, during which more people were killed by their own governments than were killed in war, we ought to take notice.

What is Pilate's great sin? His is the sin of the state down through the ages. He attempts to maintain order in Jerusalem, to preserve his own position of power; he decides between right and wrong purely on the basis of what is most expedient for the state. The modern nation has proved to be one of our most murderous inventions, appearing to have no ethic other than self-preservation at any cost. After Pilate will come Nero, and after Nero will come Henry VIII, Hitler, Stalin, Mao; Pilate is there for them all.

So as Jesus stands before Pilate awaiting judgment, Jesus judges Pilate. And the judgment is condemnation, and the face of the Roman bureaucrat is the face of the beast.

Pilate, such a powerful man, appears weak, vacillating, indecisive, jerked around by the will of the mob. Jesus, who has no legions behind him, no legal authority, no state, appears powerful, triumphant. In his work this weekend, a new polis will be formed. God's kingdom will take visible form, not with monumental state buildings, capitals, courts, military bases, but rather around the table, with a group of ordinary people; he is called to come forth and be part of God's kingdom.

At least give Pilate credit. Savvy politician that he is, he was able to see a competitor, a rival for power when one stood before him. He could see that, though Jesus did not often talk politics, what Jesus was about was, in the end, very political. Jesus is a challenge to any person or power who would attempt to take what belongs to God, to usurp God's authority to name what is going on in the world and what all of this means.

Thus, Pilate's name appears in the Apostles' Creed as one who has been defeated by Jesus, power usurped by the force of love. Thus, he is mentioned in the creed, only in passing, as a way of reflecting the triumph of God worked out before us this night.

Relating the text

Good Friday may be one of the most political days for the church. Jesus is being tried and ultimately killed as a political troublemaker. Pilate had no theological or religious interest in Jesus. He was concerned only about this talk of a "king." Anyone who believes that it is a simple matter for Christians to be involved in politics, to be patriotic and supportive of governments, even democratically elected governments, must do business with today's scripture. The ministry of Jesus was brought to an end; he was eventually killed in a most cruel and horrible way, not because of his "religious" teaching, but because of politics. Of course, today's story reminds us that there really is no sure and clear distinction between religion and politics. Pilate knew. It is of the nature of Jesus to claim lordship, to be imperialistic in his demands for all of our lives, all of our desires and dreams. This is the lordship that the state finds tough to tolerate.

Theologian Albrecht Ritschl was a champion of the kingdom cause. He announced the theme of God's kingdom as the great center of the teaching and the work of Jesus: "The kingdom of God is the *summum bonum,* which God realizes in men; and at the same time it is their common task, for it is only through the rendering of obedience on man's part that God's sovereignty possesses continuous existence. . . . The moral action demanded by the kingdom of God . . . is committed to men as God's independent and responsible subjects."

—Albrecht Ritschl, *The Christian Doctrine of Justification and Reconciliation*, trans. H. R. Mackintosh and A. B. Macaulay (New York: Charles Scribner's Sons, 1900), 30–31

In Jesus's encounter with Pilate, he establishes a pattern for prophetic, truthful encounters between the representatives of God's kingdom and those who operate the kingdoms of this world. As Kenneth Kaunda, the former president of Zambia, has written, "What a nation needs more than anything else is not a Christian ruler in the palace but a Christian prophet within earshot."

For the life of me I will never understand why many think of Christians as out of it, as people who live in some sort of fantasy world that does not relate to the real world.

Christianity is a faith that is based on history, that arises from within the facts of life. Our God did not remain aloof from the tug and pull of the real world. Jesus did not hunker down with a few religiously inclined followers and discuss high-flown spiritual matters. He stood before Pontius Pilate. He stood toe-to-toe with the principalities and powers.

In just a few days on Easter, we shall see what shall become of Jesus, of who will win, Pilate or Jesus.

Easter Day

Acts 10:34-43 or Isaiah 65:17-25
Psalm 118:1-2, 14-24
1 Corinthians 15:19-26 or Acts 10:34-43
John 20:1-18 or Luke 24:1-12

Seeing Is Believing

Selected reading

John 20:1-18 (with reference to Luke 15)

Theme

Seeing is believing. In order to believe, most of us need some tangible, visible evidence. Fortunately, the risen Christ gives us what we need to believe. He overcomes our distorted, inadequate vision and shows himself to us in countless ways. Our faith in the resurrected Christ is a gift of the resurrected Christ.

Introduction to the readings

Isaiah 65:17-25

The Lord announces new heavens and a new earth through the prophet Isaiah.

1 Corinthians 15:19-26

"If we have hope in Christ only in this life, then we deserve to be pitied more than anyone else," says Paul as he recites our hope through the resurrection of Jesus.

John 20:1-18

John tells the story of Easter and the miracle that happened as Jesus's astonished disciples are encountered by the risen Christ.

Prayer

Risen Christ, show us your glory! Come to us, reveal yourself and your will to us, be with us, prod us, lead us, and give us the vision to see you among us. Give us the guts to follow wherever you take us. Amen.

Encountering the text

When it comes to the resurrection, John's Gospel stresses the important role of vision. This is the message that Mary gives the disciples, "I have seen the Lord." When it comes to Easter, there is no knowing and there is no real believing without dramatic seeing. O. Wesley Allen Jr., in his very helpful book *Preaching Resurrection* ([St. Louis: Chalice Press, 2000], 107–8), helpfully lists the various visionary experiences characterized in the twentieth chapter of John's Gospel. Mary saw that the stone had been rolled away, but she did not know where they had taken the Lord (20:1-2). The disciple whom Jesus loved looked in the tomb and saw the linen cloths lying there (20:4-5), but not Jesus. Then Peter arrived and saw the clothes lying in separate places (20:6-7). The beloved disciple followed and saw the linen cloths and believed (20:8). Just what he believed is a bit unclear because John says, "They didn't yet understand the scripture that Jesus must rise from the dead" (20:9). Perhaps he believed that the body had been stolen. Then Mary looked in the tomb and saw two angels sitting at the head and the foot where Jesus's body had been (20:12); still she did not know where they had taken the Lord (20:13). But when she saw Jesus, she knew it was Jesus (20:14).

It was not much help to Mary to focus on the linen cloths and the empty tomb. It was only when she was able to see Jesus that she was able to believe. Just being there at the empty tomb is not enough. One must be encountered by the risen Christ.

In our sermon on this Easter we will focus on the important role of vision in the resurrection experience, taking our cues from the Gospel of John's treatment of the resurrection. We will affirm our faith in Easter as a gift of a God who comes to us and gives us what we need to believe.

Proclaiming the text

I recently heard a distinguished historian of the modern world declare that the modern world has gone downhill ever since it convinced itself "that nothing is real except what we can see, taste, and touch." The modern world is dedicated to the principle that there is no reality other than what we can sense.

This seems to be the attitude of the salesclerk who waited on me the other day. I was thumbing through the cantaloupes in the vegetable department. None of them looked appealing. So I asked, "Do you have any more cantaloupes?" The reply from the vegetable vender was, "Well, what you see there is all there is. Either take it or leave it."

I found this a grand summary of much of modern higher education. You look at the world. There are some things about the world that don't seem right to us. A number of aspects about the world, and ourselves, displease us. But growing up and becoming a mature adult means to be the sort of person who is able to say, "Well, this is all there is. What you see is what you get. Either take it or leave it."

Most of us, as we grow up, learn to take it rather than leave it. We take the world, asking only that we have the guts to take the world as it is, not as we would wish it to be. What we see is what we get. And there is a certain dignity and courage in not whining, not consoling ourselves with fairy tales. This is all there is. Live with it.

And yet this approach does not do justice to the complexities of vision. How do we see? You don't have to live very long before you realize that what you see might not necessarily be what there is. The brain filters out so many of the visual impressions we see. What we see seems to be connected to some sort of template in the brain. When sensory images are fed in through the optic nerve, the brain sorts through its collection of previously experienced images, makes matches, and fits what we see into a pattern, and then we are led to say, "There it is! That's a tree." Thus, we are somewhat justified in saying, "If you have seen one tree, that enables you to see them all."

And yet what does the brain do with things that don't fit into previously experienced patterns? What if our vision is out of focus? What if our seeing is sometimes limited by what we expect to see, or have the courage to see? What if it is not so much a matter of "you get what you see," but also a matter of "you see what you have already gotten"?

Thus, Mary Magdalene appeared at the tomb of Jesus early Easter morning. When she saw that the huge stone at the door of the tomb had been rolled away, and that the tomb was empty, she immediately saw what had happened: someone had stolen Jesus's body, and she did not know where they had put him. Even when an angel appears and asks her why she is weeping, Mary still says that someone has stolen Jesus's body.

It is not until Jesus himself appears to Mary and calls her by name that she begins to see. Even then, she at first thinks that the risen Christ is a gardener. Mary just can't get out of her mind that she is at a cemetery, a place of death and loss. She can't refocus her eyes, even when an angel, even when the risen Christ, is standing in front of her.

And then there is Thomas. When he hears the report that Jesus's body is missing and that Jesus has appeared before some of the other disciples, Thomas says that unless he sees the wounds that killed Jesus, he won't believe. After all, the one believable thing about Jesus is that he is dead, crucified, and buried, with large holes in his hands and a gaping wound in his side. That's reality.

And then the risen Christ appears and tells Thomas to touch his wounds, and Thomas exclaims, "My Lord and my God."

I don't think it's fair to call him "Doubting Thomas." It wasn't that Thomas refused to believe. He believed. But he believed in what he could see. And what he could see was death, failure, annihilation, and destruction. Mary was the same. Until Jesus called her by name, her vision was out of focus. Until the risen Christ asked Thomas to touch his wounds, Thomas could not see.

What does it take to get us to see what is there? It is not enough simply to say, "Well, what you see, is what you get." There is a matter of failed vision, inadequate perception. We've all had that frustrating experience of seeing something at some distant point across the landscape. And then we say to the friend beside us, gesturing as we speak, "Look, over there!"

The friend looks, squints, but can't see. "Over to the right!" we say, "Just beneath that first hill to the left of that house."

It's a frustrating experience. The thing is so obvious, so apparent. But the friend just can't get it. We attempt to point to certain landmarks, hoping that the friend will move from seeing those apparent objects to this less apparent thing we are trying to show. It is very frustrating.

What enables us to see? What is it that can grab our heads, turn our eyes in the right direction, and bring everything into focus?

For Mary and for Thomas, it was the risen Christ. He did not leave them to their own devices. He did not expect them to build upon their past experiences. He did not rely on their misperceptions, but rather he came to them. He spoke to one and then he encouraged the other to touch his very body. He turned their gaze away from what was expected and accustomed toward what was being revealed.

Maybe that is why we call Christianity a revealed religion. You can't see it until it is revealed, given to you, until one has experienced the gift of the presence of the risen Christ, and then one's eyes get in focus.

Most of the time we "see in a mirror dimly," as Paul put it in 1 Corinthians 13:12 (RSV). Occasionally, by the grace of God, things come into focus and we see, face-to-face.

That's Easter. It wasn't just that Jesus was raised from the dead. It was that he was raised for us. He returned to his friends, revealed himself to them, and enabled them to see and to believe.

I know a man who, through his thirty-third year, lived a rather dissolute life. We always thought him to be a person of high intelligence and great gifts, but he really seemed to have difficulty focusing that intelligence and developing those gifts. I knew him during his college years. He was quite the party animal. We thought that when he got married that might make a difference, but it didn't. He and his wife spent far too many evenings carousing. He had a good job, but he seemed uninterested in his job and unable to get his life moving.

Another friend of mine was able to say of him, "He has really wasted his life."

But a couple of months ago, he and his wife had a little baby girl. I had never thought of him as the parental type. But there was this baby.

The change was dramatic. He totally settled down, settled in, and focused. If you met him on the street, you hardly knew you were talking to the same person. The main pleasure he now sees in life is in providing for his child's future, in being a great father, and living a good family life. What happened?

Well, I think he got encountered. I think in a moment his life was intruded upon, and it got refocused, redirected. It was as if in an instant everything came into focus and he saw. He got a vision of who he was meant to be, of who he could be. His world changed. For the first time he saw true reality.

I think it was something like Easter.

Relating the text

You've seen those images that, when you first look at them, look like a black and white picture of the head of a cow, some sort of black and white cow staring back at you. But when you linger a bit longer, you see that it is the head of Christ.

Or somebody has shown you a card that seems to have some scrambled black and white letters on it. You look at it, and it is hard to recognize any familiar letter of the alphabet. But when you focus on it again, you see the word *Jesus*. Philosopher Ludwig Wittgenstein drew a simple round head with two long ears sticking up. At least that is what it looked like to me. What is it? Well, of course, it is a rabbit.

But then the philosopher says, "No, that's a duck." And the minute he says it, suddenly the drawing is transformed and it really does look like a duck, looking up. What was earlier perceived to be the ears of a rabbit, as the rabbit looked down, now appears to be the beak of a duck, looking up.

Our perception is conditioned, warped, constricted, and unreliable.

I've tried to argue people into believing in Christ. I have found it a frustrating experience. If I had the wits to argue someone into belief in the risen Christ, someone smarter than I could just as easily argue them out of belief.

I believe that deep, life-changing Christian belief is based not upon arguments and reasons but upon encounter with the risen Christ. We believe simply because he comes to us and gives us that which we cannot give ourselves—a reason to believe, a way to go on, a path out of doubt toward faith.

I had to laugh. Joe had just been involved in an accident just down the street from his home. It wasn't too serious, but his car was broadsided by another car coming down the street.

Joe said, "I looked down that street before I pulled out of the driveway and there was nothing coming down the street. Nothing! I go down that street a dozen times a week and there are hardly ever any cars on the street. I looked! Not a car in sight!"

Well, there must have been at least one car in sight. But it was not a sight that was given to Joe on that fateful morning.

- 261 -

Acts 10:34-43 or Isaiah 65:17-25

Psalm 118:1-2, 14-24

1 Corinthians 15:19-26 or Acts 10:34-43

John 20:1-18 or Luke 24:1-12

Holding on to Easter

Selected reading

John 20:1-18

Theme

Mary Magdalene, unlike the other disciples, stayed at the tomb and was personally addressed by the risen Christ. Sometimes we, like Mary, need simply to stay, to remain close to Jesus until we come to believe in Jesus, until we are given the full Easter faith that we desire. Christians are those who stay close to Jesus in order that the risen Christ may come close to us.

Introduction to the readings

Isaiah 65:17-25

The Lord announces a new heaven and a new earth through the prophet Isaiah. When God acts, there is newness.

1 Corinthians 15:19-26

"If for this life only we have hoped in Christ, we are of all [people] most to be pitied," says Paul as he recites our hope through the resurrection of Jesus.

John 20:1-18

John tells the story of Easter and the miracle that happened, as Jesus's astonished disciples see the empty tomb. But Mary Magdalene lingers at the tomb, and there she is encountered by the risen Christ.

Prayer

Lord Jesus, we gather today loudly, lovingly, lavishly to celebrate your great defeat of death, your grand victory over the forces of sin. We give thanks that you loved us enough not only to die for us but also to rise for us and our salvation.

Enable us to lay aside our doubts, our misgivings, and misunderstandings and bask in the light of your resurrected glory. Sweep up your church in a great shout of glorious praise this day, this triumphant day that is your great gift to us and the world. Help us so to live that others may see your Easter victory in us. Amen.

Encountering the text

It's Easter. We are in the Gospel of John, a Gospel whose testimony is thick and rich with preaching possibilities—sometimes too rich. There is a sense in which it's always Eastertime in John's Gospel. The Christ in John is an energetic, majestic, lively figure from the beginning of the Gospel to the end. Nothing can stop the Johannine Christ from realizing his mission.

I propose that we focus on the story within the story—the story of Mary Magdalene. We read about Mary while we are reading about the actions of Peter "and the other disciple, the one whom Jesus loved," going out to the cemetery in the darkness of the first Easter morning. In some Easters past we have reflected upon the footrace of these two disciples out to the tomb, the way they tried to outrun each other getting to Easter.

Let's not focus on that. Let's focus on Mary Magdalene, the first follower of Jesus who was personally encountered by the risen Christ. Note that encountering the risen Christ was not in itself enough for Mary; she had to get hold of Jesus. The fact that Mary was out at the tomb in the Easter darkness is amazing in itself. After all, it had been a particularly violent and bloody week in Jerusalem, particularly bloody for Jesus. And if the authorities did what they did to Jesus, what might they do to Jesus's followers?

Nevertheless, despite the threat and the danger, there is Mary out at the tomb. I wonder if Mary might have thought that some people might say (and what they say is an expression of their obvious or not-so-obvious sexism) that Mary was a "pushy woman." She was even "aggressive." But if Mary Magdalene was that way, in pushing her way out to the cemetery on Easter, let us take that in a very positive sense. For most people, it might have been enough to let a couple of the men go out to the tomb on Easter. But not for Mary. She was determined to go out there herself and brave any dangers in order to be close to Jesus, even if it was to be close to the dead Jesus, even if it was to pay her respects to the dead body of Jesus.

Someone Mary thinks is a gardener approaches her and speaks to her in the darkness. A light goes on in Mary's mind. She hears a familiar voice. She hears her name called. She responds, "Rabbouni!" She is about to embrace this one who has somehow come back from the dead and who, throughout his ministry, embraced her. But there she learns that she cannot hold on to the resurrected Christ.

Jesus has not only been sent to the world by the Father. Jesus, at the day's dawning, is a sender. And Mary is the one who is being sent. All the rest of the disciples (including those men who were too cowardly to come out to the cemetery in the darkness) will be sent out on the way, too.

But we ought to notice that Mary stays awhile before she goes. Before being sent out in the name of Jesus, she comes close to the person of Jesus. The disciples who raced out to the tomb on Easter morning, ran back to their fellows in Jerusalem almost as quickly, not fully understanding what was happening. They seem to have believed on the basis of just seeing the empty tomb. They saw, they believed, and they left. But Mary is different. She stays. Yes, she is confused. Yes, she is fearful. No, she does not fully understand. Still, Mary stays, and because she stays, she is met by the risen Christ.

You can call it by whatever name you like—courage, hard-headedness, stamina, determination—but why don't we call it faith! Mary stayed. And therefore, we have her dramatic testimony of the first Easter. In her testimony, there is fear, confusion, and misunderstanding, but there is also glorious recognition.

Let us take Mary as an Easter parable, a resurrection parable for each of us.

Let us consider the reason Christ is on the move. Maybe we don't see a great deal of him, except for momentary glimpses, as he moves through our lives. His presence is a gift that he gives to us. But it is difficult for us to receive the gift if we do not take time, if we do not stay, if we do not have stubborn determination to receive that blessing. He is beyond our grasp. We cannot hold him in one place forever. But we can wait. We can do what Mary Magdalene did. We can stay.

Mary got moving. She ran back and told the others what she had experienced. And we are grateful to have her testimony. But before she was sent, before she moved, she stayed.

Proclaiming the text

Our Gospel for this Easter begins with an account of a group of disciples who went out to the tomb on the first Easter morning. They must have been a sad lot, going out to pay their respects to the body of their now-dead teacher and master. Mary Magdalene was one of the women who was there in the group going out to the cemetery that morning. Her great friend Jesus had died. The one who reached out to her and loved her had died. Mary went out with the rest of them in grief to pay her last respects to the memory of her friend.

When people go through grief, they often report what a huge achievement it is just to put "one foot in front of the other." To keep on keeping on becomes a great achievement. Perhaps that's the way Mary went out to the tomb that first Easter.

When people go through a great trauma, like a great grief, we don't expect them so much to triumph, as simply to survive. Simply being a survivor is a triumph.

There are so many times in life when the greatest virtue is to simply keep on keeping on, to stay, to take up accustomed rituals again, to get up and go out to work, even though you just want to give up.

Well-meaning friends sometimes tell us when we are in grief, "You must get up and get going. You need to get moving! Get up! Get dressed." Mary did that on the first Easter, yet she also didn't do that because she stayed at the tomb.

The other disciples came, saw the empty tomb, and raced back to Jerusalem to preach, "He is risen!"

But Mary lingered. She stayed. And because she stayed, Jesus met her and she saw the risen Christ for herself and believed.

I was appointed to a troubled church that had lost hundreds of members in the last decade. Like a lot of inner-city churches, this church had lost touch with its neighborhood and had been in decline.

By the grace of God, eventually things got better and started to change. We grew. One day, I had the occasion to thank one of our loyal, older members for her support and for her leadership. I thanked her for simply staying with the congregation during its rough times, and, because she stayed, she helped lead the congregation forward.

"I stayed here because I couldn't get out of my mind that God had a purpose for this church," she said. "I stayed because I was convinced that God would one day bless us and use us. You came to us as our pastor and, despite first impressions (!), you turned out to be that blessing that we needed. I am glad I stayed, because if I had left, I would have missed out on a resurrection!"

Maybe that is what Jesus expects of us this morning. I don't know if you greet the resurrection proclamation, "He is risen!" with strong, firm faith and with strong belief in the resurrection reality. But maybe you don't have to. Maybe all that you need is simply to be here. And you are!

You need to stay here, linger for a while before the mystery of the crucifixion of Jesus, as well as the empty tomb and the resurrection of Jesus. You need to keep on keeping on, to follow the rituals of the church, to put one foot in front of the other in the grand Easter procession, to keep receiving the body and blood of Christ, and just to hold on, until you have the faith you hope to have.

As Mary was reminded, we can't hold on to Jesus. He is on the move. But before Jesus heads to somewhere else, he addresses Mary by name, and he allows her to reach out to him. We can hold on to Jesus. But the beautiful thing is that Jesus, the resurrected Christ, keeps holding on to us, keeps reaching out to us, embracing us, and holding us.

A woman reported to me (I think her name was Mary Magdalene!) on a dramatic conversion that she had experienced in her life. She said that belief had always been a problem for her. Since she was young, she had greeted the faith of the church with nothing but doubts, questions, and misgivings. Yet here she was, mid-life, being given the faith that she did not have. She said that she had a vivid experience of the presence of the risen Christ. She said that it was if a "light came on in my life and things fell into place and I finally understood, I saw, I believed."

I asked her if she knew why she had been given this gift of faith now, at this particular time. She responded, "I have no idea why the light finally came on and things fell into place, right now at this specific time. I just know that I kept standing up every Sunday and saying the words of the Apostles' Creed, saying them over and over again, saying them from memory but not really in my heart. If you had stopped one Sunday and asked me, 'Do you really believe what you are saying about the resurrection, about the virgin birth and all the rest?' I don't know that I would have been able to answer affirmatively.

But one day, I did believe. I am so very glad that I stood up, for all these hundreds of Sundays, and affirmed what I believed before I believed it."

I am so glad that she stayed.

A pastor reported to me that his church went through a traumatic battle over sponsoring an interracial daycare center in the basement of his church. Two families left the church in opposition to the opening of the daycare center. But most of the members stayed.

One of those who stayed reported a conversation a couple of years later with one of the people who left in opposition to the daycare center.

"She asked me how things were going at the church. I proudly told her that things were going great, that we had experienced more growth in membership last year than in any previous year of the decade. I explained to her how the daycare center had been the key to getting back in touch with our neighborhood. I told her that it was a miraculous thing to behold. And then, God forgive me, I said to her, 'Aren't you sorry that you didn't stay to see the miracle? When you left, you cheated yourself out of experiencing one of the most miraculous works of God that I've ever seen.'"

Jesus calls people to "follow me." He takes people on a journey. But sometimes Jesus must be happy if people just stay. I don't know how you have come here this Easter morning. I don't know if you are here bearing strong faith. Maybe you've got your questions and doubts. That's okay. The point is you stayed. You have therefore put yourself in a great place for the risen Christ to reach out to you, to call your name, to hold on to you, so that you may, by faith, hold on to him. Amen!

Relating the text

John Wesley, founder of the Methodist movement, used to advise his traveling preachers (who sometimes confessed to a certain weakness of faith), "Preach faith until you have it." By that, I think that Wesley meant that it is important to keep reiterating the faith that we have until it becomes the faith we want. Of course, we don't "have" this faith. It's more accurate to say that this faith "has us." But sometimes, when it comes to believing in Jesus, the first thing is just to believe that Christ desires our faith, that he will come to us and give us the faith we need, if we just stay.

I remember when I was in seminary hearing a lecture by an Orthodox priest. He lectured on the creeds of the church and their development. At the end of his lecture a student friend of mine rose and asked, "But what do you do when you have trouble believing some part of the creed? What can you do when you, in integrity, cannot affirm the whole creed?"

The priest replied simply, "You can keep saying it until you believe it. Give yourself some time; it will eventually come to you."

I thought it a very wonderful Wesleyan view of belief.

Second Sunday of Easter

Acts 5:27-32
Psalm 118:14-29 or Psalm 150
Revelation 1:4-8
John 20:19-31

Lockout

Selected reading

John 20:19-31

Theme

The predominant response to the resurrected Christ among his closest followers is fear. We fear the new life and demanding discipleship that he brings us in his resurrection. Yet the good news is that he comes to us, and he breaks down our locked doors and shows himself to us, empowers us, and sends us forth.

Introduction to the readings

Acts 5:27-32

Peter and the disciples, called before the temple authorities for interrogation, testify to their faith in the resurrection of Jesus.

Revelation 1:4-8

The book of Revelation opens with a great hymn of praise to the One who is coming with the clouds.

John 20:19-31
The disciples of Jesus, hiding behind locked doors, are surprised by a stranger who comes and stands among them.

Prayer

Living Lord, not only did you rise from the dead and defeat sin and the powers of death and evil. You also came back to us, you broke through our locked doors, you overcame our doubts and reservations, and you called us to follow you into eternal life. Keep coming to us, Lord Jesus. Keep raising us from the dead. Keep empowering us with your life-giving Spirit! Amen!

Encountering the text

John's Gospel ends in a series of three resurrection stories. Our Gospel today comprises the second and third resurrection appearances. We had the first one last Sunday.

The opening verse sets the tone. The disciples are hiding behind locked doors. We are told that they are locked in because of fear. We are not told of the reason for their gathering, except fear of the Jews. This is curious. Perhaps the Jews that the disciples feared were their friends and relatives who were now mocking them because their messiah had died such an ignominious death.

I wonder if they are full of fear because of Mary Magdalene's announcement to them (in the preceding verse, 20:18) that Jesus has been raised. Only the beloved disciple and Mary Magdalene have seen and believed up to this point.

Rather than delve into the various aspects of Jesus's appearance to his disciples, let us ponder two points of this passage: (1) The disciples of Jesus react to his crucifixion with fear, hiding behind locked doors; (2) Jesus seeks out those fearful disciples right after his resurrection. He comes to them, appears before them, and empowers them to do his work.

Let us not focus just on Thomas and his doubts. Let us focus upon the disciples as a whole and what Jesus does to them and for them. The ones locked in fear become, in John 20, the ones locked in the loving embrace of Jesus.

Proclaiming the text

A man was telling me about how his "security business" had skyrocketed after the September 11 terrorist attacks in the United States. That seemed rather strange to me because, so far as I know, this man's security business is limited to locks, burglar alarms, and things like that. But he told me, "For some reason, after September 11, everybody needed to go out and buy a better set of locks, a better set of security alarms." Of course, none of this offers any protection in the least from a terrorist. But those terrorists put us in a mood in which we desired security above all else.

Years ago, after I proudly self-installed a new set of deadbolt locks on the parsonage, a member of my church who is a policeman said to me, "Preacher, unfortunately those locks are mainly for you, not a potential thief. Any serious thief has got lots of ways to get around those locks. If it makes you feel better, fine." Those locks did make me feel better until the policeman said what he said!

Locks come in all shapes and sizes, and not just in the hardware store.

It is quite natural when you have suffered some trauma in life, when you have been violated by some injustice in life, to lock yourself away. That's always my worry when someone in my church suffers the breakup of relationship or is pained in romance. Rather than risking being pained again by love, better close the door and click the lock, and, if you can't have love, at least you can have some degree of security from pain.

A teacher at an inner-city school told me that her greatest challenge was, day after day, looking into the eyes of her high school students and seeing students who had simply shut down. They had failed so often, had experienced so often the door slamming in their faces, that they had withdrawn; they had locked the door and thrown away the key, so to speak.

"My whole teaching is involved in desperately searching for some key that can unlock that mind and give me some entrance into their soul," she said.

Now I've got all of this on my mind because of this Sunday's scripture. Here, on the Second Sunday of Easter, our Gospel tells us about a group of people who are cowering behind a locked door. But this isn't just any group of people; they are the disciples of Jesus. It is night, which is a dangerous time in nearly any city, but in the city of Jerusalem, after the weekend of terrible violence worked against Jesus, his disciples have lots of reasons to be fearful. Perhaps they were also fearful of the scorn of their friends and families. Here were the disciples of Jesus, those who had come forth to follow him, who had risked all, who believed that he was the one who would redeem Israel. No doubt they were fearful of the mocking of all those who said, "Some Messiah! Where is your Lord and savior now?" I wouldn't blame them for locking the doors against their mockers.

In a former parish, we got excited about evangelism. They realized that our church had lost touch with its neighborhood. Declining membership was a problem. So we put ourselves through a program of evangelistic training, and then, on an appointed Sunday afternoon, we moved out. We systematically began working down each street, knocking on doors, giving people some material, asking them if they had a church home, and telling them about our church.

I won't go into details, but I will simply say that a number of our visitors had doors slammed in their faces. Many people were none too happy to be disturbed on a Sunday afternoon. Our program of evangelism did not last very long. Click, click, click. And it was not simply that some people in our neighborhood closed their doors to us, but in giving up on the evangelism, our church closed its doors to these people.

Which brings us back to the Gospel for today. It is no small matter that those who have closed the door and locked the locks are Jesus's own disciples. This is not a story about all the ways the world locks its doors against the claims of the Christian faith. This is a story about the way that those of us who are Christians lock our doors. And in locking our doors out of fear of the world and what it might do to us, the irony is that the disciples have locked their doors to Jesus and what he might do to us. The irony of the Gospel today is that the soldiers of Caesar were not trying to get to the disciples, and their critics among their friends and family were not attempting to get the disciples in order to mock them. Jesus was trying to get to the disciples in order to bless them, to give them peace, to forgive and empower them.

Our securely locked doors are not a problem for Jesus. That is the good news of Easter. Just as death could not hold him in the tomb, so our various locks cannot keep him from getting to us.

He gets through the locked doors. He shows his wounds and scars from the cross to them. He says to those who may be fearful of the possibility of his retribution against them, "peace be with you."

There is thus a traditional irony here. The doors have not only been locked against the possibility of intrusions by the governmental authorities, not only been locked against the unwanted knocking of family and friends, but also the doors have been locked (albeit unintentionally) against the intrusions of the risen Christ. The risen Christ will not be locked by death in the tomb, nor will he be locked away from his people, the church.

I expect that all of our attempts to lock Jesus out and to secure ourselves against his incursions are unintended. We didn't know that we were locking him out when we stayed away from church, when we avoided signing up for the Bible study, when we found other things to do rather than pray. But we were.

We didn't know that we were locking him out when we kept our faith safely tucked away within ourselves, when our religion became something that we practice only in the safe confines behind the closed doors of the church, rather than out in the world where we work and spend so much of our lives. But we did.

But my sermon ends in an attempt to be faithful to this Gospel text, not with an exhortation for you to unlock your door, to throw wide the portals of your heart, to let Jesus into your life. No, my sermon ends with a promise. Here is the good news. Just as the risen Christ was not stopped by locked doors, so I promise you that the risen Christ will not be deterred by any locks that you have put on your doors. Our God is wonderfully resourceful, imaginative, persistent, and determined to have us. Even in our lostness, even in our betrayal, the first thing he does at Easter is come out to get us.

I believe even now, even in this sermon, in this service, here at this church, as you go forth in your daily life, he is coming out to get you. There is no sure defense against Jesus. There is no way to secure yourself against his intrusions. He is coming.

Jesus Christ is risen! Alleluia! Jesus Christ is coming for you and to you. Hallelujah!

Relating the text

When I was a campus minister I loved for students to tell me their stories of divine intrusion. They told of late-night encounters, of sleep disturbed, of a strangely moving comment they picked up in a class or something a friend said to them casually, but something that really grabbed them.

Upon hearing such stories, I found myself exclaiming, "That's amazing!" Why, I can't even get in the dorm to get to you without a magnetic card and permission from the Dean of Students. Here, despite all of our defenses against Jesus (the philosophy department is so effective!) Jesus has found you, has come out for you, intruded into your life. The risen Christ really is amazing!

Many Easters ago, we were talking about the strengths and weaknesses of Mel Gibson's *The Passion of the Christ*. Some of the people who had seen the movie liked it, and some didn't.

One of the people in the discussion said, "My brother has been alienated from church for over a decade. He is now a third-year law school student. The other night he called me and asked me to recommend to him a good church in our area. I was shocked. I wondered why he had now developed this interest in the church. So I asked him. And he replied, 'I went to see that movie, *The Passion*. And it really got to me. I can't describe what happened to me, but now I just know that I am being drawn back to the Christian faith.'"

As I have said, the risen Christ is infinitely resourceful, determined, and imaginative in coming out to get us.

I have been in a church that, for all the best of reasons, bought themselves an expensive security system in order to keep thieves and vandals out of their building. Trouble was, the security system also secured the church building against the intrusions of the congregation! Congregation members were reluctant to enter the building to arrange the flowers or to prepare for a Sunday school lesson or to meet for a Bible study, for fear of tripping the security system.

Which suggests to me that the great challenge of big locks is to be sure that you are locking out the criminals while at the same time not imprisoning yourself!

But please note that, in today's Gospel, locked doors, frightened disciples, and fear is not how the story ends. The story begins with a group of disciples, hunkered down behind locked doors like a bunch of frightened rabbits, gathered not for Christian fellowship or the praise of God, but "for fear." The good news is that they are the very ones to whom a resourceful and risen Christ appears. None of them is looking for Jesus, but Jesus, wonder of wonders, is out looking for them. This Sunday is the Sunday when the church reminds itself not only that Jesus rose from the dead, but that he also came looking for us. He returned to the very ones who had forsaken and betrayed him in his crucifixion, came out to bless them in his resurrection, and give them his work to do.

Third Sunday of Easter

Acts 9:1-6, (7-20)
Psalm 30
Revelation 5:11-14
John 21:1-19

Surprised by God

Selected reading

Acts 9:1-6, (7-20)

Theme

In the resurrection, not only did Jesus rise from the dead, but the living Christ came back to us. Scripture testifies that God comes to us; we don't come to God. And when God comes to us, touching our lives, flooding into our beings, we are changed. Our transformation is not something that we do; it is the miraculous turnaround that God works in us, in spite of us. "Conversion" is when God's transformative love comes to us, when we become vividly aware of that love and are transformed by it.

Introduction to the readings

Acts 9:1-6, (7-20)

The Acts of the Apostles recounts the stirring story of Saul's call by God to be the chosen instrument of mission to the Gentiles.

Revelation 5:11-14

John is given a vision of heaven in which, at the center, the Lamb rules from the throne at the center of heaven.

John 21:1-19

The risen Christ appears by the sea before his astonished disciples and commissions them to do his work in his name.

Prayer

Living Christ, meet us as you met the disciples who walked to Emmaus. Surprise us as you surprised the women who came to the tomb that first Easter. Appear to us and speak to us as you spoke to the disciples gathered behind locked doors on Easter evening. Do not leave us as we are. Come to us, appear to us, speak to us, change us into the disciples you would have us to be. Amen.

Encountering the text

Our text is the story of Saul's conversion to Paul. Most commentators are agreed that this is not so much a "conversion" story as it is a vocation story. Paul is called to be a missionary to the Gentiles.

Yet even as a call story, this is a story of a radical transformation. Perhaps to be called by God is to be transformed by God—a transformation signified by the change of name from Saul to Paul. This is a story of wrenching, dramatic movement from darkness to light, from being "church enemy number one" to the great leader of the church in its mission into the world.

Yet it is also a story of what happens when God calls, when God touches a life. Years ago the great scholar and churchman Krister Stendahl wrote an influential article on Acts 9 called "The Apostle Paul and the Introspective Conscience of the West." In the article Stendahl noted that most of us think of the story of Paul's conversion in terms that are more indebted to

Luther's account than to the text itself: we think of Saul as a man in search of something, a person who finally finds what he is looking for there on the Damascus Road.

Stendahl notes that nothing in the story says that Paul was searching for anything other than Christians to persecute! This is not a story of a man who is miserable and tormented until he finds a gracious God (Luther's account), but rather it is a story of someone who, quite without warning, is encountered by the living Christ. Stendahl says that to read the story otherwise is to read it from the point of view of the introspective, subjective conscience of the Western mind, not to read it as it meets us in scripture.

We will read Acts 9 as a story of how a life is affected by the living Christ, a story that has relevance for our own stories of our lives today.

Proclaiming the text

When we think about ourselves, most of us think that our selves are the result of what we have managed to make of our lives. My self is whatever I have chosen, worked, decided, and strived to be.

The Bible has a very different take on who we are. Who we are, says scripture, is not what we put together for us but what God puts together in us. Scripture knows nothing of our earnest, agonized search for God; rather more typical of the Bible is to assert God's search for us, as illustrated so well in today's lessons from Acts 9.

We meet this man Saul earlier in the Acts of the Apostles. He is an infamous persecutor of the church. And on his way to Damascus to persecute Christians, the living Christ enlists him as the great missionary to the Gentiles. In just a few verses, this persecutor becomes the preacher, the one who testifies of Jesus before kings and hostile mobs and brings the Christian faith into the Roman Empire. Quite a change. And where did that dramatic change come from?

I think of another dramatic transformation—that of C. S. Lewis. Lewis wasn't really searching for anything in his life at the time when, in Lewis's words, "God closed in on me." Lewis exclaimed with surprise, "So, it was you all along." He didn't find a new life; a new life found him. God met him and it wasn't the same C. S. Lewis afterward.

How did I get here? How did I come to possess the self that now possesses me? Note how I am trained to narrate myself: "It all began in a small town in South Carolina. I was born to two loving, but often inept parents, and raised in a middle-class environment plagued by racial segregation that even at an early age I began to question."

See? Modernity teaches us to describe ourselves as mostly self-contrived. Our lives are the result of historical, psychological, genetic development that occurs within the self. Everything unfolds developmentally from some historical beginning. This is the story we have been taught to tell about ourselves.

Now if you study C. S. Lewis's self as it developed from not much of a believer to a believer in some vague "theism" to the robustly orthodox "Christian" who forever touched the world with his writings, you will be disappointed. Lewis's biography is singularly unrevealing.

Lewis grew up negative about Christian faith in his grandfather's church in Dundela, where he said, "We were offered dry husks of Christianity." The main point of Protestantism in Northern Ireland was to demonstrate that whatever it was that they believed in was not what Roman Catholics believed. College, army, the war for Lewis—all were negative experiences of Christian faith.

He read G. K. Chesterton and concluded that "Christianity was very sensible—apart from its being Christianity." As a bright young scholar he knew that the Gospels were ahistorical nonsense. Yet in rereading the Gospels he felt that they were so appallingly unimaginative and artless that they must be historical fact! They certainly weren't great literature.

Then, as if out of nowhere, in 1931, Lewis wrote to his lifelong friend Arthur Greeves, "I have just passed on from believing in God to definitely believing in Christ." Also in 1931, he received communion at the church in Heddington for the first time since boyhood.

Where did this come from? In the most famous passage of *Surprised by Joy* he writes: "Picture me alone in that room in Magdalen, night after night, feeling, whenever my mind lifted even for a second from my work, the steady, unrelenting approach of Him whom I so earnestly desired not to meet. That which I greatly feared came upon me. . . . I gave in, and admitted that God was God, and knelt and prayed: perhaps, that night, the most dejected and reluctant covert in all England" (p. 228).

I think this is why Lewis deliberately made *Surprised by Joy* nonautobiographical. From the first, this disappointed some critics. (His doctor and friend, Dr. Humphrey Havard, said the book should have been called "Suppressed by Jack.") From out of nowhere comes this dramatic turn toward faith. Yet we search in vain for something in the earlier life of Lewis that leads to this, and we find nothing in his biography that accounts for his conversion.

It is as if Lewis wants to make clear that his "self" in Christ was not the result of earlier influences, not the end of some earnest intellectual search (and not the result of attending a conference on having a more meaningful self); it was a divine gift. It came from outside the self, reforming the self, transforming the self in ways the self did not previously intend.

Lewis's great moment of spiritual insight came as he rode sidecar to Whipsnade Zoo on a sunny morning in September of 1931. This has always struck me as the most ridiculous of situations for a religious conversion—stodgy C. S. Lewis, bobbing along in a motorcycle sidecar on his way to a second-rate zoo. At least St. Paul was on a road going somewhere to do important business. Yet of that moment Lewis wrote, "When we set out I did not believe that Jesus Christ is the Son of God, and when we reached the zoo I did." That's it? This is rather uneventful spiritual stuff, even for an English professor!

In modernity, the self becomes an exclusively human construct, something we fabricate through our astute decisions and adventurous choices. "I choose, therefore I am." Lewis illustrates a very different conception of the self: the self as surprising gift of a creative God.

Christians believe that there is no "self" there until God makes a move, until the embrace, the intrusion, the surprise. Of course, we are modern women and men who have had years of education designed to insulate ourselves from even considering the possibility that something's afoot other than that of our own devising. We do not expect to be addressed by voices other than those that are self-derived.

So the story of C. S. Lewis—who wasn't worrying about the meaninglessness of his life, who wasn't searching for anything, whom God surprised by joy—is a jolt to our sense of self. What if the life I'm living is not my own? What if I am not only the sum of my choices and decisions but also the result of "the steady, unrelenting approach of Him whom I so earnestly desired not to meet"? Lewis's conversion is akin to today's scripture about Saul, who had a wonderfully fulfilling life as "Pharisee of Pharisees" and therefore wasn't looking for more meaning but rather for more Christians to persecute.

In the story of Saul's conversion there is no development, no history, no precedent, nothing but a God who shows up and transforms the self into that which the self could have never been on its own.

Only God knows the self I'm meant to be. Only God knows the self I will, by God, become. Only God can give me a self that is worth having. And God does, in those surprising moments, when we're proceeding down our accustomed ruts, just busy looking after ourselves, and there is, as if out of nowhere, light, a voice, a summons, and we know we have been cornered, and we mutter with C. S. Lewis in astonishment, "So, it was you all along."

Have you known such a surprising, disrupting, transforming encounter with the Living Christ?

Here's the promise of Easter: you will.

Relating the text

In Harold Ramis's endlessly rewatchable movie *Groundhog Day*, Bill Murray plays the most superficial of men engaged in the most inane of jobs (reporting the weather). One drab morning in a Pennsylvania town he awakens to the radio blaring Sonny and Cher's whining rendition of their most pointless song, "I've Got You Babe." He then plods through his day, encountering a group of wearisome people along the way.

The next morning the radio awakens him at the same time, with the same song—Sonny and Cher all over again—and the same weather report, which he thinks is a bit odd. But things become even stranger as he stumbles through exactly the same day with the same boring people as yesterday. And then the next day and the next. After the twentieth repetition of the same meaningless day, Murray realizes he is in hell. In a number of vain attempts to end it all he tries to commit suicide, leaping from a building, falling in front of a speeding truck. But after each attempt, he awakens the next day to the same song, same day. He becomes desperate to find some sense of meaning amid the boredom. He engages in a life of crime, doing all those things that he was reluctant to do before his days became gruesome repetition. After even the worst of crimes, he awakens the next morning to "I've Got You Babe" and begins his day all over again.

Realizing that he has no way of escaping the humdrum of the same day, he launches into a program of self-improvement. He takes up piano. He memorizes poetry. He makes love like a Frenchman. He transforms himself into an interesting person. And in the process, the people around him, for whom he once had such contempt, become meaningful to him. Only then is he freed from the wheel of the eternal return.

This is the story that the modern world thinks it is now living. Take charge of your life and transform yourself into someone worth loving and use your time to make a life worth living. You can have meaning if you choose to have meaning.

Christians believe that story to be a lie. Christians believe another story than that of *Groundhog Day*.

Today's account of the conversion of St. Paul shows a person who receives a different life, not as the result of his choices or striving, but rather as the result of God's intervention. Our lives are what they are as gifts not of our devising.

This was her third semester traveling overseas. Why on earth did she not simply act like most of our students and stay in her dorm at the college? Why was she so determined to do so much travel?

I asked her. She responded, "Well, I'm a student, I'm twenty years old. I figure my major task at this time in my life is to grow up, to be a different person than I was when I arrived here. I've found that there is no way to live in a different country, speak a different language, and stay the same old me."

Take this as a sort of parable of the Christian life. There is no way to live in a whole new world and remain the same old you!

I love the writing of C. S. Lewis. But I believe that Lewis would back me up when I declare that C. S. Lewis is not as interesting as the God who took an interest in C. S. Lewis.

The "god" of American popular Christianity is the utilitarian, instrumental god who is moderately helpful and never disrupted, the god who is sometimes useful in getting whatever it is we happen to want in life other than God. Therapeutic deism reigns. We are told that God loves and cares—mainly about me, my family, and my felt needs—but this urbane, deistic therapist of a god never actually gets around to doing anything. Not the sort of God to show up and strike someone blind. Lewis called it "surprised by joy." Theologian Robert Jenson says that's how you can tell the difference between a true, living God and a dead, false god. A fake, noninterventionist god will never surprise you.

Fourth Sunday of Easter

Acts 9:36-43

Psalm 23

Revelation 7:9-17

John 10:22-30

Arise

Selected reading

Acts 9:36-43

Theme

The resurrection isn't only what happened when crucified Jesus was raised from the dead. The resurrection also continues in the faith and work of the church as God continues to defeat death and evil. Christ is raised. And we are being raised as well.

Introduction to the readings

Acts 9:36-43

Tabitha, a prominent and benevolent disciple at Joppa, is raised from the dead by Peter's prayer. Apparently, after Jesus's resurrection the life-giving power of God continues.

Revelation 7:9-17

Revelation gives a vision of a great multitude from every nation all standing before the throne of the Lamb.

John 10:22-30

"If you are the Christ, tell us plainly," people say to Jesus as he walks into the temple. Jesus responds that people ought to be able to see his works and know who he is.

Prayer

Lord Jesus, on Easter you were raised from the dead. You rose and you returned to us in your resurrection.

Living Christ, we confess that we sometimes become discouraged. It seems that our victories are so few. Your church continues to believe and to witness and to work, and yet we are still confronted by a mostly disbelieving world. We are disappointed by the meager results of our efforts. In the end it seems as if the powers-that-be are greater than the power you have entrusted to us.

Reigning Christ, inspire us anew with your life-giving word. In this time of worship, stir up in us renewed commitment to follow you wherever you lead. Strengthen us that we might doubt our doubts and not be defeated by our disappointments. Rise to us, Lord; return to us anew that we might faithfully follow you as your disciples. Amen.

Encountering the text

The resurrection of Jesus was something that happened to Jesus and no one else. Many in Israel believed in an eventual general resurrection of the dead in which those who had died in Israel, particularly those Jews who had suffered an unjust death at the hands of Gentiles (and there were many), would be raised in a grand act of God that would set right so much of the wrong that Israel had suffered here in this age.

No one believed in the resurrection of an individual. Yet that was exactly the early church's claim from the very beginning: God raised Jesus, unjustly crucified, from the dead.

But no one said, "God raised Jesus from the dead and all of us Jesus followers will be raised as well." That was an affirmation that had to come later as the church lived into the truth of the resurrection. In a short period of time, the followers of Jesus said not only that Jesus was resurrected but also that they would be raised too.

Further, the early Christians asserted that resurrection was the remarkable sign of the beginning of a new age in which resurrection had disrupted and changed everything. Now that Jesus has been raised, not only will we be raised, but also, in a deep and life-changing sense, we are being raised. And to say that we are being raised is not simply a statement that has relevance when we die. It is an act of faith here, now. The resurrection is a sign that the world is being reclaimed, that the forces of death in the world are being defeated among us. To shout and to live before the world the truth, "He is risen!" is to make a claim about reality now that Jesus Christ is raised from the dead.

That is the astounding new claim that lies behind this Sunday's reading from the Acts of the Apostles.

Proclaiming the text

As you have probably noted, in the Sundays after Easter we often do not have the usual first lesson from the Old Testament. We typically have a lesson from the Acts of the Apostles, Luke's second volume after his Gospel.

And this practice makes sense, as if the church means to say, "You know the resurrection that occurred in the raising of Jesus Christ? Well, it continues. Easter is not just something that happened to crucified Jesus; resurrection is a power let loose among Jesus's followers."

Here's today's story. At Joppa there was a woman whose name was Tabitha. Interestingly, Tabitha is called a disciple, one of the few women so explicitly designated. And Tabitha is a very good disciple because Luke says, "Her life overflowed with good works and compassionate acts on behalf of those in need."

But all that good work ends when Tabitha becomes sick and dies. The many poor widows whom Tabitha helped with her good words stand by her body mourning. They pitifully hold up the garments that she has made for them.

Peter, premier disciple, arrives at the side of the body. He kneels and prays, speaking to the dead woman, "Tabitha, get up!" In saying "get up" Peter uses much the same word that is used to speak of Jesus's resurrection.

And Tabitha rises, restored to life.

Of course, what happened to Tabitha wasn't exactly a "resurrection" because eventually Tabitha died and was buried. Yet after Easter it is impossible to hear a tale like this without thinking of resurrection. Jesus was resurrected. And after his resurrection, a good woman, through the good offices of Peter, is raised, brought back to life.

I'll admit it's a strange story. But maybe that's part of Luke's point in telling it to us today. After Easter, after dead Jesus is raised, you had better become accustomed to some strange stories! The world after Easter is not like the world before Easter. Before Easter, everyone who lived died, and all who died stayed dead. Before Easter, poor people are totally at the mercy of external forces over which they have no control. Before Easter there is much grieving as we bid farewell to those dear saints who depart us in death.

But after Easter, after God's great defeat of death in the raising of Jesus, death is not given the last word. After Easter, those who are poor and vulnerable have hope because there is a power for good let loose in the world that is greater than the powers of evil. After Easter, we are able to have hope that the future is not totally constrained by the past.

This is one reason why we refer to the message of what happened in Jesus Christ as "gospel," as "good news." It is particularly good news because what happened in Jesus Christ in his resurrection still happens. Here. Now.

Easter is a promise not only that death does not have the last word but also that God will not be defeated by evil and death. And those disciples who do

God's good work in Christ's name will not be defeated. Certainly there will be sickness, setbacks, and even death and mourning. But don't you see? All those once all-powerful forces have received a great blow. Death, the great Defeater, has been defeated. And thus we have hope.

In my own ministry I have found that to be true. Here is the church, a little body of believers, commissioned by Jesus Christ to be his people in the world. Here is the church with a sweeping, seemingly impossible mandate, to show Christ and his kingdom in all that we do and say to an unbelieving world. Therefore, to be in the church, to be a disciple like Tabitha or Peter, is to experience lots of disappointments, lots of defeats. Our church, as faithful as it is, continues, like any church of anytime, to fall short of Christ's mandate to us.

And yet we have hope. Tabitha's fledgling little congregation, a tiny fringe group on the edge of the mighty Roman Empire, was up against greater odds than our church. Yet they took heart. They had hope because they heard this story and they believed it to be a true account of what God was really up to in the world.

In John Masefield's book *The Trial of Jesus* (New York: Macmilan Publishers, 1925), the character of Longinus was patterned after the centurion in command of the soldiers at the foot of the cross. Some of the Gospels tell the story of a centurion who looked up and said, "This was certainly God's Son" (Matt 27:54). In Masefield's novel, Longinus returned with his troops from Calvary on Friday. That evening he was summoned by Pontius Pilate to give his daily report. When he finished, Pilate's wife begged him to tell her more about the crucifixion and how the prisoner had died. After Longinus told her, she said, "Longinus, do you think he is dead now? Is he dead and gone?" "No, ma'am," he replied. "Then, where is he?" she asked. "Let loose in the world, where neither Roman nor Jew will ever stop his truth," he said.

That is the truth of the resurrection. It is our truth, our hope. In life, in death, in life beyond death, Jesus Christ has been let loose in the world. Anything can happen now.

Relating the text

In the church, we continue to care about those who have died. In fact, that we are today reading a story about a woman, Tabitha, who died over two thousand years ago, is very typical of the church. We honor the dead by letting them speak to us in scripture. In *Animal Dreams* (New York: Harper Perennial, 2013), Barbara Kingsolver tells about the town of Grace, where each year they celebrate the Day of the Dead. Everyone gathers in the village cemetery; they elaborately decorate the tombstones, strewing flowers all over the ground. They bring food, the children run, and they all sing and play games. It is a great festivity, all done with tender care. "It was a great comfort to see this attention lavished on the dead," Kingsolver notes. "In these families you would never stop being loved."

Christians honor the saints, remember their stories, and submit to their teaching any time we read and listen to scripture. In the story of Tabitha, we have an account from the very first days of the church. You can almost feel the church attempting to adjust to the shock of the resurrection, the surprise that, in them, God was defeating evil and death. In a way, that's always been the reaction of the church; it takes us a long time to adjust to the shock of resurrection.

I couldn't believe it. For ten years our congregation has been serving food to the homeless. We set out to solve the problem of hunger in our city. We had some generous initial gifts that got the ministry started.

But the problem of hunger and homelessness kept growing. We raised more money, but the money was never enough to fund all that we needed. The more people we fed, the more people there were who showed up each year looking for food.

And this year the board has voted to increase our budget by 10 percent. Ten percent! Are they crazy? We were behind in last year's budget. In fact, we have failed to make the budget every year for the last ten years and they want to raise the budget even higher!

Of course, after God raised crucified Jesus from the dead, who knows? Maybe it's not crazy to expect another resurrection right now, here in our city as God shows the hungry homeless—and us—what God can do.

Fifth Sunday of Easter

Acts 11:1-18
Psalm 148
Revelation 21:1-6
John 13:31-35

A Heavenly Vision

Selected reading

Acts 11:1-18

Theme

Only God can do most of the work that needs to be done among us. We have not within ourselves the power to transform ourselves, our church, or our world. Easter says that there is a power unleashed in the world, the power of God in Jesus Christ, the power of the Holy Spirit transforming everything. One of the powerful works of the Holy Spirit is to leap over our humanly imposed boundaries with miraculous, heavenly power. In our church today, that same Easter power is still at work.

Introduction to the readings

Acts 11:1-18

Peter receives a vision from heaven of all sorts of animals let down in a sheet. He is told to prepare the animals for food. "Never consider unclean what God has made pure," Peter is told. Later he will find that the vision is not so much about unacceptable food as about acceptable members of the church.

Revelation 21:1-6

The Revelation to John concludes with a vision of "a new heaven and a new earth," in which the pain and the tragedies of earth are healed by the one who is "the Alpha and the Omega."

John 13:31-35

Christ gives his followers a new commandment to love one another as he has loved us.

Prayer

Almighty and Everlasting God, here we are after Easter, still trying to come to terms with the miracle that has met us in the risen Christ. When Jesus came forth from the tomb everything changed for us. A whole new world met us.

Forgive us for all the ways we attempt to live in the same old world of sin and death. Beckon us to that transformed new life that we have yet to embrace in its fullness.

O God who leaped over the boundary between life and death, continue to leap over our boundaries, continue to surprise us with where you show up next, continue to keep working on us, transforming us so that we might be your faithful people, miraculously transformed by you. Amen.

Encountering the text

For the past two Sundays we have been reveling in heavenly visions, presented so dramatically from the Revelation to John. It has been as if we have had the curtain pulled back enough to see where all this leads, to see the consummation of our faith. Heaven is where the journey ends, when God gets what God wants.

Well, you will note that we've got Revelation again this Sunday—again a vision of the end. Our first lesson from the Acts of the Apostles also is a heavenly vision, or at least a vision that descends from heaven (Acts 11:5-6).

Behind the Acts of the Apostles is the pressing question, "How did salvation come even to the Gentiles?" Few boundaries were more rigid and honored than the boundary between Jews and Gentiles. Through centuries of persecution, diaspora, and difficulty, Israel had remained faithfully Israel by carefully distinguishing between those who were part of the covenant to Israel and those who were not. The survival of a scattered, besieged minority (Jews) was accomplished only through the faithful honoring of the boundaries between Jews and Gentiles. It is therefore important for us (a Christian majority, a Gentile majority) to read Acts 11:1-18 as best we can from the standpoint of the minority (Jews).

Now, in the Way, that boundary between Jews and Gentiles is broken. Gentiles were being baptized. How did that happen? That is surely a question that lurks behind today's scripture from the Acts of the Apostles.

That move is defined, not as an event of human inclusiveness, openness to the "other," or any other sociological, humanly derived phenomenon. It is described as the result of a visionary experience "from heaven" (11:5).

The inclusive, boundary-breaking quality of the church, of salvation in Jesus Christ, is divinely derived. It is a miraculous event that is "from heaven."

Proclaiming the text

The congregation was a rainbow of colors. So many races, nationalities, and languages had found a home in this congregation. "How did this happen?" I asked the pastor of this multicultural throng. "God only knows," was the reply of the pastor.

"No, I'm serious. How did this happen?" I persisted. I sure wanted to know what program, what technique, what styles of leadership accounted for such a rich, rainbow-colored church.

"I'm serious," said the pastor. "God only knows because this congregation is not something that I produced. It's what God miraculously gave."

I immediately thought of today's lesson from the Acts of the Apostles 11:1-18. Peter had some explaining to do when he got back to Jerusalem.

The church council said to Peter, "You ate with them! You had the nerve to baptize them! How dare you violate the boundaries established by scripture?"

Peter's defense? He recounted a vision: In a dream, he saw a large sheet let down from heaven, a sheet full of all kinds of animals. A voice said, "Get up, Peter! Kill and eat!"

Peter replied, "Nothing impure of uncleans has ever entered my mouth." And God said, "Never consider unclean what God has made pure." The vision was repeated three times just to be sure Peter got the point. Then the sheet was pulled back up to heaven.

Peter didn't get the point. Why such a heavenly fuss about dietary restrictions?

Immediately Peter is called to go to the house of a Gentile. The Holy Spirit descended and then the penny dropped. Peter figured out that the vision from heaven was not about unclean food, but about "unclean" people. Even the Gentiles, who had no part of the promises of God given to Israel, were received into this new Jesus movement, "the Way."

The whole church marveled that "God has enabled Gentiles to change their hearts and lives so that they might have new life."

I think this story is a parable for the church. Whenever boundaries are broken, whenever the "other" is embraced by the church, then that is "from heaven." Someone has obeyed the vision. It is an act of God, miraculous.

The church itself is a miracle, a kind of protest against the way the world gathers people. In the world, "like attracts like." The church is whomever Jesus Christ calls to himself. In the world, we gather mainly on the basis of affinity, on the basis of similar racial, economic, educational, or other worldly unifying characteristics. The church, however, is a miracle, an act of God.

Let's look over our congregation and ask ourselves, "Are we true to that vision? Could people look at the composition of our church and say, 'that gathering of folks is nothing less than a miracle'"?

Can you imagine what it felt like to be Jewish, to have suffered injustices at the hands of Gentiles, to have been trained from birth to carefully make proper distinctions between our group and theirs now to find themselves in this new family that contains both Jews and Gentiles, insiders and outsiders?

It's sort of heaven on earth.

Relating the text

A friend and I entered a dingy diner in rural South Carolina at lunchtime. Nothing but pickup trucks parked out front. At nearly every table sat working people, almost all of them wearing baseball caps, having lunch. Almost every table seemed equally integrated racially, white and black. There was much laughter and conviviality. My friend, surveying the scene said, "We've walked into God's kingdom."

Then he said, "Don't you wonder what this crowd talked about at lunch the day after the O. J. Simpson verdict?"

In racially divided America, a racially inclusive diner is a glimpse of the hope that moves us. Here is church as it's meant to be—that gathering convened by God where we are forced to be in conversation with those whom we might have avoided had God not brought us together. To be sure, God's kingdom is more than a bunch of diverse people having a meal together. But Christians believe that while just eating together and talking about difficult subjects is not the end of the kingdom, it could well be its beginning. That's what we do every Sunday. When Christians enact, celebrate salvation in Jesus Christ, we do it with a meal, the Eucharist. This holy meal preserves salvation from being intellectualized by us, made a matter of our feelings, our decisions, our projects. Salvation is when we come to the table, with those whom we do not necessarily like, and we hold out empty hands, receive a gift, obeying Jesus's command. We "do this" rather than think about it; we share, and we ingest, and Jesus becomes our life.

Of course, neither I nor my friend would know any of this without Jesus. Jesus teaches what "God's kingdom" designates, Jesus who first implants in us the hope that there is such a time and place that is our destiny, Jesus who is host at the table. Salvation is literally inconceivable apart from him: "Salvation can be found in no one else. Throughout the whole world, no other name has been given among humans through which we must be saved" (Acts 4:12). Peter wasn't speaking to the question of other faiths at this point in the Acts of the Apostles; he was testifying before his fellow Jews about Jesus. Still Peter's statement does represent what the church has always and has everywhere believed about the name of Jesus. It was an implication that would become clearer to Peter in the heavenly vision in Acts 11.

Alas, too many of us church leaders have been content to hunker down in the vineyard (Matt 20) with the few faithful who have been bequeathed to us by the evangelism of previous generations rather than to join the "master of the vineyard" in his forays to the unemployment office. Inversion, obsessive concern with internal ecclesial matters, rather than constant reaching out to the world in Jesus's name, is the death of the church. John Wesley knew enough about the expansive quality of salvation in Jesus's name to ask prospective preachers not only about their vocation, their gifts, and graces, but also about their "fruit." When we settle down and become parochial, the Holy Spirit drifts elsewhere; Jesus leaves us as his miraculous, heavenly inspired movement keeps on the move. There is something about Jesus that refuses to bed down with the sheep who are either too unimaginative or decrepit to wander. I once closed a church after a seventy-year run. Their dying words were, "There is no one anywhere near our church who might join our church." What they meant is, "We are in the middle of great population growth that is all of a color and a language other than our own." Church growth is an expected, essential by-product of a savior who is relentlessly out on the prowl for fresh disciples. Church decline is an expected result for a church that refuses to follow a savior who is relentlessly out to grow God's reign.

I love the image of the Holy Spirit and the church that I see in the Acts of the Apostles. Evangelism, church growth occurs in Acts, not as some program or plan, but rather in a sort of breathless attempt to keep up with the pace of the Holy Spirit. Today's lesson from Acts 11 is no exception. Peter did not plan or decide to be where he was, out baptizing Gentiles. Rather the Holy Spirit put Peter there.

Perhaps this is the real beginning of faithful evangelism. Perhaps mainline Protestantism particularly needs to hear this message. The goal is not to be inclusive, open, hospitable, affirming of others, inviting, or any of those other virtues. The challenge is to be determined to worship, to obey, and to follow the Holy Spirit!

I remind you that we are in Easter, still in that time (maybe the church is always in that time) when we are still exploring the radical implications that crucified Jesus was raised from the dead.

Gentiles put Jesus to death on the cross. Crucifixion was a specifically Roman punishment, often saved for Jews who caused trouble for the Romans who occupied Judea.

And yet, when Jesus is raised, in the aftermath of Easter, the Holy Spirit, the power and presence of the risen Christ, leaps even over to the Gentiles, making them disciples, followers of the Way.

It is a miracle of a different kind, but of the same magnitude as the resurrection itself.

How do we know for sure that Easter is true? Well, how do you explain the church? How do you explain the spread of the gospel even to the Gentiles, even to us Gentiles?

Because of a horrible traffic jam on the way to the theater, we missed almost the whole play. Our friends waited for us, then went ahead and entered the theater, wondering what on earth had happened to us (this was before cell phones).

We didn't get there until the last ten minutes of the play, the last of the last act of the play!

Afterward, when we were having dinner with our friends, my friend said, "Actually, if you didn't get here until the last act, you got most of the play. At least you know all that is really important."

The drama involving us with God is not yet over. The play continues. But Christians are those who have been given a privileged glimpse of the last act of the play, the grand finale, the conclusion. That enables us to live now with faith and confidence. We've seen the end.

Sixth Sunday of Easter

Acts 16:9-15

Psalm 67

Revelation 21:10, 22–22:5

John 14:23-29 or John 5:1-9

You Don't Need to Be a Disciple by Yourself

Selected reading

John 14:23-29

Theme

Jesus makes great demands upon us as his disciples. He doesn't expect us to be disciples on our own. He doesn't expect us to do anything on our own. We are graciously given the Holy Spirit—guide, interpreter, counselor, and advocate. In our weakness, the Holy Spirit helps us. We don't have to try to follow Jesus on our own. The Holy Spirit helps us.

Introduction to the readings

Acts 16:9-15

Paul has a vision in which he sees someone pleading, "Come over into Macedonia and help us." Thus the mission of the early church expands to a pious woman named Lydia.

Revelation 21:10, 22–22:5
The Revelation to John continues with a vision of the holy city of Jerusalem, a place now flooded with the light of the Lord.

John 14:23-29
Christ says that he will not leave his disciples without help. The Father will send "the Companion, the Holy Spirit" who "will teach you everything and will remind you of everything I told you."

Prayer
O Holy Spirit, active, fertile, powerful spirit of the living God, blow upon us this day your breath of life.

When our spirits flag and our bodies droop, blow gently upon us, lifting us up, refreshing us, restoring us to your service.

When our spirits grow cautious and cowardly and we are hesitant to speak up and to speak out, blow mightily upon us, filling us with new determination to be faithful to you, giving us a fresh portion of courage, teaching us to step up and say things that we would never say on our own.

When our spirits are dry and dusty and we find ourselves alone and bereft in some desert of a place, blow your holy wind through our death valley, give life to our dry bones, knit us back together, and send us again on your way, resurrected, newborn, and empowered for work for you and your kingdom. Amen.

Encountering the text
Verses 23-24 of John 14 are a response to Judas's (not Judas Iscariot) question about why Christ has not fully manifested himself in glory to the world. This is a repeat of some of the issues that arose in the first part of this chapter. The disciples are assured of God's love for those who love Christ and they are as-

sured that God in Christ will come and make a "home" with them. The coming of Christ is thus a parallel to the arrival of the Companion in verse 16. We are reminded of the way John's Gospel opened with the announcement that the "Word" would come and tabernacle with mortals.

This Companion is the presence of Christ with his followers after the ascension. The concern here is that Christ has come to be present with believers and that, if he leaves, if he assumes another mode of presence in his absence from them, he will still be with them as Companion.

Although Christ has done much talking in the Fourth Gospel, more talking, more revealing will be done through the work of the Companion. Thus, Jesus attempts to reassure his troubled disciples at his departure. He ministers to their fears and uncertainty by promising them a continuing, vital, revealing presence.

The Fourth Gospel is the Gospel of the incarnation. In Christ, God has become flesh and moved in with us. That movement from heaven to earth is now being consummated in the gift of that presence of God that speaks to us, empowers us, reveals God's will to us.

We will hope, in today's sermon, to offer a word of pastoral care: in our struggles to be faithful, we are given the gift of the Holy Spirit.

Proclaiming the text

We were going around the room, sharing the reasons why we had joined our church. One man replied, "I grew up in a very strict religious environment. Basically, what that meant was that I spent thirty-five years of my life thinking that God was mad at me. My conversion, if you could call it that, was when I figured out that God, whom I thought was my enemy, turned out to be my friend."

Jesus is on his way to his death, and on his way, he bids farewell to his disciples. It is a long scene that we witness here in the Gospel of John. And the scene is made all the more poignant because the ones to whom he speaks—his disciples, his twelve closest friends—are also ones who have a hand in his betrayal. They have not only disappointed Jesus through their repeated misunderstanding (in the Gospel of John, nobody ever seems to "get it" when Jesus is talking) but also actively betrayed him when the soldiers came to arrest Jesus. Despite their declarations of fidelity, all of the disciples flee into the night, says Matthew. The disciples, who have been so close to Jesus during sunnier times in Galilee, are nowhere to be seen when Jesus is dragged into court, whipped until he is almost dead, and then brutally crucified.

Time and again, throughout the story, these so-called disciples are anything but disciples. Jesus has given them his words of life, and he has shared with them the deepest truths of God. He has not only spoken to them but also enacted signs and wonders before them. He has revealed to them the depths of the heart of God. Still, even here at the end, they just don't get it. Jesus speaks to them, in this last speech, about the way that he is going. "We don't know where you are going. How can we know the way?" the disciples say, true to form, ignorant all the way to the end (14:5).

And I guess you would have to be a contemporary disciple of Jesus to know the peculiar comfort that comes to contemporary Christians by listening to these stories of the stupidity, the failure, and even the betrayal of these first disciples. Let's face it, if we were sitting there that night with Jesus, and he was giving us our final exam, who here could hope to pass?

I know that I have flunked the exam so many times. Repeatedly Jesus told us not to put our trust in riches, not to attempt futilely to heap up treasures here on earth. And yet I do. When I meet with my stockbroker concerning my pension, I disobey Jesus's word to "stop worrying about tomorrow" (Matt 6:34). No. I ask my stockbroker, "What have you done to accumulate enough stuff for me in my stock portfolio so that I might be able to buy eternity for myself?"

Jesus told us to turn the other cheek when struck. Yet when I'm struck, I try to strike back hard enough to knock the purse thief, my aggressor, down, at least figuratively speaking.

Jesus told us to take up our cross and follow, but for me, religion is mostly a cushion rather than a cross, something to soften the blows of life, a comfort amid the storm, something palliative, to make life go down a little easier. Am I the only one? Did you come here this morning hoping that Jesus would make your life a little more difficult and complicated? Not I.

And so, as Jesus speaks his strange words about a peace that passes our understanding, about love, but love that is quite different from our love, about glory that has a cruciform shape, forgive me for having greater sympathy with the disciples of Jesus than with Jesus. Stupidity, their coming betrayal when the soldiers arrive, all of that is a great comfort to me. They just don't get it. It's good for my self-image that they are as dumb as I, maybe even dumber.

And yet, it is to these disciples that Jesus promises an "Advocate" (14:26 NRSV). He gives them the sad news that he is leaving them. The world that he came to save is attempting to push him out of the world. The darkness that he came to enlighten will attempt to engulf him. He is being dragged away to a humiliating end.

But before he goes, he tells his disciples that this is not the end. He will continue to be with them, though he is away from them. Though he will no longer teach them face-to-face, he will continue to teach them. Although they will no longer walk the roads of Judea together, he will walk with them. They think the door is about to close between them and Jesus, and yet Jesus says he is now opening another door for them. This is the end of the way, and yet he tells them that he is still the way. They are horrified at the prospect of his death, but Jesus tells them that in this death is life.

To those who could not give Jesus proper understanding, faithful discipleship, courageous obedience, he gives them an Advocate. He promises never to leave them. He pledges to be close to them, even closer than he is now. He is going to send an Advocate. He, who has been so frustrated with his disciples' lack of comprehension when he taught them, is going to send an Advocate who will be their teacher, who will instruct them and show them everything.

One of the things that the Holy Spirit does is teach us and advocate for us. The Holy Spirit is the power of God. God the Father—and God the Son—speaks to us, instructs us, advocates for us, in the Holy Spirit.

Put simply, this means that God knows the Christian life is too difficult to be done alone. We are not to try to understand the Bible, to have community here in the church, to take up our cross, to witness for Christ, to live the Christian life alone. When it comes to following Jesus, nothing is done alone.

That's why when you are baptized we always have a prayer for the Holy Spirit. At your baptism, we promise you that God will give you the Holy Spirit to teach you, strengthen you, guide you, and equip you to be a faithful disciple. Nobody expects you to do this alone. You have an Advocate.

I had a summer job in a factory and was given only a couple of weeks to learn the job. The foreman warned me that he was going on a two-week vacation and that I would be in charge while he was away. I did all I could to learn the job as best I could. Still, on the day that the foreman prepared to leave for his vacation, I was filled with anxiety. On the day before he left, the foreman said to me, "Son, here is my operations manual. This has everything that I have told you. Any problem that will come up, you can turn here and figure out how to handle it. This little book is your Bible in this job."

Some people have thought of the Bible as that sort of thing. Here is life's little instruction book. If you've got questions about how you are to live as a Christian, just open up the Bible and it'll show you how.

No, that's not what Jesus says here. He doesn't say, I'm leaving you a book of instructions. He says, *I am leaving you a teacher, a guide, a friend—the Advocate.* This Advocate will tell you all that you need to know.

The Advocate is more like that foreman saying to me, "I'm getting ready to leave on my vacation, but kid, here is my e-mail address, my cell phone number, my GPS location, and I want you to feel free to call me day or night if you've got any questions, or if this job gets to be too much for you."

Sometimes, when you consider the huge tasks to which Jesus calls us, his great expectations for us, you get the impression that the Christian life is a heroic affair; that is, only the very best and brightest could aspire to be a disciple. But, look who Jesus called to be his first disciples; they were ordinary people who were really not at all quick on the uptake. How on earth did he expect twelve losers like these to be faithful?

Jesus didn't expect them to be faithful by themselves. He didn't expect them to do anything by themselves. In fact, in the Gospel of John he tells them that they can't do anything by themselves.

Therefore, he sends them an Advocate, the Holy Spirit. The Holy Spirit strengthens them to do that which they could never do by themselves.

Relating the text

The seminarian had just completed the course "War and Peace" with Dr. Stanley Hauerwas. In the course of his study, he had become convinced that Jesus was utterly nonviolent and that it was impossible to follow Jesus without being a pacifist.

"I'm from Texas!" protested the seminarian. "Guns, guts, and glory are a part of my culture. I believe in the nonviolent way in my brain, but I'm not sure that I can pull it off in my life."

I found his honesty refreshing. Then I reminded him that Jesus doesn't expect us to follow him on our own.

The night I was ordained was one of the most humbling experiences of my life. Looking out over the gathered congregation, I was suddenly overwhelmed by the faces of the people whom I would serve as a pastor. I caught a vision of all my inadequacies and limitations, all the things I didn't know and couldn't do well. How could any mere human being undertake such a mission?

Then, in the ancient rite of ordination, when the bishop laid hands on my head, he prayed the ancient prayer, *Veni Creator Spiritus*, "Come Holy Spirit." I realized that the church had no intention of sending me out alone. I would be given the gift of the Holy Spirit to help me do the ministry to which I was called. I would not have to be a pastor by myself.

While today's Gospel deals with the Holy Spirit in the Gospel of John, my model is for the Holy Spirit as depicted in the Acts of the Apostles. The Holy Spirit in Acts is an ever-present reality, taking the lead in almost every major move of the church in Acts. In fact, some commentators have suggested that the Acts of the Apostles might better be entitled "Acts of the Holy Spirit." In Acts, the Holy Spirit keeps prodding and pressing the church to move out into the world, keeps preceding a reluctant church into new areas of mission and outreach.

Seventh Sunday of Easter

Acts 16:16-34
Psalm 97
Revelation 22:12-14, 16-17, 20-21
John 17:20-26

The Glory of God

Selected reading

John 17:20-26

Theme

Jesus is our glorious savior. Yet Jesus has a very strange definition of glory. He is a crucified savior who reigns from a cross. Even after Easter, the risen Christ still bears the scars of the cross. He calls us to share in his glory and in his ministry, promising us only that where he is, we will be also. Jesus has a peculiar definition of *glory*.

Introduction to the readings

Acts 16:16-34
Paul and Silas, imprisoned for their preaching, convert their jailer and his whole household.

Revelation 22:12-14, 16-17, 20-21
The risen Christ promises, "I'm coming soon," as the vision of Revelation ends in a group "Amen!"

John 17:20-26
Jesus prays to his Father, promising that "the glory that you have given me I have given them."

Prayer

Lord Jesus, we want to follow you where you are going. You have promised that you are going to prepare a place for us, that where you are, we might also be.

Prepare for us a place, dear Lord, where we may spend all of glorious eternity with you. This is our hope after Easter.

Prepare for us a place, dear Lord—when you enter human suffering and pain, when you are the victim of this world's cruel injustice, when you stand beside people in their hour of deepest need—that where you are, we might also be. This is our hope after Easter.

Make us worthy and willing to be where you are. Amen.

Encountering the text

We are listening in on Jesus's prayer before his crucifixion (17:13, "Now I'm coming to you") and also of the glorified Christ (17:11, "I'm no longer in the world"). In the first part of this prayer (17:1-5) Jesus speaks of his return to glory. Throughout the Gospel of John, Jesus speaks of his "hour of glory." In one sense, we all know what *glory* means. But in the Fourth Gospel it also has a specifically Johannine meaning. When Jesus speaks of seeking his own glory in John 8:50, or of glorifying himself in 8:54, we are justified in thinking that he is speaking of our common sense meaning of *glory*.

When Jesus says that the Father is going to glorify him, the meaning is different. This means that the Father reveals himself to Jesus and specifically through his death (12:23-25). Thus, two poles of the meaning of *glory* are found in the Gospel of John. When Jesus turned the water into wine at Cana of Galilee, it was said that his disciples believed in him because "he revealed his glory" (2:11). The Gospel of John is a story of the growing manifestations of Jesus's glory in word and deed; but it is a glory that culminates in his death. Jesus in John's Gospel often refers to his death as his glorification (12:23). It is only from the viewpoint of the cross and his death that we see the true glory of Jesus.

In today's Gospel, Jesus makes a rather amazing statement about his disciples: "The glory that you [the Father] have given me I have given them, so that they may be one, as we are one." On the face of it, it is a wondrous statement that the same glory that is manifested in Jesus is handed over to his followers. In Jesus we see the glory of the Father, and through Jesus we participate in that glory. Jesus says that it is a glory "which you have given me because you loved me before the foundation of the world."

But a hint of the double meaning of *glory* comes when Jesus says that "the world does not know you," but "I will make [your name] known."

Note the context of Jesus's prayer. He is on his way to crucifixion and death. And in praying this prayer he manifests his glory. But it is a cruciform of glory. Further, when he says that his followers will participate in that glory, he means that we are to participate, at least to some degree, in the glory that is his cross.

The world looked at Jesus and expected a glorious Messiah. The world got a glorious Messiah in Jesus, but not the kind of glory the world expected or thought it wanted.

Here, after Easter and just before Pentecost, let us meditate upon the peculiar glory of Jesus and the peculiar glory that he calls us to bear.

Proclaiming the text

Just before he ended his earthly ministry, Jesus prayed to his Father, giving his disciples the glory. Now is the time when Jesus at last gives us the glory.

Glory was what we expected of him. And glory is what we got from him, but not the sort of glory we expected.

I've got a friend I accuse of verbal inflation. He tends toward linguistic extravagance. I might say, "This was a really good book." He says, "This book was a work of genius, a marvelous, splendid book!"

I might look at a sunset and say, "Beautiful!"

My friend says, "The most splendid, magnificent sunset in the history of the world!"

But I have been with him at times when even his verbal skills cracked under the strain of the moment. Recently we participated in a worship service with glorious music and glorious preaching in a glorious old church and, when the service was over, he simply turned to me and said, "Glory!"

We may say something is wonderful or marvelous, but we do not call something "glorious" unless it really is, unless we have gone to the summit, the apex, the very height of human experience. When are you in your glory?

I flew to a large convention center in the Midwest. I gathered with a couple thousand fellow believers. I marched in a grand procession to the music of a great orchestra. At the appointed time I mounted the pulpit and preached. My sermon ended in a grand crescendo, the singing of a great hymn, accompanied by the orchestra. We marched out with banners unfurled and trumpets blaring. It was my hour of glory.

There were only four minutes left in the game. The L.A. Lakers actually did everything possible to keep the ball away from Michael Jordan in the last moments. But Jordan defied the laws of physics, grabbed the ball, plunged in toward the net, twirled in midair, and dunked it, winning the game for the Chicago Bulls! It was Jordan's time of glory.

She had labored in the back woods of Minnesota for thirty years, working her craft as a poet. Finally, thirty years into her labors, she began to get recognition. A book of her poems had become a bestseller in the poetry world. In June her college summoned her for an honorary degree. And this once quiet, unknown English major at the college at last stood on the stage, receiving a standing ovation from the assemblage. She wept with tears of joy to finally have her work validated in this way. She was in glory.

Throughout the Gospel of John, Jesus speaks of glory. Right at the beginning of the Gospel of John, Jesus and his disciples go to a wedding (John 2). You know the story. The wine gives out. The mother of Jesus comes to him saying, "They have no wine." Jesus tells the servants to fill the water jars up to the brim with water. And wonder of wonders, the water is turned to wine. There was an overflowing of graciousness, a miraculous abundance.

And right there, in Cana of Galilee, John says that Jesus's disciples see Jesus's glory.

It usually takes a moment like that for us to see glory. We plod along in our accustomed ruts, victims of the ordinary and the everyday. And then there comes, in some shining moment, an outbreak of glory. The ordinary veil of the everyday pulls back, the light shines, and everything is transformed into golden hues, and we see glory. In the Olympics, after the race has been run, there is that time when the three winners come to the stage for the medal ceremony. After all the work, and all their sweat and determination, all those long hours of practice on the track, this is their hour of glory.

And so there is among us a quiver of excitement, a growing anticipation, when Jesus speaks of his glory. We have been with him on a long road, through all of the twists and turns of his earthly ministry. There has been rejection and threat. But at last, Jesus speaks of his coming glory. In today's Gospel, deep in the Gospel of John as Jesus prays, we overhear Jesus talking to his heavenly Father about the glory that has been given to him. He is one with the Father; therefore, he shares in the Father's resplendent glory.

Further, Jesus speaks not only of the Father having given him glory but also of Jesus giving glory to his followers. For this ragtag group of sometimes-faithful, often-faithless followers to be told that they are to share in his re-splendence, this is, well, glorious.

Earlier in this Gospel Jesus said, when pushed by his followers, that his hour had not yet come. That is what he said to his mother back in John 2 at the wedding of Cana, "My time hasn't come yet." It was only the second chapter of the Gospel of John. Jesus had done no teaching or preaching or healing. It was not yet his hour. But now, we are moving with him close to his hour of glory. We are moving with him toward the cross. In other words, Jesus has a very peculiar definition of *glory*.

I know a man, a banker, who is a wonderfully pious, deeply Christian person. In the loan department of his bank, he became aware of a systematic, though completely quiet and unstated, practice of denying loans to people in ethnic minorities. Of course, there are federal laws against such discrimination. But he became convinced that, through subtle pressures, and a corporate culture of noncompliance, his bank was violating the spirit, if not the letter, of the law.

Through prayer, he decided to complain about this practice to bank management. He came up with the figures and documented his case. He was not making a big deal out of it, not trying to start trouble; nevertheless, he wanted the management to change their practices.

Exactly one month after he went to management, he was fired. The bank said that they were going through some reorganization. But he knows why he was fired.

He was out of work for more than seven months. When he finally got a job, it was much less of a job than he had at the previous bank. People in our congregation said that he had had a period of bad luck. Many told him, during his time of unemployment, "I know this is a hard time for you."

Jesus might have said, "This is your hour to share in my glory."

We Christians believe that Jesus as the embodiment of God's love was never a more glorious and self-evident sign of God's resplendent love than when he was hoisted up on a cross. This was his hour of glory. And in today's lesson, Jesus promises us a share in some of that resplendence.

Have you had a glorious moment recently? A major reason why we come to church is to share in the glory of God, to have some of God's splendor shine upon us. And fortunately, in many of our services in this church, we partake of great glory.

In the Gospel of John Jesus says that he is going to prepare a place for us, so that we will go where he goes. Today he says that the glory of God is his glory as well and we will be privileged to share in that glory. Are you prepared to share in the glory of a crucified God?

Relating the text

Her church had sent her, when she was a young woman, to work as a nurse in a mission in Japan. I knew her in her eighties when she was a resident in a church-sponsored nursing home where I occasionally visited.

She had a tough time in Japan in the 1940s. Her youthful idealism quickly wilted as she encountered racial, cultural, and political resistance to her work and message. The missionaries worked long and hard to win the trust of the people, giving them free medical care, food, and clothing. But when the missionaries gathered for church on Sundays, only two or three local people ever attended.

She was jailed at the beginning of World War II by the Japanese government. No one in the community where she worked as a nurse spoke up for her. After a year of deplorable treatment and abuse, she was released. She returned home sad, defeated, and disillusioned.

Yet when she returned, her church welcomed her home with open arms, had a great banquet in her honor, celebrated her ministry, gave her a home to live in, and gave her a place to work in a mission hospital among Native Americans.

She said to me, "I came back to America thinking that I was a complete failure as a missionary. Fortunately for me, the church has an odd definition of success."

Korean theologian Chung Hyun Kyung tells of the tremendous courage of a Korean comfort woman who lived through unimaginable hardships and survived. In her old age the woman learned to forgive all her tormentors. How could she do this? Chung Hyun Kyung only says that "she cut the vicious cycle of violence and revenge with her power, which I cannot easily name."

She goes on to say that it was this Buddhist woman who brought the lotus flower to bloom out of her suffering. She was not a Christian, but one could still say that the lotus flower was a sign of holiness that emerged not as an explanation, but as a blessing and hope for her renewed life.

—Sharon G. Thornton, *Broken Yet Beloved* (St Louis: Chalice Press, 2002), 108

At the end of his earthly ministry, Jesus gathered with his disciples at a table for a meal for which Jesus was the host (Luke 22). There, while Jesus was serving them food, "an argument broke out among the disciples over which one of them should be regarded as the greatest" (22:24), a supreme irony considering what Jesus was doing for them at that very moment. Jesus contrasted the leadership of the Gentiles who love to lord over people with that of his followers: "The greatest among you must become like a person of lower status and the leader like a servant. . . . I am among you as one who serves" (22:26-27). Jesus thus pushed a peculiar definition of *greatness*.

The earliest biblical designation for Christian leaders in the early Christian congregations was *deacon*, which means something like "butler" or "waiter." Christians did not call their leaders "priest" or "president" or "master." Christians called their leaders "servants."

The church has to relearn in every age the scandalous quality of Christian leadership. We honor our leaders by calling them "servants." We have a peculiar definition of *honor*.

Scripture Index

**Page numbers in bold indicate the passages that
are the selected readings for each week.**

CPSIA information can be obtained
at www.ICGtesting.com
Printed in the USA
LVOW03s0735040418
572192LV00001B/1/P